First Along the River

A Brief History of the U.S. Environmental Movement

THIRD EDITION

BENJAMIN KLINE, Ph.D.

ROWMAN & LITTLEFIELD PUBLISHERS, INC.
Lanham • Boulder • New York • Toronto • Plymouth, UK

ROWMAN & LITTLEFIELD PUBLISHERS, INC.

Published in the United States of America
by Rowman & Littlefield Publishers, Inc.
A wholly owned subsidiary of The Rowman & Littlefield Publishing Group, Inc.
4501 Forbes Boulevard, Suite 200, Lanham, Maryland 20706
www.rowmanlittlefield.com

Estover Road
Plymouth PL6 7PY
United Kingdom

British Library Cataloguing in Publication Information Available

Library of Congress Cataloging-in-Publication Data:

Kline, Benjamin, 1955–
    First along the river : a brief history of the U.S. environmental movement /
Benjamin Kline.—3rd ed.
        p.   cm.
    Includes bibliographical references and index.
    ISBN-13: 978-0-7425-5853-3 (pbk. : alk. paper)
    ISBN-10: 0-7425-5853-3 (pbk. : alk. paper)
    1. Environmentalism—United States—History.   2. Environmental policy—
United States—History.   3. Nature—Effect of human beings on—History.
4. Green movement—United States—History.   I. Title.
GE195.K578   2007
333.720973—dc22
                                                                        2007002773

Printed in the United States of America

♾ ™ The paper used in this publication meets the minimum requirements of
American National Standard for Information Sciences—Permanence of Paper for
Printed Library Materials, ANSI/NISO Z39.48-1992.

First Along the River

Contents

Preface

I have been told that a history book, especially one on such an emotional topic as environmentalism, is judged more by what is left out than by what is included. This fact is particularly true with an introductory study such as this. It has now been three years since the publication of the first edition of *First Along the River: A Brief History of the U.S. Environmental Movement,* and what I was told has certainly proved true. Although the response to the book has been very favorable, even my most ardent supporters have suggestions for what should be added, expanded, rephrased, or removed from the second edition. I have tried to respond in the most constructive manner possible without affecting the reasons for writing the book in the first place. The reasons are as they were for the first edition: (1) to discuss the historical foundations of the environmental movement in the United States, (2) to introduce the important facts and themes essential to understanding the development of the movement, and (3) to supply the tools and resources needed to pursue more in-depth studies of the topics presented. Whenever possible, I have included quotations from numerous primary sources, including the voices of prominent environmentalists such as Henry David Thoreau, George Catlin, Franklin Roosevelt, Rachel Carson, and Gifford Pinchot. The chapter notes along with the bibliography and suggested readings list provide complete references for further study of the material introduced in *First Along the River.* The extensive glossary contains historically and environmentally relevant terms, events, and people.

First Along the River is intended for anyone who is interested in or active in the environmental movement, environmental issues, or environmental history. Educators in a number of disciplines who want to introduce their students to this subject will find that the book complements their reading list. This book can be used as a supplemental reader for many general courses, including those in history, environmental studies, political science, sociology, biology, geography, natural sciences, and social science.

Acknowledgments

There are so many people who contribute in so many ways to a project like this one. First and foremost are my family. I appreciate their help and patience—they have put up with much. I also owe a debt to Guy Wilson, Tina Sidlow, Owen Woodward, and Lori Heathorn for their assistance in all the little things that went into the compilation of this book. Laura Sutton did a great deal to assist in the editing of this second edition, and I want to thank her for being there. The time and effort contributed by Brian Romer and Robin Romer at Acada Books cannot be overstated. They made this book possible and I thank them. Special thanks to Victoria Ruelas and the McNair Scholars Program at San Jose State University. I was fortunate to have her assistance, and I thank the McNair Scholars Program for the opportunity.

My name is on the cover, but the success of this book belongs to all these people, and I thank them sincerely.

Introduction

If we ignore history we are bound to repeat the mistakes of the past. This age-old axiom is true enough, but knowledge alone will not help us avoid those mistakes. Perhaps a more practical reason for exploring the past is to better comprehend how and why we got where we are today. For example, the United States environmental movement is the result of numerous historical events, many of which occurred long before the nation was established. In fact, historians can trace the environmental movement to the beginnings of Western culture, particularly since the advent of Christianity. These past beliefs and thoughts have influenced the philosophical foundations of today's environmental movement. By understanding our link to this past, we can better see how those experiences shaped the United States and perhaps find the insight to act more wisely.

Innovation, invention, and a reverence for the power of technology have enabled Western culture to improve the material well-being of its population on a scale without peer in world history. However, the damage to the environment has been severe, even excessive, and is a regrettable legacy of this materialistic philosophy. The United States, as a product of Western culture, rigorously applied this philosophy and achieved a material standard of living for its people that is higher than that of any other society, past or present.

Although environmental causes are important public issues in our modern world, they are rooted in history. Americans are a product of the conquered wilderness, and the nation's relatively short history is irrevocably connected to this fact. The age of exploration, colonialism, Native Americans, cowboys, robber barons of the industrial age, social reform of the Progressive Era, and the ascension of the United States to a global power are only a few of the topics that have become part of our nation's environmental lore.

The historical fortunes of the United States have influenced our society's changing attitudes, values, and relationship to the environment. One key issue is the right and power of people to alter and manage the environment. Before the twentieth century, this debate was monopolized by the argument that people had a God-given right to exploit nature for the resources they needed to survive. Americans gave little thought to conservation as

1

they strove to achieve their national goals from the colonial period through the nineteenth century. Still, some people suggested caution and warned not to take the "unlimited" frontier for granted. Among those who had an early influence were George Catlin, George Perkins Marsh, Frederick Law Olmsted, and John Wesley Powell; many of these people had been influenced by Henry David Thoreau. Although they were not able to halt the sometimes irresponsible use of the environment, they were essential in shaping the unique relationship Americans have with nature.

Ecology did not command public and private attention until the twentieth century when the frontier was gone and the need to conserve what wilderness and resource remained became a priority. During the Progressive Era, Americans tried to halt through conservation the rapid exploitation of nature that had prevailed throughout the Industrial Revolution. In 1908 President Theodore Roosevelt warned that "the natural resources of our country are in danger of exhaustion if we permit the old wasteful methods of exploiting them longer to continue."

As the United States entered a period of governmental management and regulation during the Theodore and Franklin Roosevelt eras (1900–1945), the protection of the environment also became a legislative issue. Encouraged by ecology groups, legislators responded to public concerns and instituted such reforms as creating national forests, fostering urban development, and protecting the waterways in an effort to conserve nature's resources. Conservation was seldom done with the energy environmentalists might have wanted, but some action did take place and created a foundation from which to work.

In the modern era, many people have forwarded the environmental message through political and private means. In government, the efforts of President Lyndon Johnson, the Environmental Protection Agency, and Vice President Al Gore have enhanced public awareness of environmental issues. Rachel Carson's book *Silent Spring* (1962) marked the start of the modern environmental movement. Environmental organizations, both traditional and alternative, advocate and lobby government for the responsible use of the environment.

However, this debate is not one sided. Other people oppose what they consider the radical or misplaced priorities of environmentalists. They argue that human needs must take prominence over those of nature. They claim that warnings of environmental disasters are exaggerated. The discussion is one of degree; both sides recognize that the destruction of the environment is everyone's concern. Still, the debate remains firmly entrenched in U.S. history and the close relationship Americans have always had with their environment.

Nature is an infinite sphere
whose center is everywhere and
whose circumference is nowhere.
—BLAISE PASCAL

1

Philosophical Foundations

We are products of the society in which we are raised. Our views of our identity, purpose, and place in the universe are shaped by our experiences. Consciously or unconsciously, these experiences in turn shape our relationship with nature. Western society assumes that humanity and nature are essentially disconnected and that the environment is subordinate to human needs, whether explained by Judeo-Christian tradition or by scientific rationale. As a result, Western history is the story of struggle and gradual domination of nature by people. The events that mark this history are the foundation of our society, and understanding them helps us trace the roots of the environmental movement in the United States.

Biblical Justification for Dominating Nature

In 1967 the historian Lynn White, Jr., published a short essay in *Science* called "The Historical Roots of Our Ecological Crisis." White contended in this essay that Western society's relationship with nature is based principally on the exploitative philosophy of its Judeo-Christian tradition.[1] Several scholars and theologians sharply challenged White's argument. The scholar Rene Dubos was particularly critical, maintaining that the people of pre-Christian Egypt, Mesopotamia, and Persia had equaled Western society's capacity for exploiting and damaging its environment.[2] Although it is true that many non-Western societies abused their environments to various degrees, White's argument provides some explanation for the West's energetic exploitation of nature and for its technological developments as well.

3

Christianity inherited from Judaism a faith in the continual progress of humanity. Change, the core of this belief, is considered part of the existing order of nature. Altering the environment is a key to this relationship, and change is an expected result of human development. We measure time as depicted in the book of Genesis in the Bible, where God took six days to bring his creation into existence. God first created light and darkness, and then the heavenly bodies, the planets, and all the other lifeforms except man. Finally, Adam was created in God's image and given Eve to keep him company. Their position in this new world was made clear when God commanded,

> be fruitful, and multiply, and replenish the earth, and subdue it: And have dominion over the fish of the sea, and over the fowl of the air, and over every living thing that moveth upon the earth.

Adam and Eve named all the animals, establishing their dominance over them. Although they were a special creation, Adam and Eve remained harmonious with nature, and peace and abundance pervaded the Garden of Eden. However, after Adam and Eve ate the "forbidden fruit" of self-knowledge, they were cast out of Eden. As punishment, they were no longer in harmony with nature.

> now, through thy act, the ground is under a curse. All of the days of thy life thou shalt win food from it with toil; thorns and thistles it shall yield thee, this ground from which thou dost win thy food. Still thou shalt earn thy bread with the sweat of thy brow, until thou goest back into the ground from which thou wast taken; dust thou art, and unto dust shalt thou return.

Adam and Eve's actions destroyed the peace of Eden. The lamb no longer sat peacefully with the lion. Even after Noah saved the creatures of the earth during the Great Flood, humanity and nature did not find a bond of understanding. God commanded Noah,

> All the beasts of earth, and the winged things of the sky, and the creeping things of earth, are to go in fear and dread of you, and I give you dominion over all the fishes of the sea. This creation that lives and moves is to provide food for you.

The word *dominion* is significant in this passage. Humanity may have been punished for its misbehavior, but it nevertheless remained the dominant species on earth. Western society embraced this concept of humanity's superiority over nature.

By the fifth century, Christianity had spread throughout the Roman Empire and was the predominant faith. By the sixth century, most western Europeans had converted to Christianity from paganism. A nature–based religion, **paganism** taught that people and the natural world were spiritually connected, were dependent on each other, and had a common bond. Pagans believed spirits inhabited all of nature and were accessible to humanity. Spirits took many forms: trees, rivers, mountains, fairies, centaurs, elves, and so forth. Out of respect, humans placated each spirit before taking an ax to it, damming it, or mining it for ore. Christianity, by contrast, commanded people to exploit nature in their ongoing struggle for sustenance and life. Because both Adam and Noah had been commanded to dominate nature, Christians felt justified in their efforts to harness nature.

Throughout the Middle Ages, circa 500–1500, humans applied innovation and technology to overcome natural obstacles and to tame nature. In the more populated areas of the Mediterranean basin, where the soil was semiarid, farmers used crude plows to scratch the earth into small, squarish fields. By the seventh century, northern farmers developed a new plow with a vertical knife, horizontal share, and moldboard that cut deeply into the often wet and solid soil.[3] This innovative plow, found nowhere else in the world, provided a tool to help people assert their dominance over nature. That humanity was winning the struggle over nature is evident in the way many artisans began to depict this relationship. As Lynn White, Jr., describes it,

> The same exploitive attitude appears slightly before 830 A.D. in western illustrated calendars. In older calendars the months were shown as passive personifications. The new Frankish calendars, which set the style for the Middle Ages, are very different: they show man coercing the world around them—plowing, harvesting, chopping trees, butchering pigs. Man and nature are two things, and man is master.[4]

A quick succession of technological inventions followed, as western Europeans strove to use and exploit their natural surroundings. Faced with constant and unrelenting force, nature succumbed to humanity's needs. Early industries, such as grain mills, used water power by the eleventh century and wind power by the late twelfth century. Labor-saving devices, including new harnesses, shoulder collars, wheeled plows, and power trains with cranks, appeared at a remarkable pace. Agricultural production increased as improved methods of tillage and animal husbandry were combined with new seed types and animal breeds. With the ability to cultivate more land and produce higher yields, the population of western Europe rose from 27 to 73 million people between 700 and 1300. By the fourteenth century, the surpluses generated by agricultural expansion required entrepreneurial skills, managerial ability, and technological skills and inventiveness, which in turn stimulated trade and industry. Technologically, western European society had become a global leader.

Seeking New Land

In the fifteenth century, western Europeans began to seek new lands, launching an age of exploration that would ignite one of the largest and most momentous global migrations in history and forever change the world. Western European technological and materialistic values played an important part in this movement. They had the tools and motivation to escape their exhausted and increasingly overpopulated lands. And their Christian religion encouraged them to inhabit and cultivate new regions of the earth. Inspired by this belief and determined to subdue whatever land they encountered, Europeans eventually traveled and settled the globe. With them they carried their belief that humanity must struggle to overcome nature and assert its authority over it. One of their destinations was what would later become the United States. Therefore, in order to understand American views toward the environment, we must first understand the attitudes of the Europeans who colonized the area.

The catalyst for Europe's age of exploration was the desire to exploit the rich markets of the East. This commercial growth, which had begun before the Crusades, was immensely stimulated by these Christian holy wars in the Middle East that occurred between the tenth and thirteenth centuries. In their effort to "recapture" the holy lands from the Moslems, who had conquered the region in the seventh century, Christian knights from all over Europe often used the navies of the Italian city-states for transportation. As one army after another traveled this way, the Italians found themselves shipping both passengers and supplies. They made enormous profits, which transformed many of their city-states into wealthy communities. However, the real riches came after the Crusades ended. During the Crusades, generations of European nobles and com- moners had enjoyed Eastern luxuries, such as spices, silks, drugs, and perfumes, and were determined to continue using them after they returned home. Thus arose a demand for these new commodities. Italy, initially because of its location on the Mediterranean Sea and its estab- lished trading routes, monopolized this trade, while Western merchants, eager to share in the profitable trade, contemplated an alternate route to the East.

Motivated by economic ambition and the potential wealth of their Eastern trade, Europeans began to improve their ability to travel. Thus, they left their communal societies and sought the rewards found in other lands. Europeans employed technological advances such as the magnify- ing lens, gunpowder, movable type, the printing press, clocks, and new navigational aids (such as the compass and the astrolabe) to aid this ambition. These advancements contributed to the sense of capability and opportunity, which in turn reduced ignorance and superstition. Simulta- neously, as innovation and technology enabled Europeans to overcome the obstacles that had limited past generations, a new age dawned that celebrated individual accomplishment and encouraged a belief in the ability to fashion one's earthly fate. The result was the **Renaissance** of the fourteenth and fifteenth centuries, which transformed western Europe by generating a rebirth of learning and a fresh enthusiasm for scholarship.

During this period, commercial capitalism, with its reliance on money rather than service, soon supplanted the feudal system and its stagnating agricultural economy, which had dominated medieval Europe. Nation-states emerged from alliances between merchants and feudal monarchs. To obtain stability and security, political and commercial leaders worked together to strengthen secular laws as well as to undermine the influence of the powerful Roman Catholic Church.

The church, centered in Rome and long supreme in western Europe, found its religious assumptions and temporal influence more frequently challenged. The commercial society disputed doctrines that emphasized position in the community, advocated the authority of the church, and frowned on excessive profiteering. Criticism reached a climax in 1517, when Martin Luther (1483–1546) nailed ninety-five theses denouncing papal abuses and deceptions onto a church door in Wittenburg, Germany, launching the Protestant Reformation. Luther insisted on salvation through faith, rather than through what the church called "good works." He argued for direct communication with God through the Bible, rather than through the intercession of church authorities. Luther was immediately excommunicated.

Fifteen years later, John Calvin (1509–1564) presented a radically different theology in *Institutes of the Christian Religion*. According to Calvin, people were sinners tainted by Original Sin (the fall from Eden). However, the death of Christ had redeemed a select few who were predestined for salvation. It was impossible to tell who these people were, but Calvin believed there were clues. If a person worked hard, lived righteously, and put nothing before God, he or she would be rewarded. A successful life was a sign that you were likely one of the predestined.

Calvin considered wealth evidence of a productive and godly life, and poverty a badge of sin; "idle hands" became the devil's playthings. Calvin taught that wealth should never come between an individual and God, and therefore riches should be sought but never flaunted. Calvinism stood as a religious justification for material gain while emphasizing labor over consumption. Not everyone seeking material gain was motivated by this belief, though it did influence the Puritans and others who settled the British colonies of North America.

A significant result of this philosophical change and technological progress was the migration of Europeans and the exportation of their culture on a global scale never seen before. Europeans had been exploiting and transforming their continent for more than two thousand years. In fact, a primary motivation for expansion overseas, besides a growing population and monetary gain, was the realization that their own wilderness had all but vanished from most of the European continent. The vast natural abundance the first Europeans encountered in North America was unlike anything they had experienced. The New World contained temperate forests sweeping from the Atlantic coast to the Mississippi, endless grasslands in the Great Plains, the awe-inspiring Rocky Mountains, magnificent forests in the Northwest, and deserts in the Southwest that stretched to the Pacific. Millions of beaver, bison, pronghorn antelope, elk, white-tailed and mule deer, wolves, mountain lions, bears, birds, and other assorted wildlife roamed this virtually untouched or undeveloped land.[5] Everywhere life prospered in what many newcomers viewed as a natural paradise.

With their background and philosophical values, European colonizers began to shape this New World into the image of the Old. This meant that nature must succumb to the human needs and supply the growing hordes with the material goods they sought. As John Steele Gordon explains, the resulting excessive and irresponsible use of nature was a normal response, considering the context of the times.

> Because the supply seemed without end, the value placed on each unit was small. It is only common sense to husband the scarce and let the plentiful take care of itself. Caring for the land, an inescapable necessity in Europe, was simply not cost-efficient here. After all, the settlers could always move on to new, rich land farther west. For three hundred years they did exactly that, with ever-increasing speed.[6]

Rational Nature of the World

By the seventeenth century, western Europeans and their colonial societies were in the midst of a **scientific revolution**—an age that emphasized the rational nature of the universe, but that gave humanity more credit for its ability to understand God's creation than did Christian tradition. The scientists of the age, such as Johannes Kepler (1571–1630), Galileo Galilei (1564–1642), and Isaac Newton (1642–1727), opposed the medieval European belief in nature as an ever-changing living organism, replacing it with the concept of a great machine driven by mechanical certainty. Kepler, Galileo, and Newton, basing their efforts on the findings of Nicolaus Copernicus (1473–1543), established the concept of the solar system as a complex and orderly instrument. Kepler discovered that the planets' orbits are ellipses. Galileo built one of the first telescopes in 1609 and confirmed the Copernican theory that the earth revolves around the sun. Newton, whose *Mathematical Principles of Natural Philosophy*, first published in 1687, synthesized the work of the past and showed that motion can be described by a mathematical formula. Newton's theory that gravity moved matter remained a basic law of science until Albert Einstein showed in 1916 that this theory does not apply to subatomic structures. The work of these scientists made it possible for humanity to believe that universal laws controlled the natural world with mathematical precision. Further, they laid the foundations of a view in which the spirituality of nature no longer played a role.

The French philosopher René Descartes (1596–1650) developed coordinate geometry, which led to the further domination of nature. He believed that nature could be reduced to mathematical formulas, just like the workings of a great machine. Descartes concluded that living things acted and reacted according to set principles that could be observed and defined. People, however, possess conscious thought that gives them free will and choice, unlike nature. Humanity was still dominant, not because of God's will, but because of its ability to reason and define nature.

Francis Bacon (1561–1626) formalized the inductive method of acquiring knowledge. He took a more practical approach to scientific knowledge, which he believed would enable humanity to assert its authority over nature and solve its most troublesome problems. Like his colleagues, he concluded that humanity was superior to nature.

> Man, if we look to final causes, may be regarded as the centre of the world, insomuch that if man were taken away from the world, the rest would seem to be all astray, without aim or purpose.[7]

Using this new science, humanity could now define, explain, and understand nature for the benefit of society. The universe was no longer based on spiritual or mythical forces, but rather worked according to natural laws. Controlling nature was now within the realm of humanity's understanding. Nature could be manipulated, without God's help, by the power of human intelligence.

The **Enlightenment,** during the eighteenth century, marked the end of the medieval period and the birth of modern humanism. The Enlightenment was an age when reason, nature, happiness, progress, and liberty were the dominating themes of intellectuals and progressive thinkers. Since the time of the ancient Greeks and Romans, Western culture believed that the universe was controlled by order and law: natural laws of economics, politics, and morality, as well as physics and astronomy. In fact, they believed that modern humanity had progressed both materially and spiritually and had become equal to, if not better than, the ancient Greeks and Romans. In 1750 French economist and statesman Anne-Robert-Jacques Turgot (1727–1781) argued that history was humanity's slow struggle to discover the scientific method. Enlightenment thinkers believed that humanity was progressing consistently, if slowly. The goal had become happiness, not salvation. By combining new scientific thinking with the concept of an absent or uninterested God, humanity and society could perfect themselves without holy intervention. Devoid of this religious element, humanity maintained its superiority, and nature became just one more machine to take apart and analyze.

One of the major religious influences during the Enlightenment was Deism. Also known as the Great Watchmaker Theory, **Deism** is the belief that God is the creator of the world but not its redeemer. The basic idea is that God created everything, comparable to the assembly of a greatly complex and beautiful watch, and then left the completed work unattended for nature to operate. At some point, humanity, one cog in this watch, fell out of place. Because humanity was no longer in harmony with nature, humanity must use its ability to reason and the scientific method to discover how the machine worked and to find its natural place in the mechanism. God would not help. Prayer was useless. Miracles were not forthcoming. Humanity had only itself, and those who followed this thinking were confident that that would be enough. Deism further encouraged the view that nature is essentially mechanical, is absent of spirituality, and could be used like a machine if its various parts were properly understood.

Deists believed that morality was common to all people, that good behavior made people happy, and that people would act in this natural way if they were free from ignorance. According to this belief, a major source of this ignorance was the dogma and ritual created by superstitious people who relied on the fear of metaphysical powers to limit humanity's baser behavior. Some people took this thinking to the extreme. They became atheists, convinced that a god was no longer necessary in a scientific age when people themselves could solve humanity's problems. Many Protestants tried to combine Christian beliefs with rationalism and created Protestant liberalism, which understood scripture as metaphors for moral living rather than as a factual account of God's word and which abandoned traditional, literal interpretations. Many Protestants also could not understand the intellectualism and cold rationality of a philosophy that held little hope for the poor, uneducated, socially limited, or spiritually hungry. Deism did nothing for those who felt that any philosophy or religion should meet the emotional needs of humans. Catholics had fewer questions because church officials simply forbade them to listen or adhere to such doctrines.

Persuasive and difficult to refute, Deism gained many followers. It was firmly based on rationalism, a belief in what one knows, rather than on the more-difficult-to-prove concept of faith. Still, the link to the Christian tradition was not entirely severed. Humanity remained dominant and held nature subordinate to its needs; only now, this relationship resulted from human ability instead of God's will.

Social and Political Thought in the Eighteenth Century

By the eighteenth century, because of the influence of the scientific revolution, many people accepted only what they could observe and shunned metaphysical explanations. Nature was now a set of physical laws that had to be discovered and then used to support human endeavors. This approach reinforced the belief that the universe worked according to mechanical principles, which determined human behavior.

The views of the American colonists were influenced by Europeans, the most influential thinkers of this time. In 1776, the same year that

Great Britain's thirteen colonies in North America declared their independence, Adam Smith (1723–1790), who wrote *Inquiry into the Nature and Causes of the Wealth of Nations,* built the foundation of science and political economy. His support of free trade—a system of natural liberty of trade and commerce—became authoritative in politics as well as in economics. Such concepts as supply and demand formed the basis of this natural law of economics. Montesquieu (1689–1755) applied the methods of natural science to the study of society and in 1748 published *The Spirit of the Laws,* which suggested that the differing forms of governments throughout the world arose as reactions to the environments in which they exist. Thus, different penalties for the same crime exist in different climates. In 1762 Jean-Jacques Rousseau (1712–1778) wrote *The Social Contract,* in which he argued for a new politics of democracy, upholding the principle that a nation's rightful authority is the general will of the people. He based his argument on the idea that humanity had lost the perfection it once enjoyed in a precivilized world. Society could fabricate only a less ideal condition by instituting a majority rule system. These philosophers believed that human conduct was determined not by spiritual influences but, as in the material world, by scientific principles.

The more radical of these thinkers formed "Les Philosophes." A key member of this social group was Baron Paul Henri d'Holbach (1723–1789) who, in his book *The System of Nature* (1770), presented an extreme philosophy of atheism and materialism. For d'Holbach, humans were machines, not even blessed with free will, and should accept the basic cause-and-effect dynamics of our personal natures. There was no sense in attempting to explain our ignorance with superstitious and mythical explanations. d'Holbach wrote,

> Let us, then, be content with an honest avowal, that Nature contains resources of which we are ignorant: but never let us substitute phantoms, fictions, or imaginary causes, senseless terms for those causes which escape our research: because, by such means we only confirm ourselves in ignorance, impede our inquiries, and obstinately remain in error.

The key to the beliefs of d'Holbach and the other philosophers is that humanity towers above nature because of humanity's capacity for thought and rational decision making. With these abilities, people could decode nature's laws and more efficiently tame it for the betterment of society. The certainty of science was more useful than the superstition of religion.

During the nineteenth century in both Europe and the United States, the philosophical basis of the relationship between humanity and nature was a product of the Enlightenment and the scientific revolution. Human reason replaced the mystery of God, and scientific principle replaced spiritual intervention. Nature could and should be subdued to ensure the progress of humanity. Although this concept denied many of the older

Christian assumptions that God controlled and intervened in human affairs, it shared the belief that nature and humanity were separate. This relationship was still based on struggle and the need to exploit nature in order to supply humanity's needs. Although John Stuart Mill (1806–1873) was part of the nineteenth-century **utilitarian movement,** which judged actions as right or wrong according to their consequences, his beliefs echo those of the Enlightenment and demonstrate that its influence remained strong long after its most important thinkers had died. Mill was a committed social reformer who viewed nature as an obstacle that must be overcome to improve human existence. In his *Three Essays on Religion,* he wrote of nature that "Her powers are often towards man in the position of enemies, from whom he must wrest, by force and ingenuity, what little he can for his own use."

Conclusion

By the time the United States was established with the Declaration of Independence in 1776, western European culture had developed a philosophy toward nature that emphasized materialism and humanity's right to dominate its environment. Throughout the Middle Ages and the Enlightenment, this attitude was expanded on the basis of either biblical interpretation or scientific reasoning. The means differed, but the conclusion was the same: it was natural for humanity to continue its struggle against nature. The technological advancements of this time helped people overcome their environment and reap a higher standard of living from it. Using technology to tame nature was a lesson that Europeans brought with them to the New World—and one they would energetically apply in taming their new environment.

Chapter Notes

1. Lynn White, Jr., "The Historical Roots of Our Ecological Crisis," *Science* 125, March 10, 1967, 1205.
2. Philip Shabecoff, *A Fierce Green Fire: The American Environmental Movement* (New York: Hill and Wang, 1993), 126.
3. White, "Historical Roots," 1207.
4. Ibid.
5. John Steele Gordon, "The American Environment: The Big Picture Is More Heartening Than All the Little Ones," *American Heritage,* Oct. 1993, 34.
6. Ibid.
7. Clive Ponting, *A Green History of the World* (London: Penguin Books, 1991), 148.

The Indian and buffalo—joint and original
tenants of the soil, and fugitives together
from the approach of civilized man.
—GEORGE CATLIN

2

The 1400s through the 1700s: Inhabiting a New Land

*B*ritish colonization of North America began in the seventeenth century and continued well into the nineteenth century. The colonists' belief that they had a God-given right to inhabit the continent was a driving force as they created a new nation—the United States of America.

From the Atlantic Ocean to the Pacific, these **Euro-Americans** increasingly organized their ownership of the land as they established settlements, territories, and eventually states. In their way stood natural challenges and the Native American people. They overcame both through ingenuity and determination. They completed their conquest with such speed and single-mindedness that by 1860 Americans had reached the Pacific Ocean, effectively subduing the Native Americans and much of the environment of North America in their wake.

The values and attitudes these Euro-Americans displayed during the colonial period set a precedent for how nature should be treated that continues to influence both pro-environmentalists and antienvironmentalists to this day. The communities and frontier explorers debated whether nature exists simply to supply humanity with its material needs, or has a spirituality that benefits humanity but should be respected for its intrinsic value; that is, "Nature for Nature's sake." This question became the inheritance of later generations.

Euro-Americans initially answered this question with **Old World** attitudes and traditions. Their Judeo-Christian tradition and materialistic philosophy also played an important role. As Daniel Friedenberg describes it,

> They shared an obsessive desire to succeed, prodded forward by burning memories of hunger or social abasement at home. They felt free of the

constraints of Europe but, paradoxically, wanted to succeed in establishing values that were imitative of Europe.[1]

Native Americans as Prototypical Environmentalists

The aboriginal residents of North America, or Native Americans, played a significant role in the development of the environmental movement in the United States. They not only fought against Euro-American colonists' efforts to occupy their land, but they also provided an alternative to traditional Old World values. Over the years people have romanticized the Native American lifestyles and beliefs, viewing Native Americans as prototypical environmentalists—a people in harmony with nature, who, like the wild animals, occupied their environment without resorting to the excesses commonly attributed to Euro-American culture. Environmental historians, however, challenge the myth that all of the many Native Americans tribes lived in perfect harmony with their environment. Arthur McEvoy, of Northwestern University, argues that preindustrial societies, like the Native Americans, exploited nature to the limits of their technology.[2] University of Wisconsin historian William Cronon agrees, stating, "Environmental history reminds us that the landscape we take to be eternal has been heavily altered by people."[3]

Native Americans were multicultural, with a variety of customs, values, and social practices. Their relationships with the environment also varied. Some tribes were hunters and gatherers, others semiagriculturists, and many, like the Iroquois and the Creek, had mixed economies. They obtained from their environment the sustenance they needed by the most efficient means available to them. Sometimes this meant that waste or the destruction of nature occurred. Yet the harm Native Americans did to nature seems almost inconsequential compared with the destructive behavior of Euro-Americans. This perception has influenced the thinking of many nature lovers and made the Native American an icon of today's environmental movement.

Despite the diversity of their societies, Native Americans did share a respect for their environment. In a practical sense they had a limited ability to alter their environment, neither possessing nor developing the necessary technology. Their lifestyles also contributed to an ingrained appreciation of nature's gifts. The trees, rivers, mountains, and wildlife were essential to their existence, and this dependence bred reverence. Like those of nontechnological societies, Native American philosophies and religions emphasized a sense of interrelationship between humanity and nature, one that does not exist in the Judeo-Christian tradition. This view is consistent with the ancient and widespread Native American religion of **animism**, which believes that the spirituality of nature inhabits everything. This same belief appears in the holy writings of the Hindus, in African traditional religions, as well as in Native American oral traditions. Standing Bear, of the Lakota, described this belief among his people.

> The Lakota was a true naturalist—lover of Nature. He loved the earth and all things of the earth, the attachment growing with age. The Old people came literally to love the soil and they sat or reclined on the ground with a feeling of being close to a mothering power. . . . The Lakota could despise no creature, for all were of one blood, made by the same hand, and filled with the essence of the Great Mystery.[4]

This conviction greatly influenced Native Americans' behavior as well as their relationship to the environment. However, this is an ideal Native Americans sought to achieve, not a reality practiced on the grand scale often attributed to them. Native American beliefs and lifestyles remain an important and relevant example for the environmental movement, though stripping away the myth shows the complexity of their societies and places them more realistically in the history of the United States.

The first humans arrived in North America when a temporary land bridge from Asia formed across the Bering Strait during the last ice age, circa 40,000–15,000 B.C.E. Groups of hunters and gatherers quickly followed the herds that migrated over the land bridge and, through hunting and agriculture, they contributed to the eventual extinction of Pleistocene fauna and wildlife throughout North and South America. They were not quite the prototypical environmentalists often depicted in modern lore, but instead actively affected their environment. These early Native Americans continued to alter and control their environment long before Europeans arrived in 1492.

Native Americans quite adeptly altered the land to suit their needs. They burned forested areas inhabited by elk, deer, and turkey to facilitate hunting. They also used fire to communicate, drive off enemies, and increase agricultural yields by burning away old growth so that they could cultivate the land more easily. In precolonial California, Native Americans annually burned fields to remove old stock to make grass seeds, an essential food source, more plentiful. In the south Atlantic region, they used "farming in conjunction with hunting and gathering, demonstrating a remarkable ability to blend agricultural innovation with traditional means of acquiring food."[5] Many Native Americans east of the Mississippi River grew large quantities of peas, beans, potatoes, cabbage, Indian corn, pumpkins, and melons as an important staple of their diet. Thanksgiving is a reminder of how much the early European settlers appreciated the surplus corn provided by Native Americans.

Although Native Americans had a closer relationship to their environment than did the European settlers, their methods were at times wasteful, if more out of necessity than intention. For example, hunting bison on foot was very dangerous and by no means assured success. Additionally, food was not so plentiful that hunters could chance an unsuccessful

hunt. So Native American hunters often stampeded bison over cliffs or
herded the animals into corrals, killing more than they needed. In 1804
Meriwether Lewis, the explorer of the Northwest, encountered

> mangled carcasses of Buffalo which had been driven over a precipice of
> 120 feet by the Indians & perished; the water appeared to have washed
> away a part of this immense pile of slaughter and still there remained the
> fragments of at least a hundred carcasses, they created a most horrid
> stench.[6]

A significant reason for this behavior may have been, ironically, the religious beliefs that gave the Native American such a reverence for their
environment. Myths and legends often implied that nature's abundance
was unlimited and nurtured by mystical powers. Historian Dan Flores
quotes a nineteenth-century observer who reported,

> Every Plains Indian firmly believed that the buffalo were produced in
> countless numbers in a country under the ground, that every spring the
> surplus swarmed like bees from a hive, out of great cave-like openings to
> this country, which were situated somewhere in the great "Llano Esta-
> cado" or Snaked Plain of Texas.[7]

This situation was further complicated by the horses imported by
Europeans. Horses became extinct in the Americas about eight thousand
to ten thousand years ago and reappeared only after Christopher Columbus brought several to Española in 1493. As the Spanish spread throughout the land, so did their horses. Many of them escaped and ran wild until
Native Americans domesticated them once again. The horse made the
Native Americans much more efficient hunters and enhanced their ability to cull the bison herds. By the time Euro-American culture reached
the Native Americans of the southern plains (by the early nineteenth century), they had been using horses for more than two hundred years. Furthermore, Euro-Americans arrived in large numbers and brought a
demand for bison robes, creating a profitable market in which the Native
American participated willingly. At the same time, Native Americans tried
to increase the size of their communities as a way to protect their lands
from the onslaught of settlers. Fighting for their very survival, the Native
American was in no condition to contemplate the enigma of the horse or
the advantages of conserving the bison. As Dan Flores concludes,

> Did the Southern Plains Indians successfully work out a dynamic, ecologi-
> cal equilibrium with the bison herds? I would argue that the answer
> remains ultimately elusive because the relationship was never allowed to
> play itself out.[8]

Still, Native Americans usually did not waste what their labor managed
to reap. They used every part of the bison: meat for food, hides for clothing and shelter, muscles and sinew for thread and bowstrings, bones for

tools, horns for eating utensils, and dung for fuel. In comparison to the European settlers, the efforts of Native Americans to modify their environment were minuscule. Their example, even stripped of its mythical trappings, continues to influence environmentalists who seek a philosophy more compatible with an environmentally "friendly" lifestyle.

Early Colonial Environmental Attitudes

Most colonists came to the New World for the power to practice their religion without persecution, the right to have a say in their government, the ability to obtain wealth and improve their material well-being, and the security they lacked in the Old World. Their attitudes and values, particularly the concepts of landownership and its use, continue to be a philosophical benchmark in this nation.

In eighteenth-century Europe, the key to power and wealth was landownership, which was generally monopolized by the nobility. Colonial America, without a traditional aristocracy, had a more liberal social class system. Although colonists brought their ambitions from the Old World, they fulfilled them in their New World, where they could seek nobility without having to meet the birth qualification. Landownership became the recognized path to riches and high office—creating the New World nobility.

This concept of landownership was new in North America. If white people did not occupy an area of land, the colonists considered it empty and available and eagerly staked a permanent claim to it. In contrast, Native Americans viewed the earth, sky, and waters as communal possessions, precluding the right to own or trade them. They measured the land's worth by its usefulness rather than the material value of personal ownership. This philosophical difference, which would further exacerbate relations between Native Americans and Euro-American settlers, not only is relevant to colonial history, but also remains a strong influence throughout United States history.

Besides the concept of land ownership, Euro-Americans also inherited from the Old World the tradition that land, and nature in general, exist to benefit humanity. They assumed that the environment must be tamed, and to do so they descended on the abundant frontier. The settlers exploited nature whenever possible and by whatever means available. As environmental historian Roderick Nash explains,

> A massive assault was directed at the New World environment in the name of civilization and Christianity. Progress became synonymous with exploitation. Men slashed the earth in pursuit of raw materials. The strength of individualism and competitiveness in the American value system supported the pioneer's (and his descendant, the entrepreneur's) insistence that the land he owned could be used as he willed. The long

term interest of society made little difference. Consideration of immediate profit dictated the relationship with the land. A scarcity of natural resources? Absurd! Over the next ridge was a cornucopia of wood, water, soil, and game![9]

It is still a popular belief that nature will replenish itself or, if necessary, that humanity will find a way to replace nature's losses.

The establishment of the British colonies in North America shows how colonists brought with them the Old World tradition that nature existed solely for the purpose of supporting human needs. The London Company established the first successful English settlement in North America at Jamestown, Virginia, in April 1607. Its primary motivation was a quest for gold and the long-sought northwest passage to Asia. The settlers also had a pious interest in converting what they termed the "pagan" Indians to Christianity. Initially, poor leadership, futile attempts to find gold, and sickness killed more than half the hundred settlers. Eventually John Smith, one of the survivors, provided the leadership the settlers needed to survive that first winter, although the colony remained unstable for the next decade.

Almost from the beginning, the Virginians were fixated by the desire to own land. In response, the Virginia Company granted a charter to settle the colony. This charter gave fifty acres of land to colonists for each person they brought to Virginia. Still this was not enough, and colonists often reported immigration of nonexistent settlers. By 1650 some Virginians had amassed estates measuring thousands of acres.

This **land jobbery**, illegally manipulating the system to obtain extra land, could not fulfill all the colonists' ambitions. Not until the "Siamese twins of tobacco and slavery" were fully established did the colony became secure.[10] John Rolfe, a Virginia colonist, found an economic base for the colony's future growth and prosperity in tobacco. Virginia exported 2,500 pounds of tobacco in 1616, 30,000 pounds in 1618, and 500,000 pounds in 1627. Settlers planted tobacco seeds everywhere, including the streets and graveyards of Jamestown. At first, labor was generally supplied by white indentured servants, but in 1619 a Dutch trader sold some twenty black slaves and set in motion the future economy of Virginia. By the 1680s the British Royal African Company was efficiently supplying black slaves from Africa to Virginia. This trade became particularly important as new regulations in Britain were making it more difficult to obtain white indentured labor.

The plantations of the Virginia "aristocracy" continually required new injections of fertile land to replace the soil depleted by tobacco, a crop notorious for its consumption of nutrients. The aristocracy also joined speculative ventures aimed at profiting from the resale of fertile land to immigrants, who in turn grew tobacco and speculated.[11] (In fact, gambling on the profitability of land was common throughout the colonies. Such noteworthy northerners as Benjamin Franklin made fortunes from land speculation.) In the South, the **plantation system** and the initial over-planting of tobacco caused **monocultural husbandry**, which emphasized **cash crops** and depleted the soil. By the eighteenth century Virginia began suffering low yields, as the best lands were exhausted and eroding from overuse. Some colonists were clearly aware that the damage and overuse of land was a serious problem. The famous revolutionary orator and Virginian Patrick Henry quipped, "The greatest patriot is he who fills the most gullies."[12] Yet the southern plantation owners continued to believe that nature's losses could always be replaced. The same attitude existed in the north.

The Pilgrims arrived at Plymouth, Massachusetts, on December 26, 1620. They had originally secured an unincorporated joint-stock company to settle in Virginia, but spotted Cape Cod after a stormy voyage and instead disembarked from the *Mayflower* at Plymouth Rock. They drafted the **Mayflower Compact**, a preliminary form of government based on majority rule. Fewer than half survived that first winter, and at one time only seven people were healthy enough to care for the sick and bury the dead. However, they survived with William Bradford's leadership, Native American help, and their strong religious dedication. By 1691 Plymouth settlers numbered seven thousand.

The Massachusetts Bay Colony was established in 1623 as a small fishing post at Cape Ann financed by Dorchester businessmen. The venture failed and some settlers returned to England while others moved to Salem. When economic depression and religious persecution increased in England, John Winthrop and eleven other Puritans joined in the 1629 **Cambridge Agreement** and pledged to go to Massachusetts. Thus began the so-called Great Migration: seventeen ships and some two thousand settlers crossed from England to the Massachusetts Bay Colony in 1630. By 1642 about sixteen thousand people had immigrated and founded many towns radiating outward from the main settlement at Boston. These Puritans had come to the New World to obtain religious freedom, but their hunger for land was no less than that of their southern compatriots. Roger Williams, a founder of Rhode Island, observed of the Bay colonists,

> They have a depraved appetite after . . . great portions of land, land in this wilderness, as if men were in as great necessity and danger of want of great portions of land, as poor, hungry, thirsty seamen . . . after a long and starving passage.[13]

By 1750 the thirteen established British colonies had a dynamic drive to inhabit and exploit the North American continent. The settlers, beginning with the earliest colonists, assumed that they had a God-given right to subdue both nature and any Native Americans they encountered, all for the benefit of Christian society.

Paradoxically, the first Pilgrims had been saved during that first harsh winter by the generosity of the local Native Americans, who had shared their surplus corn. But the Pilgrims were not as generous when the first recorded epidemic of smallpox, brought to the New World by the colonists, appeared among the Algonkins of Massachusetts in the early 1630s. The disease ravaged the Native American communities, leaving villages littered with the sick and dying and "in some not so much as one soul escaping Destruction."[14] The colonists reported that God was preparing the land for his chosen people. John Winthrop, first governor of the Massachusetts Bay Colony, noted on May 22, 1634, "For the natives, they are neere all dead of small Poxe, so as the Lord hathe cleared our title to what we possess."[15] The disease reportedly swept through New England and reached the St. Lawrence-Great Lakes region, reducing the Huron and Iroquois confederations by half through the 1630s and 1640s.

Disease was not the only outcome of taming and occupying the land. The Euro-Americans were a teeming population, who, although sometimes hesitant about the wilderness dangers, inevitably took the challenge. Edward Johnson, an early colonial historian, wrote in 1653 that nature was being successfully subdued "as God's providence that 'a rocky, barren bushy, wild-woody wilderness' was transformed in a generation into 'a second England' for fertileness."[16] These attitudes soon expanded into the settlers' belief that all of North America must be tamed to fulfill God's will. This view remained strong even after the colonists won their independence from Britain in 1776. In 1779 George Washington argued that the proper cultivation of the wilderness was a priority for the new nation, for "Nothing in my opinion would contribute more to the welfare of these states than the proper management of our land."[17] It did not, however, keep Washington from supporting the destruction of Iroquois crops and land by the military as a means of defeating that people.

Society was progressive during the Revolutionary period in United States history. The population was highly literate: 90 percent of New England's males and 40 percent of its women could write well enough to sign documents, while in other colonies it varied from 35 percent to more than 50 percent among males. In particular, the upper classes lived in a world of print and were greatly influenced by the ideas of the Enlightenment. The seaboard cities where the latest books and ideas from Europe circulated formed the main centers of Enlightenment thinking. The educated established small societies to investigate the mysteries of nature and discuss these ideas. They believed that understanding the laws of nature would enable humans to better exploit their environment.

Thomas Jefferson was a product of this society. A model of the **Renaissance man**—a successful dabbler in many fields—Jefferson was an amateur scientist who became involved in many fields of study, including architecture, botany, urban development, anthropology, music, and political science. He was pro-agrarian, pro-individual rights, and anticentralization. He wrote the Declaration of Independence and foresaw an America inhabited by the common man on small farms that reached across the continent. Accordingly, Jefferson's nation was essentially rural, supported by the cultivation of land, without the problems of cities and a large industrial base.

As the third president of the United States, Jefferson purchased the vast Louisiana Territory in 1803. Without a legal precedent, he took advantage of the opportunity to increase the nation's possessions and allocated the $15 million demanded by Napoleon Bonaparte before either Congress or that French emperor had a chance to review the deal. Then, with typical American alacrity, he sent Meriwether Lewis and William Clark to survey and map the nation's newest acquisition. Their expedition from 1804 to 1806 became a symbol of Americans' adventurous spirit and thoroughness. Lewis and Clark recorded their observations of nature; catalogued the animals, birds, and fish they saw; described the Native Americans they met; and incessantly propelled themselves toward the Pacific Ocean.[18] Jefferson opened the continent to the nation's citizens and acted as a catalyst for further expansion.

However, even an accomplished and far-seeing man like Thomas Jefferson could not imagine the speed at which North America would be settled. He thought it would take a thousand years for his fellow Americans to reach the Pacific Ocean. The immensity of the intervening wilderness appeared overwhelming and the challenge of subduing it daunting. Still, as the United States entered the nineteenth century, its people were fiercely optimistic, determined to conquer the frontier, and sure that its vastness was their new nation's greatest asset. Albert Gallatin, Jefferson's secretary of the treasury and a land speculator, wrote, "The great happiness of my country arises from the great plenty of land."[19] During the 1796 debates on public land he argued, "if the cause of the happiness of this country was examined into, it would be found to arise as much from the great plenty of land in proportion to the inhabitants, which their citizens enjoyed, as from the wisdom of their political institutions."[20]

Conclusion

During the colonial period, Americans were caught in a frenzy of expansion and growth that became the symbols of the age. Nothing could stand in the way of progress as the nation confidently set its sights on the achievements of tomorrow. In the New World, Old World attitudes about nature persisted, leading the colonists to believe that the environment existed solely to support human needs. The abundance of the North American continent encouraged this belief as colonists assumed the wilderness was not only limitless, but also that, once tamed, it would continually provide for their growing needs. This shortsighted approach still influences the thinking of many Americans today. The virtue of growth and expansion—at any cost to the environment—remains a popular doctrine.

The colonial period in United States history is important to the environmental movement not because such a movement existed then (it did not), but because many presumptions about nature's subservience to human needs, which today's environmentalists oppose, were established during these years. Long after Euro-Americans reached the Pacific and the frontier forever became a memory, the achievements of the first settlers would be honored. Their perseverance, ingenuity, and strength enabled them to establish a great nation. However, in their efforts to tame a wilderness, they perpetuated the belief in humanity's right to dominate their environment. This concept was a natural, even necessary, philosophical assumption within the context of their society. Without it, they might not have had the fortitude and conviction to overcome the many obstacles they faced.

Chapter Notes

1. Daniel M. Friedenberg, *Life, Liberty, and the Pursuit of Land* (New York: Prometheus Books, 1992), 23.
2. Alvin P. Sanoff, "The Greening of America's Past," *U.S. News and World Report*, Oct. 19, 1992, 69.
3. Ibid., 68.
4. Standing Bear, *Land of the Spotted Eagle* (Lincoln: University of Nebraska Press, 1978), 192.
5. Timothy Silver, *A New Face on the Countryside: Indians, Colonists, and Slaves in South Atlantic Forests, 1500–1800* (Cambridge: Cambridge University Press, 1990), 38.
6. James West Davidson and Mark Hamilton Lytle, "The Invisible Pioneers," *After the Fact* (New York: Alfred A. Knopf, 1986), 124.
7. Dan Flores, "Bison Ecology and Bison Diplomacy: The Southern Plains from 1800 to 1850," *Journal of American History*, Sept. 1991, 483.
8. Ibid., 482.
9. Roderick Nash, *The American Environment: Readings in the History of Conservation* (London: Addison-Wesley, 1968), 3.
10. Friedenberg, *Life, Liberty, and the Pursuit of Land,* 36.
11. Ibid., 99.
12. John Steele Gordon, "The American Environment: The Big Picture Is More Heartening Than All the Little Ones," *American Heritage*, Oct. 1993, 36.
13. Friedenberg, *Life, Liberty, and the Pursuit of Land,* 73.
14. Alfred W. Crosby, *Ecological Imperialism: The Biological Expansion of Europe, 900–1900* (Cambridge: Cambridge University Press, 1986), 202.
15. Ibid., 208.
16. Philip Shabecoff, *A Fierce Green Fire: The American Environmental Movement* (New York: Hill and Wang, 1993), 13.
17. Frank Graham, Jr., *Man's Dominion: The Story of Conservation in America* (New York: M. Evans, 1971), 14.
18. Stephen Ambrose, *Undaunted Courage: Meriwether Lewis, Thomas Jefferson, and the Opening of the American West* (New York: Simon and Schuster, 1996), 96.
19. Shabecoff, *Fierce Green Fire,* 25.
20. Friedenberg, *Life, Liberty, and the Pursuit of Land,* 359.

I wish to speak a word for nature,
for absolute freedom and wildness,
as contrasted with a freedom and
culture merely civil.
—HENRY DAVID THOREAU

3

The Early 1800s:
Destroying the Frontier

*I*n the zealous rush to expand west during the colonial period, the
settlers simply ignored the damage they were inflicting on nature.
At the time, such reflection was unthinkable. The environment and
the riches it bestowed were considered part of God's bounty: a means for
the American people to spread their civilization and religion and to build
a great nation. The problem for these nation builders was not how to
preserve or conserve their resources—for nature was abundant wherever one looked—but how to succeed in the struggle preordained by biblical scripture. The task had seemed overwhelming to most observers at
the beginning of the century. As American frontiersmen and the pioneers who followed continued to move westward, however, a new philosophy was forming in Europe and America that would challenge the belief
that nature existed only to supply humanity's needs.

The colonists' relationship to nature was patterned significantly on the
experiences they had in the Old World. Yet their experiences with the
vast and abundant American wilderness in the New World also shaped
their views of nature. The colonists were not simply exploiting their surroundings, but trying to transform their world as well. Yet what is so
important about this period is that the earliest few voices of protest could
be heard among the clatter of national growth. These were the voices of
Ralph Waldo Emerson, Henry David Thoreau, George Catlin, and others.
They rejected the narrow, materialistic conception of nature's value,
maintaining that America's wilderness must be preserved for the spiritual
benefit of all. Their warnings grew slowly, as a response to the uncontrolled abuse of the environment during the nineteenth century.
Although these men's protests did not curb the aspirations of the

colonists, they slowly stirred the conscience of many—and became the
roots of the environmental movement.

Manifest Destiny

The drive to move west and conquer the North American wilderness has
been a basic theme of United States history since the first settlers arrived
on the Atlantic coast. The frontier held the promise of renewal, betterment, and the freedom to throw off the shackles of established society. In
1851 Henry David Thoreau expressed the expectations of many Americans when he extolled the virtues of the West.

> Eastward I go only by force, but westward I go free. Thither no business
> leads me. It is hard for me to believe that I shall find fair landscapes or suf-
> ficient wildness and freedom behind the eastern horizon. I am not excited
> by the prospect of a walk thither, but I believe that the forest which I see
> in the western horizon stretched uninterruptedly toward the setting sun,
> and there are no towns nor cities in it of enough consequence to disturb
> me. Let me live where I will, on this side is the city, on that the wilderness,
> and ever I am leaving the city more and more, and withdrawing into the
> wilderness. I should not lay so much stress on this fact, if I did not believe
> that something like this is the prevailing tendency of my countrymen. I
> must walk toward Oregon, and not toward Europe.[1]

It was a movement that Thoreau would later regret, as the wilderness
he loved quickly dwindled in the face of the onrushing frontiersmen.
Manifest Destiny was a term Americans coined in the 1840s to describe
the zeal and righteousness with which they pursued their goal of expanding westward. They believed God had ordained them to spread American
civilization and culture throughout the land. In the first half of the nineteenth century, no longer restrained by British colonial policy, settlers
rushed across the mountains, plains, and deserts at a pace that would
have amazed the founding fathers of this nation.

Western expansion became an unrestrained dynamo, sweeping before
it the obstacles of nature, Native Americans, and even the political powers of great European nations. People flooded to the Northwest and
Southwest after the American Revolution. Mountain men opened trails,
trapping and hunting the high country. They were followed by pioneer-
farmers who staked out homesteads in the valleys and clearings. The
farmers, in turn, were followed by townsfolk—shopkeepers, bankers, doc-
tors, lawyers, preachers, land speculators, and others. Settlers bent on
fulfilling their personal Manifest Destiny quickly filled the "empty" spaces
on the map. Urban centers arose from the wilderness at a remarkable
pace. For example, population, trade, and wealth turned Chicago, a small
town of 500 people in 1830, into a robust metropolis of 4,000 within ten
years. Rising land prices symbolized the vitality of the new city and, as

historian William Cronon explains, created a very confident attitude about the future: "What could be more certain than real estate investments at a site so clearly marked for greatness?"[2]

The expansion of the population and the rise of cities created new markets, which demanded products, food, and land. Chicago and St. Louis became centers for the railroad and cattle, enabling eastern producers to reach customers in the West, and westerners to supply eastern communities with products in return. Throughout the nation, exploitation of the environment became the most convenient and obvious way to supply these needs. Industries grew in the East, farms were cultivated in the Midwest and the South, ranches and orchards multiplied in the West as the nation eagerly sought a great purpose—the civilizing of North America.

By great leaps and bounds, through purchase and annexation of lands, and then the removal of Native Americans from these lands, the United States was stretching its sovereignty across the continent. Texas was added to the Union in 1845 followed by the acquisition of Alaska in 1867. After the Mexican–American War of 1846–1848, the United States gained New Mexico and California. The timing could not have been better for the United States, as the discovery of gold in 1848 ignited the California gold rush and catapulted thousands of forty-niners across the continent. San Francisco became a minor metropolis overnight and a booming new market for businesses throughout the nation. Utah became a territory in 1850 and the continental boundaries of the United States were completed in 1853 with the Gadsden Purchase from Mexico: 50,000 square miles of the Gila Valley obtained for the purpose of facilitating the construction of the transcontinental railroad. In fifty years, from the Louisiana Purchase to the Gadsden Purchase, the United States had successfully achieved its Manifest Destiny. However, little thought had been given to the environment, which nurtured this growth by supplying the food and shelter needed by an expanding population. Instead, the belief was reinforced that God had granted Americans the bounty of nature for the purpose of establishing their nation.

The young nation turned its energy to reaping the rewards for subduing nature. In 1783 the new republic had a population of 3,250,000 people, about one-third of whom (not including Native Americans) were either slaves or in jail. By 1850 the total population reached 30 million people. Between 1851 and 1860 some 2,598,000 immigrants arrived in America. The greatest number came from Ireland and Germany and supplied the labor that the nation needed to take its place among the industrial nations of the world.

Between 1820 and 1837 investment in industry rose from $50 million to $250 million. The Midwest became the leading manufacturer of agricultural machinery, which ranked higher in quality than any available in the world. The steel plow, invented by John Deere in 1837, quickly helped cultivate the Midwest, which would become the breadbasket of the world. In an 1854 thresher competition, an American machine threshed 740 liters of wheat in a half-hour, an English machine 410, and a French machine 250. The 1840s and 1850s saw the introduction of the sewing machine, the vulcanization of rubber, and the production of inexpensive steel and petroleum. By 1860 the United States was the fourth-ranked industrial country in the world.

Urbanization was an immediate result of this industrial revolution. Meanwhile, the population blossomed. More than a million people lived in New York by 1860; the populations of Philadelphia, Baltimore, and Boston lagged behind. Chicago had 110,000 residents, while St. Louis and Cincinnati counted 160,000 each. All this expansion was interpreted as progress—a progress the country did not want to slow by worrying excessively about its impact on the environment.

The railroad went hand in hand with this industrial progress and invention. The steam engine freed energy from natural restraints, such as water and wind, providing energy wherever it was needed. The steam engine was soon adapted for many purposes, most notably for transportation. With these tools, the young nation was now able to overcome nature's obstacles, moving its population and products across the Great Plains, over the mountains, and through the deserts. In 1840 the United States led the world with 3,000 miles of track; by 1850, 5,500 miles of track were added, and by 1860 another 21,000 miles. By that time, $1.5 billion had been invested; fifty-four railroads were granted 10 million acres of land; and Chicago was the railroad hub of the United States. With transportation and energy,

> forests could be cut, fields cleared, dams built, mines worked with unprecedented speed. As a result, in less than a single human lifetime an area of eastern North America larger than all Europe was deforested. Virtually uninhabited by Europeans as late as 1820, the state of Michigan by 1897 had shipped 160 billion board feet of white pine lumber, leaving less than 6 billion still standing.[3]

Domesticating the Wilderness

The plants and the animals that European colonists imported altered permanently the North American environment. Native plant life was particularly susceptible to the hardier European stocks and suffered a fate similar to that of the Native Americans—isolated for thousands of years, many were quickly felled by disease and competition for land. The new plants were so successful that today many European stocks, such as Kentucky blue grass, the dandelion, the daisy, white clover, ragweed, and plantain, are wrongly believed to be native to North America. Seeds often arrived by accident, in settlers' baggage or clothing, or stuck to any number of places, and then were strewn across America as the march westward progressed. The immigrants also intentionally brought trees, fruits, and seeds to transform the wilderness into a re-creation of the natural world they had left behind. Henderson Luelling, an Iowa Quaker, hauled seven hundred trees, vines, and shrubs (including varieties of apple, cherry, pear, plum, black walnut, and quince) along the Oregon Trail in 1847. Efforts such as his eventually created a multimillion-dollar orchard business in California and Oregon.

Nearly a quarter of a million settlers crossed the overland trails during the 1840s and 1850s, distributing new vegetation and depleting the natural resources readily at hand. Timber was especially valuable for firewood, wagon repairs, and other assorted purposes. By the beginning of the Civil War in 1861, many of the timber sources along the trails had been destroyed to such a degree that shortages often caused serious difficulties for later immigrants.[4] The abundant wildlife was similarly diminished.

People living in Europe often interpreted early tales of North America's bountiful animal life as fanciful or exaggerated stories. Yet once they reached the New World, their doubts were quickly squelched. Early explorers reported red deer and fallow deer congregating in the hundreds along the coast of Virginia. In Pennsylvania, gray and black squirrels ate so much of the colonists' grain that a bounty was put on their heads: colonists killed more than six hundred thousand squirrels in one year. Beaver-filled streams were common from the eastern forests to the Rockies, and as early as 1700 the North America beaver constituted more than half of England's total fur imports. Other fur-bearing animals, including bear, coney, otter, mink, marten, raccoon, fox, and hare, formed nearly 40 percent of England's imports.[5] As the frontier moved farther west, the natural marvels of the continent continued to astonish the pioneers. The famed frontiersman Daniel Boone remarked, "No Populous city, with all the varieties of commerce and stately structures, could afford so much pleasure to my mind, as the beauties of nature I found here."[6] Herds of bison roamed as far east as Pennsylvania, Kentucky, and along the Potomac River in Virginia; on the Great Plains they numbered as many as 30 million.[7]

The belief that all the earth's creatures existed to benefit humanity became a frontier maxim encouraged by this apparently limitless supply of wildlife. The early settlers viewed the forests as a rich commodity to be exploited, hunting fox, marten, otter, muskrat, and the ever-popular beaver. Furs for hats and other clothing became the rage of western society and the source of a vast international market. Often with the paid cooperation of the Native Americans, New Englanders managed to **trap out** the local streams and rivers by the end of the seventeenth century. The western pioneers' abuse of the environment reflected the habits of their eastern compatriots, and by the mid-nineteenth century game was becoming scarce in western waters.

The North American bison is the classic case of a species rapidly driven to near extinction. Many Native Americans depended on the bison for subsistence. Their hunting methods were sometimes wasteful, and on occasion they too overhunted these animals—once the horse had made hunting more efficient and commercial markets turned the bison into a more profitable commodity. This attack on the bison herds was intensified by Euro-American pioneers and hunters who not only killed the bison for food and skins, but wantonly killed them for souvenirs and simple sport. By the midcentury a traveler who witnessed this carnage noted, "Buffalo were slaughtered without sense or discretion, and oftentimes left to rot with the hides on."[8]

By the 1860s the decline in the herds began to threaten the survival of many Native American societies and caused food shortages for wagon trains that depended on bison meat to supplement their meager diets. The building and completion of the transcontinental railroad may have tolled the death knell for the bison. Hunters, typified by "Buffalo Bill" Cody, supplied the railroad crews with buffalo meat while many immigrants relieved the boredom of train travel by "hunting" the bison from the comfort of their compartments. Historian Frank Graham describes the resulting carnage.

> Any visitor to the West might observe the destruction, or its telltale signs. The herds, already cut off from one another by the advancing railroad tracks, were harassed by tourists, who fired at them for sport from the windows of passing trains. . . . Along the tracks of the Santa Fe Railroad the bleaching bones of buffaloes could be seen in a vast pile, twelve feet high and a half-mile long.[9]

By the end of the nineteenth century, buffalo robes had become as popular in eastern cities as beaver hats once were. Professional hunters descended, further depleting the exhausted herds. They eagerly killed and skinned at such a rate that by the 1880s the bison was a rare sight on the Great Plains.

As the settlers slaughtered the wildlife, they filled the open lands with their imported, domesticated animals. Signs of this transformation appeared in many forms. By the early 1620s the first honeybees had been brought to Virginia and by 1663 were reported to be thriving "exceedingly." On the East Coast the natural habitat or deer and antelope was quickly cleared to make room for cattle and swine. Inevitably some of these domesticated animals became feral. With their ability to adapt and inbred vitality, they overtook their indigenous rivals. Shortly after Maryland's founding, settlers there complained that their cattle were being "molested by reason of several heards of wilde Cattle resorting amonge their tame." These wild cattle often moved ahead of the colonists so that by the end of the seventeenth century on the South Carolina and Georgia frontiers, cattle were migrating west "under the auspices of cowpen keepers, which move from forest to forest as the grass wears out or the planters approach."[10] With the large domesticated and feral herds constantly dominating the habitats of indigenous animals, the landscape was forever altered.

As the pioneers moved west, they brought their animals. Cattle, swine, and later sheep replaced the native species. Livestock were driven over the new trails, replacing the fast-disappearing bison, and were herded in fenced ranges. By the 1850s, before the great cattle drives of the post–Civil War period, nearly a half million domesticated animals were brought into the West. Their presence limited the lands available and helped to deplete the native wildlife. Their animals were a sign of civilization in a barbarous land. Still, the rapid propagation of feral animals, wild horses in particular, became such a nuisance that even the colonists were alarmed. In Virginia and Maryland, runty stallions often impregnated valuable mares. In an effort to reduce the number of wild stallions, statutes were passed requiring that they be penned or gelded.

The perception that wild horses hindered settlement and progress remained popular among the settlers as they moved westward. One example involves the thousands of forty-niners who swarmed westward to try their luck in the California gold rush. Their arrival created instant markets for goods, which prudent businesspeople found more profitable than the elusive gold. Fortunes could be made by raising and selling cattle and sheep to the hungry goldminers. For these livestock breeders, the wild horses, who feasted on the much needed grasslands, were competitors that had to be removed. The livestock breeders drove thousands of horses off the cliffs of Santa Barbara.[11]

Final Conquest of the West

After the Civil War, the rush west became official government policy. The aim was both to encourage and support those who braved the hardships of the frontier and to eliminate Native American opposition. Some government officials and citizens argued that the Native Americans must be "civilized," Christianized, or humanized. Many more frequently proclaimed that the Native Americans "stood in the way of progress." The first important step in the final push west occurred in 1862 with the **Homestead Act**, which granted settlers 160 acres if they lived on and developed the land for five years. For those who needed enticing, this was a bonanza, promising a new life free from the rigors of crowded, squalid cities. A new generation of pioneers seized the opportunity.

This appropriation of land did not go unnoticed by Native Americans. However, a war with the Sioux the same year that the Homestead Act was passed and the massacre of the Cheyenne at Sand Creek, Colorado, in 1864 signaled that the settlers would not tolerate opposition to white occupation of the western lands. One method the U.S. government used to defeat the Native Americans was the destruction of their environment—a strategy that can be traced to colonial times. Between 1860 and 1864 the U.S. Army destroyed Navajo livestock, orchards, and crops—effectively dismantling the basis of Navajo society. For Euro-Americans, progress meant land possession—and because the Native Americans already occupied much of it, this became the primary reason for eliminating the Native American.[12]

More than land possession, the railroads opened the frontier to occupation. Between 1865 and 1900 the Northeast railroads were consolidated into four main lines: the New York Central, the Pennsylvania, the Erie, and the Baltimore and Ohio. In the South, war-damaged railroads were rehabilitated alongside an outburst of new construction. The railroads expanded their facilities in the Mississippi Valley and began to push westward toward the Great Plains. The transcontinental railroad initiated a new era of travel and settlement.

The transcontinental railroad was the crowning achievement of government-sponsored expansion in the West. Congress donated a right-of-way (preferential access to land) across the public domain and, to encourage construction of the railroad, granted incentives for each mile of track laid. Each company received 20 square miles of land in alternate sections along the right-of-way and a thirty-year loan of $16,000, $32,000, or $48,000 for constructing in the plains, foothills, or mountains, respectively. The railroad was begun in 1862; thousands of Irish immigrants built westward from Omaha, Nebraska, for the Union Pacific, while several thousand Chinese laborers constructed eastward from Sacramento, California, for the Central Pacific. The two groups met at Promontory Point, Utah, north of the Great Salt Lake, on May 10, 1869. The completed railroad enabled the growing population of the United States to spread its culture across the continent; settle the vast plains, mountains, and deserts; and fulfill its goal of taming the great wilderness of North America.

Additional government actions followed to encourage the settlement of less favorable lands. The **Timber Culture Act** of 1873 gave western homesteaders an additional 160 acres of land if they grew trees on 40 of the acres—an attempt to improve land in drier areas. In 1877 the **Desert Land Act** offered 640 acres at $1.25 an acre in states that had little rainfall, on condition that the owner irrigated part of it within three years. The **Timber and Stone Act** sold 160 acres of forestland for $2.50 an acre in 1878. Unfortunately, speculators, lumber-company representatives, and cattle ranchers seized the opportunity to increase their investments and potential profits by exploiting these loosely regulated government policies. In a society that assumed nature's abundance to be inexhaustible, the further erosion of wilderness areas went mostly unnoticed.

In quick succession, government policies and individual initiative successfully turned the wilderness of America into a productive and well-organized supermarket to support human consumption. The great cattle drives, which created the cowboy myth, began in 1867 when Joseph McCoy organized the first drive from Texas to Abilene, Kansas. An impressive growth in head of cattle occurred between 1870 and 1900, rising from 23.8 million to 67.7 million, as access to urban markets motivated ranchers to enlarge their herds.[13] As early as 1874, newly invented barbed wire effectively partitioned the frontier into protected sections.

At the same time, Native Americans were likewise being contained by military power, fences, and reservations. The massacre of General George Armstrong Custer and his troops at Little Bighorn in 1876 was an aberration in a war that Native Americans were destined to lose. The military soon defeated the Sioux and their allies, and Sitting Bull, their most daring and famous leader, spent his final years performing in Buffalo Bill's Wild West show. The **Dawes Severalty Act** of 1887 granted Native Americans personal and private ownership of tribal lands, enabling speculators to buy or steal land that previously had been untouchable by exploiting individual owners. Two years later the Oklahoma Territory, reserved for Native Americans "forever," was opened to white settlement. The final battle between the United States and Native Americans occurred in 1890 when the Teton Sioux were massacred at Wounded Knee, South Dakota. By 1890 there was no longer any new land for homesteaders, and the frontier had essentially come to an end. Three years later, **Frederick Jackson Turner** delivered a lecture entitled "The Significance of the Frontier in American History," in which he declared "the frontier has gone and with its going has closed the first period of American history."[14] All that remained were legends, as the vast American frontier became a lamented memory.

This was a dynamic age in United States history, as immigrants and emigrants colonized and tamed the wilderness. For many, the catalysts for this colonization had been a belief that the "grass was always greener" over the next hill and the promise of a better life. They gave little thought to nature, as land and natural resources were abundant and reserved for their use. Each new settlement, town, city, or "civilized" territory was considered another advancement for the people and a fulfillment of Manifest Destiny.

Renewed Interest in Nature

Although the **romantic era** is usually defined as the period from 1770 to 1830, both Europeans and Americans felt its influence throughout the nineteenth century. During this era, nature again obtained a spiritual power and relevance. The cold, mechanical view of the universe, so popular in the scientific age and the Enlightenment, was joined by a renewed love for the wilderness. A belief emerged that nature existed not simply to be exploited for economic gain but was endowed with a divinity all its own. The interdependence between the spirit of humanity and nature necessitated respect. Humans, therefore, were not more privileged than the animals or vegetation and should act accordingly. Humanity was a product of nature and within nature achieved a harmony that it could not find in the civilized world. In James Fenimore Cooper's *The Pioneers*, Natty Bumppo, a seventy-year-old who had lived his life in the forests, expressed this belief when he found himself trapped in a frontier town and pleads, "The meanest of God's creaters be made for some use, and I'm formed for the wilderness; if ye love me, let me go where my soul craves to be ag'in!"

The works of the German philosopher Immanuel Kant (1724–1804) represent a transition between the eighteenth-century Enlightenment and the nineteenth-century romantic movement. Although Kant believed that human reason was limited by the five senses, he was uncomfortable with the idea that nature was simply a machine. He was prepared to credit nature with having an imperceptible purpose and believed that we should view nature "as if" it were purposeful, even if we could never truly understand it. This did not mean that science and humanity were again dominated by metaphysical forces. Human reason would still conquer nature and, in fact, this was the natural law of life. In short, Kant argued in 1790, in his *Critique of Judgment*, that there was a natural chain of consumption in which each level supported a higher life-form, with humanity standing firmly at the top: vegetation was a product of minerals, and in turn vegetation existed for the benefit of the Animal Kingdom. These animals became the food of the Beasts of Prey and finally,

> What are these last as well as the first-mentioned natural kingdoms, good for? For man, in reference to the manifold use of which his understanding teaches him to make all these creatures. He is the ultimate purpose of creation here on earth, because he is the only being upon it who can form a concept of purposes, and who can by his reason make out of an aggregate of purposively formed things a system of purpose.

His theory allowed room for the unknown, yet order remained the way of nature, with humanity the end product.

Writers such as Ralph Waldo Emerson (1803–1882) and Henry David Thoreau (1817–1862) represent the American view of nature in the romantic era. As leading members of the **American transcendentalist movement**, they rejected materialism and utilitarianism and espoused a philosophy influenced by European Romanticism and Native American philosophy. Social scientist Carolyn Merchant succinctly defined this holistic philosophy.

> All parts are dependent on one another and mutually affect each other and the whole. Each portion of an ecological community, each niche, exists in

a dynamic relationship with the surrounding ecosystem. The organism occupying any particular niche affects and is affected by the entire web of living and nonliving environmental components . . . the idea that the cosmos is an organic entity, growing and developing from within, in an integrated unity of structure and function.[15]

The spirituality of and the belief in the essential harmony between nature and humanity that these transcendentalist writers championed were expressed by **Ralph Waldo Emerson**, who in 1841 wrote in "The Over-Soul": "We see the world piece by piece, as the sun, the moon, the animal, the tree: but the whole, of which these are shining parts, is the soul." This philosophy emphasized the interconnectedness of life, becoming in time a major influence in the development of ecological science and the movement to conserve natural resources.

Henry David Thoreau is one of the most important influences of today's environmental movement. His writings express a deep reverence for nature, a belief that it was essential for sustaining human life, and a conviction that it embodied both spiritual truth and moral law. The core of his argument was an attempt to warn his contemporaries that they were recklessly prizing only the material possibilities of the environment. Thoreau found within nature integrity, vitality, and strength that civilized humanity needed to feed both its body and its soul. He did not merely reject materialism but argued that the preservation of the environment was more rewarding than material gain. That view was a tough sale, presented in the shadow of the Enlightenment and amid the birth of the Industrial Revolution, which forever changed the United States. However, Thoreau's efforts remain timely and continue to raise the consciousness of many Americans.

In 1845 Thoreau moved to Walden Pond, near Concord, Massachusetts. Here he enjoyed the seclusion of the woods and freedom to write, study, and live by the simple terms he preached. For him, nature and civilization were inseparable. He believed each community should have "a park, or rather a primitive forest, of five hundred or a thousand acres, where a stick should never be cut for fuel, a common possession forever, for instruction and recreation."[16] Thoreau was adamant not only that such national preserves should be created but that people should treat nature as an equal. He felt that humans should not "wantonly murder any creature which holds its life by the same tenure that he does." In his essay "Walking" (1851), Thoreau foresaw the demise of the wilderness and lamented its passing.

> I can easily walk ten, fifteen, twenty, any number of miles, commencing at my door, without going by any house, without crossing a road except where the fox and the mink do: first along by the river, and then the brook, and then the meadow and the woodside. There are square miles in my vicinity which have no inhabitant. . . .

At present, in this vicinity, the best part of the land is not private property; the landscape is not owned, and the walker enjoys comparative freedom. But possibly the day will come when it will be partitioned off into so-called pleasure-grounds, in which a few will take a narrow and exclusive pleasure only,—when fences shall be multiples, and man-traps and other engines invented to confine men to the public road, and walking over the surface of God's earth shall be construed to mean trespassing on some gentlemen's grounds.[17]

Thoreau died in 1862 at the age of forty-five, unaware that his message would one day make him a founder of the environmental movement. In obscurity he had laid the foundations for environmental ethics as well as for an individualism that opposed the conformity of the industrial age of the late nineteenth century.

Although **George Catlin** (1796–1872) cannot be classified as a member of the American transcendentalist movement because he did not share many of their metaphysical views of nature, his ideas echo and often presage those of Emerson and Thoreau. As a painter he recorded life among the Native Americans of the Great Plains, and as a traveler he argued for the preservation of the American West. On a trip from Missouri to South Dakota in 1832 he described the wonders of the frontier and deplored the rapid vanishing of the wilderness. In one passage he foretells the disappearance of the American bison and the effect its passing would have on the Native Americans.

Reader! Listen to the following calculations, and forget them not. The buffaloes (the quadrupeds from whose backs your beautiful robes were taken, and whose myriads were once spread over the whole country, from the Rocky Mountains to Atlantic Ocean) have recently fled before the appalling appearance of civilized man, and taken up their abode and pasturage amid the almost boundless prairies of the West. An instinctive dread of their deadly foes, who made an easy prey of them whilst grazing in the forest, has led them to seek the midst of the vast and treeless plains of grass, as the spot where they would be least exposed to the assaults of their enemies; and it is exclusively in those desolate fields of silence (yet of beauty) that they fled, like the Indian, towards the "setting sun"; until their bands have been crowded together, and their limits confined to a narrow strip of country on this side of the Rocky Mountains. . . .

It is a melancholy contemplation for one who has traveled as I have, through these realms, and seen this noble animal in all its pride and glory, to contemplate it so rapidly wasting from the world, drawing the irresistible conclusion too, which one must do, that its species is soon to be extinguished, and with it the peace and happiness (if not the actual existence) of the tribes of Indians who are joint tenants with them, in the occupancy of these vast and idle plains.[18]

Catlin may not be remembered by today's environmental movement with the same reverence reserved for Thoreau. Still, his arguments for preserving wilderness in the United States initiated the idea for national parks and, in particular, the creation of Yellowstone National Park in 1872.

Conclusion

Emerson, Thoreau, and Catlin marked a growing awareness among Americans that the unchecked assault on nature was destroying a part of the American character that could not easily be replaced. However, during the second half of the nineteenth century, these critics and others would remain "voices crying in the wilderness," as the United States embarked on the age of industrialism. Exploiting the environment for the resources needed by a booming nation and industrial base became a common practice during this period. Such exploitation was considered a natural price to pay for progress, as the rewards of mechanization outshone those of the diminishing agrarian past. The environmentalists' cause would take a backseat to the material needs of the nation and remain a minor social issue until the twentieth century.

Chapter Notes

1. Henry David Thoreau, "Walking," *Excursions, The Writings of Henry David Thoreau*, vol. 9 (Boston: Riverside Edition, 1893), 275.
2. William Cronon, *Nature's Metropolis: Chicago and the Great West* (New York: W. W. Norton, 1991), 34.
3. John Steele Gordon, "The American Environment: The Big Picture Is More Heartening Than All the Little Ones," *American Heritage,* Oct. 1993, 37.
4. James West Davidson and Mark Hamilton Lytle, "The Invisible Pioneers," *After the Fact* (New York: Alfred A. Knopf, 1986), 135.
5. Carolyn Merchant, *Ecological Revolutions: Nature, Gender, and Science in New England* (Chapel Hill: University of North Carolina Press, 1989), 66.
6. Philip Shabecoff, *A Fierce Green Fire: The American Environmental Movement* (New York: Hill and Wang, 1993), 20.
7. Dan Flores, "Bison Ecology and Bison Diplomacy: The Southern Plains from 1800 to 1850," *Journal of American History,* Sept. 1991, 471.
8. Cronon, *Nature's Metropolis,* 216.
9. Frank Graham, Jr., *Man's Dominion: The Story of Conservation in America* (New York: M. Evans, 1971), 18.
10. Alfred W. Crosby, *Ecological Imperialism: The Biological Expansion of Europe, 900–1900* (Cambridge: Cambridge University Press, 1986), 179.
11. Ibid., 183–184.
12. Daniel M. Friedenberg, *Life, Liberty, and the Pursuit of Land* (New York: Prometheus Books, 1992), 27.
13. Joseph R. Conlin, *The American Past* (Fort Worth, Texas: Harcourt Brace, 1993), 506.

14. Frederick Jackson Turner, *The Significance of the Frontier in American History,* ed. Harold P. Simonson (New York: Frederick Unger, 1963), 58.

15. Carolyn Merchant, *The Death of Nature: Women, Ecology, and the Scientific Revolution* (San Francisco: Harper and Row, 1980), 100.

16. Douglas H. Strong, *The Conservationists* (Menlo Park, Calif.: Addison-Wesley, 1971), 19.

17. Thoreau, "Walking," 251.

18. George Catlin, *North American Indians Select Letters and Notes on Their Manners, Customs, and Conditions Written During Eight Years Travel Amongst the Wildest Tribes in North America, 1832–1839,* London: vol. 1, 288–295.

*Man pursues his victims with
reckless destructiveness.*
—George Perkins Marsh

4

The Late 1880s:
Building an Industrial Nation

D uring the second half of the nineteenth century, the United
States rose to the status of a world power. Its people consolidated the gains of the pioneers and exploited the natural
resources of the continent to industrialize the nation. As the population
increased because of massive transatlantic immigration throughout the
period, cities blossomed and communities sprung up across the nation.
The Midwest became the heartland of farming, as cities like Chicago and
Minneapolis became hubs of commerce, while the Southwest and West
became centers for ranching, agriculture, and the lumber industry. Mineral mining boomed as the Industrial Revolution caused increasingly
greater demands for steel, construction materials, and chemicals. Partly
as a result of the exploitation of these natural resources, the United
States became an industrial giant and a global leader.

Population Growth and Consumerism

During the nineteenth century, scientific exploration and technological
achievement grew rapidly worldwide, causing the **Industrial Revolution**
and its accompanying disruption of traditional social patterns and values. Between 1865 and 1900, the American economy expanded dramatically owing to the inventive and organizational skills of its people, their
claim to the land's unparalleled natural resources, and a growing population that created a vast interior market and labor source. This period of
industrialization and mass consumption was called "The Gilded Age" by
Mark Twain, who praised the power of technology (and poked fun at the
newly rich, but unmannered, class it created). Using cheap migrant

labor, factories pumped out mass-produced commodities in an atmosphere of fierce competition, for a public whose demands steadily increased in variety and quantity. Building on the traditional belief that nature existed for the benefit of humanity, this mechanized period glorified tools as a means to further exploit the riches of nature. Use of the nation's natural resources during the Industrial Revolution followed a consistent theme—a resource was exploited until it ran out, was no longer economically attractive, was replaced by technological advancements, or was made obsolete by an alternate invention.

The United States population expanded from about 36 million in 1860 to almost 76 million in 1900. At the same time, the nation's wealth increased more than sixfold; it produced goods valued at $2 billion at the end of the Civil War and $13 billion thirty-five years later. This population growth and industrial expansion forever changed the way Americans lived and worked.

Before the Civil War, the United States was essentially an agrarian nation—seven of ten people lived on farms or in small towns; barely 1 million were employed by industry. However, as settlers moved west and new markets opened, industry needed more laborers so that it could supply consumer demands. By 1860 the United States was the world's fourth-largest industrial nation.[1]

The United States had become not only one of the world's leading industrial nations but an urban one as well. Urbanization changed the way Americans viewed nature. It replaced the everyday contact with nature of an agrarian society with the artificial surroundings of city life, and created a sense that the environment was just another source of desirable commodities. In 1830, only twenty-three towns had populations greater than 10,000, the two largest being New York with 200,000 and Philadelphia with 160,000. However, the size of cities doubled every decade, so that by 1910 some fifty cities had populations of 100,000 or more. Most of these, such as Pittsburgh and Chicago, were industrial cities, attracting immigrants and farmers looking for employment and excitement.

Some 14 million immigrants entered the country from 1840 to 1890. Unlike the earlier immigrants who had originated from western and northern Europe—Britain, Ireland, Germany, and the Scandinavian nations—this new immigrant stream began to flow from another source: southern and eastern Europe—Austria, Hungary, Bohemia, Poland, Serbia, Italy, and Russia. Poorly paid, housed, and treated, these immigrants nonetheless became the labor backbone of the Industrial Revolution.

Urbanization fueled economic growth and encouraged business leaders and politicians who viewed the United States as an "economic empire."[2] This urban empire, with its factories, crowded communities, and tenements, created many problems for city planners. One of the most crucial was how to supply water to the growing population. New technologies, which improved pumps, pipes, and irrigation, enabled city planners to devise water and sewage systems by the late nineteenth century that serviced urbanites but, consistent with the times, ignored environmental concerns. The waste of millions was swept into the nearest body of water, cleansing people's lives but steadily deteriorating the rivers, lakes, and oceans. Such shortsighted ends justified the means, it was thought, and started many of the ecological problems of water and air pollution that U.S. cities face today.

As the population increased, so did the urgency for food, products, and land development. To supply these burgeoning markets, industries exploded in number, output, and variety, more land was cultivated, and new uses for natural resources were developed. Markets and economies expanded as mass production enabled sellers to supply buyers with a vast variety of commodities. Demand increased supply, and subsequently the natural resources of the nation were further abused. With improvements in transportation, railroads, shipping, and so forth, raw materials could be brought to a factory, processed, and then delivered right to the retailer's shop or the consumer's doorstep. The distance increased between consumers and the sources of the products they bought. The person who purchased beefsteak from the local grocer or a kitchen chair at the downtown department store had little connection to the cow or tree from which the finished product had originated. Not only was nature being rapidly consumed, but as packaged consumer products nature's bounty had lost much of the reverence it had once enjoyed as the source of life.

Industrial growth also changed the environment and the way people worked. During the second half of the nineteenth century, the factory system, large-scale production, and machine tools became the norm, and increasingly larger factories required armies of faceless workers. By the end of the century men, women, and children operated machines in a variety of industries, such as in auto and textile factories, replacing the craftsperson who had constructed the product from start to finish. A worker was now only one step in the overall process, constructing the left-front leg of a table, for example. This new way of working emphasized specialization and enforced mind-numbing repetition, which resulted in boredom and injuries.

The most famous example of the assembly line system is Henry Ford's assembly line that constructed his Model T Ford in the 1920s. This system helped to establish the automobile industry. The ability to mass-produce cars at lower costs made them accessible to the general public, revolutionizing transportation in America and continuing the trend toward the mechanization of America. The assembly line meant that workers no longer needed complex skills, and in fact were de-skilled so they could be trained, fired, and replaced more easily. The workers seldom encountered wilderness in this mechanical, artificial environment in which they worked and lived. For many, the workings of nature steadily became more myth than reality.

Workers no longer produced at a pace dictated by their skill or personal ambition, but rather at a pace dictated by the machines they operated. Factory owners, with an eye toward utilizing their expensive machinery to its fullest capacity, were determined to find the most efficient melding of human and machine. In the 1880s Frederick Taylor at the Midvale Steel Works in Pennsylvania began to develop techniques that measured the performance and efficiency of workers, which were used to set production norms. **Taylorism,** or scientific management, set the standards for twentieth-century production methods and the measurement of workers as "machines." The ever-changing character of nature became mostly irrelevant to the daily realities of the common laborer, who lived in a mechanized world that emphasized regulation and made a virtue of standardization.

The Industrial Revolution altered life on the farm as well. For much of the nineteenth century, farming centered on the interdependence of land, animals, and humans. As historian Clive Ponting describes it, "Until the nineteenth century farms were dependent almost entirely upon manures and composts produced on the farm itself in order to maintain soil fertility and therefore mixed farming (combining arable and animals) was the norm."[3] Throughout the century this interdependence steadily changed, with the importation of bat guano from South America in the 1820s and the development of artificial fertilizers, such as superphosphates in the 1840s and nitrogenous fertilizers by the 1920s. It no longer was necessary to maintain an interactive relationship between the various elements of a farm.

Mechanization created a new philosophy of farming. In 1837 John Deere invented the steel plow, which quickly replaced the old-fashioned moldboard plow that had been used since medieval times. New machines, such as mechanical reapers and tractors, soon followed. These machines made it possible to more easily cultivate the rich, heavy soils of the Midwest, once the haven of bison herds and Native Americans, and turn the region into the breadbasket of the world.

With the ability to cultivate more land and produce higher yields, farmers actively participated in the Industrial Revolution. Like their factory counterparts, they began to adhere to the principles of mass production; cost, efficiency, and profits (not quality, wise stewardship, and long-term survival) measured success. Farms had become just another machine to be operated to their fullest potential. The relationship of farms to nature was now one of manipulation rather than cooperation. The toll on the land sometimes proved devastating.

Devastating the Land

The wetlands of America, once thought useless by farmers and urban developers, were being rapidly drained by engineers with improved pumping devices by the end of the nineteenth century. Part of this undertaking involved dredging rivers and building canals, all of which changed the water tables. The resulting **eutrophication**, the excessive growth of plant life, often killed wildlife through oxygen loss, and land levels dropped as the waters were drained. Historian John Steele Gordon describes the effects.

> So rapid an alteration of the landscape could only have a severe impact of the ecosystem as a whole. The loss of so much forest caused runoff to increase sharply, eroding the land and burdening the waters with silt, destroying more wetlands. Many animals' habitats disappeared. And because the ancient biblical notion that humans had dominion over each still held, others vanished entirely.[4]

In Florida, which began draining the Everglades in 1883, 90 percent of the 2.5 million wading birds were lost by the mid-twentieth century.

The successes of the Midwest set a precedent for government officials who wanted to open virgin lands of the Great Plains to farmers. Despite the experience of previous generations, which had witnessed the steady decrease of arable land in Europe and America, the U.S. Bureau of Soils claimed in 1909, in defiance of all ecological and scientific principles of the time, that "the soil is the one indestructible, immutable asset that the nation possesses. It is the one resource that cannot be exhausted; that cannot be used up."[5] Even as they made that claim, the early stages of one of the world's greatest ecological disasters were being enacted on the Great Plains. The last Indian territory, Oklahoma, was opened for white settlement in 1889. During the next four decades, about 40 million acres of virgin land were plowed and cultivated with new forms of drought-resistant wheat. Whereas the wheat may have been resilient, the thin layer of topsoil was not. From overuse, drought (the area had annual rainfall of only 20 inches), and high winds, the soil dried up and blew away, causing the **Great Dust Bowl** and resulting famines and dislocations of the 1930s.

However, at the time, the ecological consequences of the Industrial Revolution either were not yet apparent or were simply ignored. Most Americans believed that growth, progress, and profit were the signs of a healthy society, and they boasted that the conquest of nature was the crowning achievement of their society. To many businesspeople, Social Darwinism explained their own successes and the character of the society in which they operated. As expounded by the Englishman Herbert Spencer (1820–1903), **Social Darwinism** taught that struggle is a normal human activity, especially in economic life. The existence of a free people ruled by natural law inevitably leads to some who progress and others who fail—in other words, "survival of the fittest."

For those who required additional ideological reassurances, most compelling was the popular **gospel of success**, which held that the acquisition of material wealth through working hard, overtaking your rival, and applying available resources are sure measures of divine blessing. This philosophy heralded consumption and profitability as the twin foundations on which the nation's success would be built. Trees, minerals, wildlife, and other natural resources were merely raw materials to be processed and sold by the emerging industries. Nature had become a commodity whose worth was measured by the end product: a table more beautiful and more useful than a tree.

Overconsumption of Natural Resources

As historian Joseph R. Conlin notes, "No country has been so blessed with such varied and abundant natural resources as has the United States."[6] Every state possessed some natural resource that could be tapped to further industry. Nature was consumed by the most rapid and expedient means available. The result was an industrial society that could supply its population with a standard of living unmatched in the world—yet at an environmental price that would be paid by future generations.

Minerals, precious metals, and inorganic materials of all kinds were essential for industrial growth. These natural resources were needed to make steel, to burn as fuel, and to be used in numerous processes required by the flourishing factories. Mining quickly appeared in newly established settlements throughout the nation to fill the huge demand for natural resources. From the mountains of Pennsylvania, Kentucky, and West Virginia came coal; from Michigan and Minnesota came iron ore to fuel the engines of industry; and from Illinois came lead. As the settlers moved west, they found new sources of mineral wealth, including gold from California, silver from Nevada, and copper from Montana. California gold may have created the most famous "rush" of fortune hunters in U.S. history, but any site of mineral discovery was sure to attract people seeking riches and employment.

Motivated by the needs and wants of American society, miners dug enthusiastically, at times recklessly. In the 1880s miners used steam shovels in the Pennsylvania coal mines and to obtain iron ore from Minnesota's Mesabi Range. Such tools made extracting minerals easier but often left deep and permanent scars on the land.

In the effort to reach mineral riches, miners peeled away the very crust of the earth, gutted mountains with water cannons, clear-cut woodlands, and destroyed the habitat of wildlife. The waste products of these enterprises were pumped into the atmosphere or piled in remote places. But as demand increased and the mining industry grew, it became exceedingly difficult to continue this "out of sight, out of mind" habit as remote areas became less and less accessible. The scum of coal mines turned streams to acid, litter from abandoned camps covered the landscape, poisons deposited in the countryside killed wildlife, and the by-products of various minerals polluted the air. Minerals were necessary to build an industrial nation, and their extraction made many people wealthy—but again the environmental costs were high as pollution and wastes accumulated.

Resource consumption increased rapidly during the industrial age: energy requirements rose from 8 million horsepower in 1850 to 64 million in 1900 as the Industrial Revolution required more resources to fuel factories, which supplied a growing population with the commodities it needed to progress materially.

Wood was the first resource to become scarce. Before the Civil War, wood supplied 90 percent of the nation's fuel, and charcoal was used to make 50 percent of the iron produced. Early industrialization depended on wood and water for power. In 1870, 12.8 billion board feet of lumber was taken from the forests; by 1900, the amount had risen to about 36 billion. Much of this was used as fuel. As long as wood was available, it remained the major source of fuel for industry and transportation. Stoves, boilers, steam engines, and steamboats remained solely dependent on wood until the 1880s, when accessible wood sources had been depleted.

In the last quarter of the century, coal replaced wood as the major source of fuel in the United States. As historian Clive Ponting explains, "The experience of the United States showed that coal was not utilized until other more easily available and more flexible energy sources were on the point of exhaustion."[7] Coal consumption rose thiryfold between 1850 and 1900, supplying three-quarters of the nation's energy by 1910. The resulting damage to the environment was obvious to anyone who witnessed the gouging of the countryside by coal miners or who lived in urban areas where the air was darkened and fouled by the soot and waste of burning coal.

Coal was not the only resource used to replace wood as the fuel for industry and a mechanized world. Crude oil, often found oozing through the cracks of the earth and floating in the waters of America, had had few uses in the first half of the nineteenth century. Native Americans sometimes used it for medicinal reasons (as a laxative). Euro-Americans made bitumen for caulking ships from it or bought it from traveling peddlers, who mixed it with sugar, spices, and alcohol to concoct a "cure-all" potion. Then, in 1855 chemist Benjamin Silliman discovered a way to process crude oil into kerosene. The poor quickly turned to this cheap fuel for light and heat, although the wealthier classes continued to burn whale oil. But by the 1850s, overharvesting of whale herds made this source of oil scarce, and kerosene became popular among all levels of society.

Wanting to exploit this new market, **Edwin Drake** built the first oil well in Titusville, Pennsylvania, in 1859, and began pumping the "black gold." As the Industrial Revolution progressed, the demand for new sources of lubricants for machines made crude oil a popular alternative to animal and vegetable oils; once again its demand increased. In addition, more sophisticated methods of oil refining enabled industrialists to use oil as an energy resource. By the end of the century, 85 percent of refined oil was used to illuminate homes and cities, while industry consumed most of the remainder. The public was oblivious to or simply ignored the fact that this limited resource could not be replaced and that its removal permanently altered the environment. People had not learned from their experience with wood that simply substituting a depleted resource with a temporarily more abundant one was shortsighted. At some point the resource would be gone, and although an artificial substitute might be invented, that part of nature perhaps would be forever lost.

Once oil-burning furnaces were developed in the early twentieth century, and the efficiency of the internal combustion engine was improved, the use of oil, refined into gasoline, expanded and became the chosen fuel of the automobile industry. Wood, coal, and then oil had become power and energy sources in the industrial age, creating a need for resources that by their nature were limited—because, once consumed, they could not be readily reproduced. Most Americans viewed these improvements in technology and transportation as great social advancements, reinforcing their belief that nature was unlimited.

As the cities grew and markets expanded, the demand for resources incessantly destroyed North America's wildlife. Americans believed that wildlife, like the nation's minerals, woodlands, and waters, was a resource to be tapped and exploited for their needs.

The passenger pigeon is an infamous victim of the nation's reckless use of nature. Huge numbers of the blue, long-tailed, fast, and graceful pigeons filled the sky as far as a person could see, one tier above another. The birds' roosting sites were enormous, breaking tree branches with the weight. Nineteenth-century ornithologists estimated that 3 billion passenger pigeons lived in North America in 1800. Hawks, eagles, and humans were their only natural predators. The pigeons' main sources of nourishment were acorns, chestnuts, and beechnuts, but the settlers quickly cut down those trees, destroying the birds' food supplies. As play, "Small boys assaulted the close-packed flocks with sticks and killed dozens in a few minutes." City dwellers attacked the birds from their rooftops, bringing down as many as a hundred birds with a single gunshot. Commercial hunters who found in the bird a cheap source of meat for the hungry poor of eastern cities inflicted the most serious damage on the flocks. By the middle of the century the pigeons were being slaughtered for food, packaged, and shipped to the cities by the hundreds of thousands; New York alone received three hundred thousand in 1855. The last wild passenger pigeons were sighted in Ohio in 1900, and the last of the species, named Martha, died in captivity in the Cincinnati Zoo in 1914.[8]

The hunting of seals and whales also shows the nation's disregard for other species. The Newfoundland sealing industry began in the early nineteenth century, and by the 1830s hunters were killing about eighty thousand seals annually. The hunting season peaked at the end of February when the newborn seals still retained their coveted white fur. Hunters beat the seals to death with clubs to protect the valuable fur. They killed the parents for their darker fur and oil. Between 1800 and 1915 approximately 40 million seals were slaughtered in the region, reducing the herds by a fifth of their original size. In the north Pacific, from the Bering Sea to California, seals were hunted by Russian traders and, after Alaska was purchased from Russia in 1867, by Americans who by the 1890s were killing a hundred thousand seals a year. For most of the century, the seals were killed as they settled on edges of islands, but by 1910 the numbers dwindled so low that hunters were forced to hunt at sea. The depletion of the seals was so severe that in 1911 Britain, Russia, and Japan signed the North Pacific Sealing Convention, which restricted the area of pelagic sealing, and is one of the first examples of international environmental cooperation. Still, the profit for seal fur and oil was huge, and the killings continued well into the twentieth century.[9] The species was hunted to near extinction.

The whaling industry in America began in 1650 and was limited primarily to northeast towns such as Nantucket, in New England. Whalers first targeted right whales but within fifty years had so exhausted their numbers that the whalers hunted the sperm whale instead. By the end of the eighteenth century, sperm whales also were scarce, and whalers were forced to hunt juveniles to turn a profit. At this point the whaling industry was in trouble. Overhunting the young limited the whales' ability to regenerate. As their numbers dwindled, whalers found it increasingly difficult to find their prey and were saved only by technologically improved boats and weapons of the nineteenth century. As Clive Ponting states,

> The most important developments were the introduction of fast, steam-powered boats and the explosive harpoon, which detonated inside the whale. The invention of the factory ship, which processed the whales at sea and stored the oil on board in vast quantities, also extended the length of time the whalers could remain at sea.[10]

With these innovations, the whaling industry survived into the early twentieth century, finding new markets in processing blubber for soap and margarine and whalebones for corsetry. Oil had replaced whale blubber as the main source of energy and lubricants by the late nineteenth century. Yet the demand continued as nations, such as Norway and Japan, relentlessly hunted the whale, driving many species to near extinction in the 1930s. It was not until the 1960s, when hunting was less profitable and public protests were more active, that moratoriums on commercial whaling were established. Short-term economic goals, even those as limited as the uses of whales, often superseded the need to protect and conserve a natural resource.

American society proved itself resilient and innovative in an age that prized these qualities, but the growth of mechanization distressed

many who felt that the nation was abusing its most treasured asset—
the environment.

Voices for Nature

As urban life and the effects of industrialization worsened, leading to congested cities and growing environmental pollution, many people living in
these conditions sought a reprieve from the pollution, congestion, and
destruction of the environment. People developed a wilderness myth that
popularized an idealistic version of rural America and longingly recalled
an imagined cleaner, healthier past. This nostalgia, as historian Peter
Schmidt, Jr., describes it, envisioned murmuring brooks and "cattle lazily
in groups that need no care, and flowers opening that need no culture."[11]

The back-to-nature movement that developed was more illusion than
substance, popularizing nature writing, art, and travelogues. A common
example is the painting of a tranquil rural scene—for example, sheep
placidly drinking from a stream—hung on the wall of a tenement apart-
ment or middle-class home. But in actuality people didn't want to return
to this idealized rural America. According to writer Frank Stewart,

> Even though they entertained this "Arcadian myth" a dream set in an ide-
> alized rural past . . . few Americans wanted to reject all the conveniences
> of city life. Material comforts were not to be given up that easily.[12]

Yet those who spoke for nature were beginning to be heard and, while
their audience may have been prone to sentimentality, their influence
was growing. The reality of environmental decay was apparent to many
Americans—and so were the warning voices of naturalists.

Early environmentalists such as Henry David Thoreau, who observed,
"I walked through New York yesterday—and met no real and living person," felt that resource depletion and unrestricted exploitation of the
nation's wildlands were destroying the spirit that had defined the American character.[13] In particular, Thoreau drew attention to urbanization and
deplored the movement of people off the land and into the dark, sprawling, and, for him, dehumanizing cities. During the industrial age, lovers of
nature continued to demand that, amid the frenzy of mass consumption,
some consideration must be given to the preservation and appreciation of
America's natural treasures.

George Perkins Marsh (1801–1882), a Vermonter whose varied
career required extensive travel in Europe and the Near East, was one of
the first Americans to understand that the condition of the land was as
much a product of humanity as of nature. In Man and Nature; or, Physical Geography as Modified by Human Action, published in 1864, Marsh
defined the basic principles of conservation for the first time, explaining
the relationship between soil, water, and vegetation through hundreds of
examples taken from environmental history. His basic thesis was that

humanity's "power to transform the natural world should entail a commensurate sense of responsibility. That it did not, he warned, constituted one of the gravest threats to the welfare, indeed the survival, of civilization."[14]

Marsh attacked the older view that nature existed to be tamed and conquered. Cautioning Americans to curb their destructive use of the landscape, he warned the public to change its ways, for

> man is everywhere a disturbing agent. Wherever he plants his foot, the harmonies of nature are turned to discords. The proportions and accommodations which insured the stability of existing arrangements are overthrown. Indigenous vegetable and animal species are extirpated, and supplanted by others of foreign origin, spontaneous production is forbidden or restricted, and the face of the earth is either laid bare or covered with a new and reluctant growth of vegetable forms, and with alien tribes of animal life. These intentional changes and substitutions constitute, indeed, great revolutions; but vast as is their magnitude and importance, they are . . . insignificant in comparison with the contingent and unsought results which have flowed from them.[15]

Such warnings and the obvious dwindling of the wilderness began to persuade federal government officials that some action needed to be taken. Yellowstone National Park, in Wyoming, Idaho, and Montana, became the first publicly owned park in the world in 1872. States, too, began to set aside land to protect what was left of the wilderness. New York turned 5 million acres, 15 percent of the state's land area, into the Adirondack Park and Forest Preserve, to remain "forever wild."

In the 1870s Carl Schurz (1829–1906), U.S. secretary of the interior, began lobbying for the preservation of federally owned forests. Born in Europe, where forests had long since become scarce and thus precious, and where forest-management techniques were far more advanced than those in the United States, Schurz and many others helped to create a new concern for America's fast-dwindling woodlands. In particular, he strongly enforced laws protecting government timber and supported policies for forest conservation during his tenure in office.[16]

Major **John Wesley Powell** (1834–1902), a one-armed veteran of the Civil War, charted the Colorado River through the expanses of the Grand Canyon in 1869 and recorded an eloquent tribute to the grandeur of nature in *The Exploration of the Colorado River of the West and Its Tributaries,* published in 1875. He described coursing through one stretch of rapids.

> A beautiful view is presented. The river turns sharply to the east, and seems enclosed by a wall, set with a million brilliant gems. What can it mean? Every eye is engaged, every one wonders. On coming nearer, we find fountains bursting from the rock, high overhead, and the spray in the

sunshine forms the gems which bedeck the way. The rocks below the fountain are covered with mosses, and ferns, and many beautiful flowering plants. We name it Vasey's Paradise. . . . [17]

In his *Report on the Lands of the Arid Regions of the United States,* published in 1878, Powell continued to praise the unique beauty of the Colorado River. He also took the opportunity to preach a gospel of conservation, saying that Americans needed to take a more responsible approach to the use of rivers, streams, and lakes of the western terrain.

The most famous of the late-nineteenth-century conservationists and preservationists was **John Muir** (1838–1914), a Scottish immigrant who had grown up in Wisconsin.[18] Temporarily blinded by an accident, Muir went to San Francisco in 1869 for medical treatment and quickly fell in love with the redwood forests of the nearby Yosemite Valley. For the next forty years he tramped the rugged mountains of the West and campaigned for their preservation.

A romantic at heart, Muir struggled to experience the wilderness at its most elemental level. Once trekking high in the Rockies during a summer storm, he climbed the tallest pine he could find and swayed back and forth in the raging wind, howling with glee.

Muir became the late nineteenth century's most articulate publicist for wilderness protection. He shared the transcendentalists' idea that a divine spirit flowed through the whole of nature. In his concern for the wilderness, he initiated the ideas of forestry conservation and national parks, and he was one of the first to develop a conscious environmental ethic. His spirited campaign to protect the wilderness contributed strongly to the establishment of Yosemite National Park, in California, in 1890 and two years later to the creation of the **Sierra Club,** an organization committed to encouraging enjoyment and protection of the wilderness in the mountain regions of the Pacific Coast.

In his *Our National Parks,* published in 1901, Muir expressed hope that the spirit of nature might yet save the materialistically obsessed nation from the narrow priorities of the industrial age.

> The tendency nowadays to wander in wilderness is delightful to see. Thousands of tired, nerve-shaken, over-civilized people are beginning to find out that going to the mountains is going home; that wilderness is a necessity; and that mountain parks and reservations are useful not only as foundations of timber and irrigating rivers, but as foundations of life. Awakening from the stupefying effects of the vice of over-industry and the deadly apathy of luxury, they are trying as best they can to mix and enrich their own little ongoings with those of Nature, some are washing off sins and cobweb cares of the devil's spinning in all-day storms on mountains; sauntering in rosiny pinewoods or in gentian meadows, brushing through chaparral, bending down and parting sweet, flowery sprays; tracing rivers to their sources, getting in touch with the nerves of Mother Earth; jumping

from rock to rock, feeling the life of them, learning the songs of them, panting in whole-souled exercise, and rejoicing in deep, long-drawn breaths of pure wilderness.[19]

By the turn of the century the romanticism of the West and its capacity for inducing spiritual renewal was a recurring theme in American literature. Theodore Roosevelt, future president of the United States, in *The Winning of the West* (1889), described the West as a challenge to one's physical and moral character. For Roosevelt, the wilderness stripped away the tedious and artificial habits a person acquired in urban life and revealed the true nature and abilities of that person. Wilderness was the last arena in which people could discover the traditional American values of honesty, strength, and simple virtues.

Owen Wister echoed these sentiments in his novel *The Virginian,* published in 1902. For Wister, the basic physical and social environment of the Great Plains produced individuals like his unnamed cowboy hero, "the Virginian," an honest, strong, and compassionate man, quick to help the weak and fight the wicked. The Virginian was one of nature's aristocrats—ill educated and unsophisticated though upright, steady, and deeply moral. For Wister and Roosevelt, the westerner "was the Christian Knight on the Plains, indifferent to material gain as he upheld virtue, pursued justice and attacked evil."[20] The end of the wilderness could not be allowed if America was to remain a unique and prosperous nation.

Conclusion

In the second half of the nineteenth century, a pattern had become clear: as the population moved westward and methods of travel and communication improved, communities grew and began sending their products to the rich markets of the East. In turn, eastern businesspeople were eager to exploit the expanding markets of the West. It became a symbiotic relationship in which a "gospel of wealth" drove people to seek gain as a natural part of the American dream.

The accomplishments of these nation builders are astounding. However, the resulting damage to the environment was enormous. Whole species were decimated and the land was misused as economic expediency and necessity ruled the day. A slower pace might have made the environmental changes imperceptible until it was too late, but the rapidity of industrial growth and ecological damage began to shock many observers. As George Perkins Marsh foresaw in 1864, it may have been inevitable that such a frenzy of consumption would cause an environmental backlash.

the destructive agency of man becomes more and more energetic and unsparing as he advances civilization, until the impoverishment, with which his exhaustion of the natural resources of the soil is threatening him, at last awakens him to the necessity of preserving what is left, if not of restoring what has been wantonly wasted.[21]

Chapter Notes

1. Joseph R. Conlin, *The American Past* (Fort Worth, Texas: Harcourt Brace, 1993), 434.
2. William Cronon, *Nature's Metropolis: Chicago and the Great West* (New York: W. W. Norton, 1991), 45.
3. Clive Ponting, *A Green History of the World* (London: Penguin Books, 1991), 247.
4. John Steele Gordon, "The American Environment: The Big Picture Is More Heartening Than All the Little Ones," *American Heritage*, Oct. 1993, 40.
5. Ponting, *Green History of the World*, 260.
6. Conlin, *American Past*, 434.
7. Ponting, *Green History of the World*, 284.
8. Frank Graham, Jr., *Man's Dominion: The Story of Conservation in America* (New York: M. Evans, 1971), 25–28.
9. Ponting, *Green History of the World*, 183
10. Ibid., 188.
11. Peter Schmidt, Jr., *Back to Nature: The Arcadian Myth in Urban America* (New York: Oxford University Press, 1969), 6.
12. Frank Stewart, *A Natural History of Nature Writing* (Washington, D.C.: Island Press, 1995), 78.
13. Douglas H. Strong, *The Conservationists* (Menlo Park, Calif.: Addison-Wesley, 1971), 16.
14. Roderick Nash, *The American Environment: Readings in the History of Conservation* (London: Addison-Wesley, 1968), 13.
15. George P. Marsh, *Man and Nature; or, Physical Geography as Modified by Human Nature* (New York: Charles Scribner, 1864), 32.
16. Henry Clepper, ed., *Leaders of American Conservation* (New York: Ronald Press, 1971), 285.
17. John Wesley Powell, *Exploration of the Colorado River of the West and Its Tributaries* (Washington, D.C., 1875), 10.
18. Strong, *Conservationists*, 92.
19. John Muir, *Our National Parks* (Boston: Houghton Mifflin, 1901), 1.
20. Paul S. Boyer, *The Enduring Vision* (Lexington, Mass.: D. C. Heath, 1995), 379.
21. Marsh, *Man and Nature*, 48.

*The outgrowth of conservation, the
inevitable result, is national efficiency.*
—GIFFORD PINCHOT

5

The 1900s through the 1930s: Beginnings of the Conservation Movement

B y the beginning of the twentieth century a new view of nature appeared in America. This change was part of a general backlash against the excesses and wastes of the industrial age as Americans from all levels of society sought to reform the social problems characteristic of the late nineteenth century. During the Progressive Era (1900–1920), Americans attempted to cleanse the nation of the real and perceived evils that had resulted from unrestricted economic growth. Progressives, led by such notables as President Theodore Roosevelt, believed that the purity of the American soul and the simple values of the past, often sentimentally recalled and certainly mythical in proportion, were being eroded by the materialism of the industrial age. This shift in thinking was helped along by the fact that the "never-ending" West had ended. The realization that there was no longer a West to flee to or a wilderness to tame was a shocking revelation.

Correcting the reckless habits of the past would be difficult but, as a product of the Progressive Era, there grew a determined group of government officials and citizens who fought for a more responsible use of nature's resources. This was the beginning of the conservation movement. As historian Roderick Nash explains,

> Up to the late 19th century, in short, Americans experienced a population-to-land ratio unconducive to the conservation idea. But with the ratio reversed, with man in control and his needs pressing against the capacity of the earth to fulfill them, conservation made sense.[1]

After World War I (1914–1918), the United States struggled with massive technological and social changes, adapting to mass production, mass consumption, and mass culture. A metropolitan world seemed to emerge overnight. Technology, along with the many pleasures it provided, enchanted Americans, who found the automobile and a variety of other new machines irresistible. The effects these new toys might have on the environment were generally ignored as Americans sought the good life. Their continued irresponsible use of the nation's natural resources contributed to the Great Depression of 1929.

In the 1930s President Franklin Delano Roosevelt adopted the New Deal to advance economic recovery and social welfare. Federal power grew, while the government assumed greater responsibility for human needs. In particular, the Roosevelt administration increasingly regulated use of the nation's natural resources, because many people believed that managing the environment required a level of knowledge, power, and money that only the federal government could command.[2]

Conservation during the Progressive Era

The population growth at the beginning of the twentieth century was dramatic: in 1900 the population was 76 million, by 1920 it had risen to 105 million. Much of this increase resulted from immigration. Between 1900 and 1915 some 9.5 million immigrants entered the United States, and their labor and ingenuity greatly contributed to the success of the country's industrial growth. They helped make the United States a nation with material wealth and world power. However, this age of consumption and wealth came with its own problems. In particular, natural resources were overused and most Americans encountered social problems such as unequal division of wealth, congested urban life, and poor living conditions. A social backlash was inevitable as turn-of-the-century Americans sought to correct these problems with the same energy that had characterized the Industrial Revolution.

During the first two decades of the twentieth century—known as the Progressive Era—a reform movement arose. It cut across all levels of society, from worker to socialite, as the nation organized in an effort to regulate big business, clean up the cities, and deal with alcoholism, women's rights, civil liberties, and a host of other social problems.

The government became the agency for this reform movement because progressives believed private businesses and organizations to be self-serving or corrupt. Government would control the corporate world for the benefit of public needs and would offer a forum in which Americans could express their views and act on the principles of the common good. One of the most important issues to take center stage during this period was the **conservation movement**. Consistent with progressive thinking, conservationists believed that through government regulation they would be able to limit excesses and encourage both businesses and individuals to use the nation's vast natural resources more carefully. They targeted large corporations as the primary abusers of nature, exonerating small farmers and individuals. As historian Samuel P. Hays explains,

> The agency most responsible for this exploitation was not the individual farmer who typified the earlier periods of American history, but the corporation which with abundant capital at its disposal was able to appropriate large areas of valuable land and often to exact an exorbitant tribute from the people who were attempting to build up the civilization of the country.[3]

Conservation was a movement to create a policy of responsible, efficient, and planned use of resources—not a movement to protect nature for nature's sake. As Samuel P. Hays continues,

> The possibilities of applying scientific and technical principles to resource development fired federal officials with enthusiasm for the future and imbued all in the conservation movement with a kindred spirit. These goals required public management of the nation's streams because private enterprise could not afford to undertake it, of the Western lands to adjust one resource use to another. They also required new administrative methods, utilizing to the fullest extent the latest scientific knowledge and expert, disinterested personnel. This was the gospel of efficiency—efficiency which could be realized only through planning, foresight, and conscious purpose.[4]

Conservation came to mean the proper use of the nation's natural resources as determined by the scientific standards of the times and regulated by objective bureaucrats.

Debates over the proper use of the environment coincided with a wilderness vogue that swept America during the Progressive Era. In 1891 Congress had authorized the president to designate public lands as forest reserves. During the 1890s Presidents Benjamin Harrison and Grover Cleveland exercised this power to save more than 35 million acres of land. Public support for preserving wilderness areas reflected urban disenchantment with the harried, congested lifestyle of the city and a longing for the calm, spiritual pace of the country. Sierra Club president John Muir expressed this perception well.

> Awakening from the stupefying effects of the vice of over-industry and the deadly apathy of luxury, they are trying as best they can to mix and enrich their own little ongoings with those of Nature, and to get rid of rust and disease.[5]

Popular writers, such as Owen Wister, Gene Stratton Porter, and Edgar Rice Burroughs, drew evocative literary pictures of living in the wilds and being closer to nature. Groups such as the Boy Scouts and the Girl Scouts (founded in 1910 and 1912, respectively) gave city children the opportunity to experience America's wilderness areas.

As the wilderness vogue grew, it began to find a voice in politics. Questions of land management and the proper use of natural resources became important issues for local, state, and federal officials.

The most dominating figure of the progressive conservation movement was President **Theodore Roosevelt (1858–1919)**. As a young man he spent many happy hours on the western plains, camping, fishing, hunting, and developing an appreciation for nature. After he became president "by accident," as he phrased it, when President William McKinley was assassinated in 1901, he took an avid interest in the conservation movement, referring to it as "my policy."[6] In his speeches, Roosevelt made it clear that the preservation of nature would be one of his administration's top concerns, declaring "it is safe to say that the prosperity of our people depends directly on the energy and intelligence with which our natural resources are used."[7]

Roosevelt was also a practical politician who recognized that conservation must be balanced by the protection of economic priorities. He believed that the proper use of nature benefited the nation's economic health. As a result, his policies leaned toward a utilitarian approach to conservation, which emphasized the practical use of resources. He expressed this attitude when supporting the work of the U.S. Forest Service.

> The fundamental idea of forestry is the perpetuation of forests by use. Forest protection is not an end in itself; it is a means to increase and sustain the resources of our country and the industries which depend upon them. The preservation of our forests is an imperative business necessity.[8]

As a progressive, Roosevelt believed efficient regulation and practical use of nature were the best methods for pursuing a responsible conservation policy. Government, with science and proper management strategies, would be able to protect and allocate the nation's natural riches more fairly.[9] In 1902 he persuaded Congress to pass the **Reclamation Act,** which funded the construction of dams and canals and the development of water power projects in seventeen western states. It also limited federal water rights to farms of 160 acres or less, landing "the first broad blow for land reform since the Homestead Act of 1862."[10]

Roosevelt maintained an active agenda of conservation activities, keeping the issue in the public mind and pushing for legislation to protect wilderness areas. Although an enthusiastic hunter, Roosevelt had a sympathy—unusual for his times—for wildlife conservation, and he compared the extinction of a species to the destruction of "all the works of some great writer."[11]

Roosevelt, during his two terms in office, managed, by proclamation, to enlarge the national forests from 42 million acres to 172 million acres. Through his efforts, Congress created fifty-one national wildlife refuges, including six in Alaska. Furthermore, he set aside eighteen areas of special interest, including the Grand Canyon and the Petrified Forest, as national monuments.

Roosevelt's sympathy for environmental issues and those who fought for them is shown by his 1903 visit to Yosemite Valley. John Muir and Will Colby, both leaders of the Sierra Club, accompanied Roosevelt and California governor James Pardee to Yosemite Valley and the Mariposa Grove of Sierra redwoods. Muir and Colby took the opportunity to call for the return of Yosemite Valley to the federal government. Roosevelt, impressed by the valley's scenic glory, agreed to support the Sierra Club's lobbying effort. The California state and federal governments followed suit shortly after. In 1905 the "magnificent valley" was restored to federal control (although Congress reduced the park's area by 12,000 acres).[12] With such presidential support, the Sierra Club's membership rose to one thousand by 1908. Among its early achievements was the advocacy and creation of Glacier National Park, Montana, in 1910.

Perhaps Roosevelt's greatest accomplishment was organizing the first Conservation Conference, held at the White House in May 1908 and attended by state governors and officials. They recognized, for the first time, that protecting human health is the main goal of conservation. This principle remains a basic tenet of today's conservation movement and one of its strongest arguments for regulating natural resource use. The commission's report from the conference stated,

> The spirit and vigor of our people are the chief glory of the republic. Yet even as we have neglected our natural resources, so have we been thoughtless of life and health. Too long have we overlooked that grandest of our resources, human life.[13]

Roosevelt's legacy for the conservation movement was best expressed by Senator Robert la Follette: "His greatest work was actually beginning a world movement for staying terrestrial waste and saving for the human race the things upon which alone a great peaceful and progressive and happy race can be founded."[14] Although Theodore Roosevelt was the most publicly recognized proponent of the progressive conservation movement, he was not the most influential.

No one did more to define the conservation movement during the Progressive Era than **Gifford Pinchot** (1865–1946). As a friend of Teddy Roosevelt and a master of public relations, Pinchot became the catalyst and publicist for the progressive conservation movement.[15] Pinchot, after graduating from Yale University in 1889, was the first American to choose forestry as a career. Forestry may have been a unique vocation for the times, though not for Pinchot, who loved the outdoors and admired the writings of George Perkins Marsh. Because professional training in forestry was unavailable in the United States, Pinchot used some of his family's wealth to travel to Europe and enrolled at the French Forest School in Nancy, France. After returning to the United States in 1892, "fired with enthusiasm for the idea of managing forests as a crop," Pinchot was quickly hired as a forester on Biltmore, George W. Vanderbilt's North Carolina estate.[16]

By 1905 Pinchot was the chief forester of the U.S. Department of Agriculture. That same year President Roosevelt appointed him to head the new U.S. Forest Service. In his autobiography Pinchot recalled how, as head forester in America, he developed a new philosophy for the Forest Service.

> Suddenly the idea flashed through my head that there was a unity in this complication—that the relation of one resource to another was not the end of the story. Here were no longer a lot of different, independent, and often antagonistic questions, each on its own separate little island, as we had been in the habit of thinking. In place of them, here was one single question with many parts. Seen in this new light, all these separate questions fitted into and made up the one great central problem of the use of the earth for the good of man.
>
> To me it was a good deal like coming out of a dark tunnel. I had been seeing one spot of light ahead. Here, all of a sudden, was a whole landscape. Or it was like lifting the curtain on a great new stage.
>
> It took time for me to appreciate that here were the makings of a new policy, not merely nationwide but world-wide in its scope—fundamentally important because it involved not only the welfare but the very existence of man on the earth. I did see, however, that something ought to be done about it. . . . [17]

Pinchot determined that "The object of our forest policy is not to preserve the forests because they are beautiful . . . or because they are refuges for the wild creatures of the wilderness. The forests are to be used by man. Every other consideration comes secondary."[18] He campaigned not for the protection of nature for nature's sake, but for the planned, regulated use of the nation's forest lands for various public and commercial purposes. To achieve this goal Pinchot surrounded himself with scientific experts. Samuel P. Hays observes,

> Conservation, above all, was a scientific movement, and its role in history arises from the implications of science and technology in modern society. Conservation leaders sprang from such fields as hydrology, forestry, agrostology, geology, and anthropology. Vigorously active in professional circles in the national capital, these leaders brought the ideals and practices of their crafts into federal resource policy. Loyalty to these professional ideals, not close association with the grass-roots public, set the tone of the Theodore Roosevelt conservation movement. Its essence was rational planning to promote efficient development and use of all natural resources.[19]

It was Pinchot and some of these scientists who named the conservation movement. They agreed that the most efficient means to exploit the nation's natural resources was to develop them under government rather than private supervision. As historian Frank Graham describes it,

> During one of the discussions among Pinchot and his colleagues someone mentioned that the government-owned forests in India were called "conservancies," and then the talk returned to their own hopes for the forests.
>
> "The idea was so new," Pinchot recalled later, "that it did not even have a name. Of course it had to have a name. Our little inside group discussed it a great deal. Finally, Overton Price suggested that we call it 'conservation,' and the President said 'O.K.' So we called it the conservation movement."[20]

Under Pinchot's direction, conservation came to mean a belief in using the nation's natural resources to benefit humanity as dictated by objective government employees who were supposedly free from the self-interest that plagued profit-oriented commercial enterprises. Although they united to fight the common enemy of corporate excesses, they clearly disagreed about how to regulate the nation's resources. **Conservationists** believed in the regulated exploitation of nature, or "right use," while **preservationists** argued for the protection of nature for its own sake. As historian Robert Gottlieb explains,

> During the seven years of the Roosevelt administration, when conservationism emerged as the country's dominant resource strategy and when the conservationist's agencies became central to the formation of these resource strategies, the first sharp divisions between those primarily focused on "preservation" and those linked to "right use" also emerged.[21]

Political and civil service officials, led by Pinchot's conservationist views, soon dominated this debate as government policies based on their views became law. The efforts of the conservationists culminated with Roosevelt's 1908 Conservation Conference. Pinchot purposely excluded John Muir, a preservationist, from the meeting, preferring to promote and publicize only the views of conservationists. The conference became one more example of how the utilitarian principle represented the progressive conservation movement.

Pinchot's policies won further victories in the West. In that region, controversies over land use burst into the political arena as mining and timber interests, farmers, ranchers, sheep growers, city officials, and preservationists presented competing claims to the proper use of land. Whereas western business interests and their supporters preached maximum exploitation of the region's resources, conservationists argued for efficient use and preservationists fought for *non*use. That Washington and federal officials in general were clearly out of step with the western philosophy is described by Roderick Nash.

For most Westerners, conservation (they sometimes called it "Pinchotism") was the arbitrary and un-American policy of snobbish Eastern bureaucrats unsympathetic to the needs and desires of the West. Closer to what remained of the frontier, whose myth of inexhaustibility was still alive, Western resource users regarded every reservation or restriction as a "locking up" of raw material and a limitation on individual enterprise.[22]

Theodore Roosevelt was sympathetic to environmental concerns but was also swayed by political pressures. Conservationists, whose rational use of nature appeared to present a balanced approach to environmental issues, seemed to be President Roosevelt's best political choice. Thus, conservationist policies that regulated land use, water, and forestry were instituted in the West. Many western businesses and public interests protested, but had few significant victories.

Although Washington officials were predominantly conservationists, activists with alternate views found ways to influence legislators and the public. In particular, preservationist groups such as the Sierra Club sought to protect large wilderness areas for their pristine beauty and aesthetic appeal. The group's original mission was, "To explore, enjoy, and render accessible the mountain regions of the Pacific Coast; to publish authentic information concerning them; to enlist the support and cooperation of the people and government in preserving the forest and other natural features of the Sierra Nevada Mountains."[23]

Sierra Club founders had mixed feelings about Gifford Pinchot's Forest Service. The group appreciated that the Forest Service safeguarded the land against irresponsible use, but was concerned that Pinchot's conservationist policies would eventually lead to commercial misuse. Pinchot's utilitarian outlook and right-use policies, they maintained, ignored the spiritual benefits of the wilderness. Preserving nature was essential, John Muir argued, to improve human life: "Everybody needs beauty as well as bread, places to play in and pray in, where Nature may heal and cheer and give strength to body and soul."[24] Professional conservationists often retorted that preservationists were ill informed and dismissed them as sentimental amateurs.

The struggle between preservationists and conservationists continued even after Theodore Roosevelt left office. This struggle became a national issue with the bitter 1912–1913 fight over proposals to dam the Tuolumne River in Yosemite National Park. When San Francisco officials saw Hetch Hetchy Valley, a vision of natural beauty carved by centuries of glaciers and the Tuolumne River, they saw only a solution to their city's serious water shortage. A dam at the valley's mouth would create an immense reservoir, more than sufficient to supply San Francisco with the water it needed, and would pay for itself as a hydroelectric power source. But Hetch Hetchy was within the borders of Yosemite National Park, which Congress established in 1890, and the secretary of the interior refused San Francisco's application to dam the Tuolumne. The city's officials persisted and in 1908, two years after the devastating San Francisco earthquake, they applied again. This time a more sympathetic secretary acquiesced.[25]

The Sierra Club organized opponents to the dam, confident they could persuade Congress to deny the application. John Muir and his comrades alerted conservation groups across the nation and published magazine articles warning that the reservoir's waters would forever hide the valley's beauty. Muir denounced the dam's supporters.

> These temple destroyers, devotees of ravaging commercialism, seem to have a perfect contempt for Nature, and instead of lifting their eyes to the God of the Mountains, lift them to the Almighty Dollar. Dam the Hetch Hetchy! As well dam for water tanks the people's cathedrals and churches, for no holier temple has ever been consecrated by the heart of man.[26]

The project attracted powerful backers, including Theodore Roosevelt and Gifford Pinchot, who said,

> The first great fact about conservation is that it stands for development. Conservation does mean provision for the future, but it means also and first of all the recognition of the right of the present generation to the fullest necessary use of all the resources with which this country is so abundantly blessed.[27]

San Franciscans also fought strongly for the dam. They called Muir's arguments "verbal lingerie," and pointed out that, in addition to the practical benefits for the city, the dam would create a lake at Hetch Hetchy, which would make a wonderful recreational spot for swimmers, fishers, and water enthusiasts of all kinds.[28]

The conflict came to a climax in 1913 with hearings before the Public Lands Committee of the U.S. House of Representatives. With the support of Pinchot, western politicians, and land use advocates, Congress passed the Hetch Hetchy Dam bill by a large margin later that year. Muir was shocked and depressed by the loss but attempted to put on a brave front in a letter to the secretary of the Sierra Club.

> Never mind, dear Colby, the present flourishing triumphant growth of the wealthy wicked, the Phelands (sic) [mayor of San Francisco], Pinchot and their hirelings, will not thrive forever. . . . We may lose this particular fight, but truth and right must prevail at last.[29]

John Muir died a year later of pneumonia, caused perhaps by the stress and disappointment of his defeat.

The first water reached San Francisco from the new reservoir in 1934. Although the dam's opponents lost the battle, the struggle had a larger meaning. Hetch Hetchy helped put wilderness preservation squarely on the public agenda. For more than five years, the American public had debated the aesthetic ramifications of a major public-works project. Such a debate would have been inconceivable in the nineteenth century.

Despite the loss of the Hetch Hetchy Valley, preservationists won important victories during the Progressive Era, thanks in part to their skill in using magazine articles to rally public support. For example, private citizens groups campaigned and saved a large grove of California's giant redwoods as well as a lovely stretch of the Maine coastline from commercial depredation. In 1906 Congress passed the Antiquities Act to protect ancient archaeological sites, especially in the Southwest. A number of these sites eventually became national parks. The national park system also found surer footing during these years. Beginning with Yellowstone in 1872, thirteen national parks were created by 1916. The number of park visitors surged from 69,000 in 1908 to 335,000 in 1915, compelling Congress to create the **National Park Service** in 1916 to oversee these priceless preserves. Most important, environmental issues became matters of intense national concern for the first time during the Progressive Era, despite the differences between conservationists and preservationists, and those between state and federal officials. Support for conservation issues declined in the following decade as economic and technological innovations dominated public interest.

Environmental Decay during the Roaring Twenties

The decade following World War I was a time of economic growth and social change in the United States. The Roaring Twenties was the age of flappers, jazz, and bootleg liquor as many Americans rebelled against Prohibition and the traditional conventions of the past. This carefree attitude followed the prosperity that arose from tax cuts and the government's "hands-off" approach to business, during which they allowed progressive regulations to lapse or simply be ignored. For most of the decade prosperity abounded, but the price was environmental decay and the **Great Depression** of 1929.

An important example of how environmental decay contributed to the Great Depression was the damage done to the land. After the Russian Revolution of 1917, wheat exports were no longer available from Russia's vast plains. To compensate for the shortfall, Americans increased their agricultural production two and a half times the 1914 level, cultivating an additional 5 million acres of new land between 1925 and 1930. Unfortunately, much of this land was unsuitable for such intensive use and the results were disastrous—the Great Dust Bowl. As with wood, seals, and whales, Americans had overexploited a resource for short-term gain.

Unlike during the Progressive Era, the government generally ignored conservation issues during the 1920s, and they did not regain presidential support for nearly a decade. Warren G. Harding, elected president in 1920, presided over one of the most corrupt administrations in U.S. history. His lack of leadership enabled abuses of government power to permeate his administration; one scandal after another plagued his term in office. Harding was particularly uninterested in the need to conserve natural resources. Instead, he preferred the rapid development of resources as a way to improve the economy, and granted private enterprise a free hand in such matters.

One disastrous outcome of President Harding's poor leadership was the Teapot Dome Scandal. In 1924 a congressional investigation found that the secretary of interior, Albert Fall, had leased naval oil reserves at Teapot Dome, Wyoming, and Elk Hills, California, to petroleum companies in return for donations of cash, bonds, and a herd of cattle. Harding's successor, Calvin Coolidge, avoided such scandals, but was as indifferent to conservation issues as his predecessor.

Presidential neglect of environmental issues changed dramatically with the arrival of President Herbert Hoover in 1929. As secretary of commerce during the Harding and Coolidge administrations, President Hoover had displayed a keen interest in resource management, supporting legislation to regulate the Alaskan salmon fisheries, limit water pollution, establish fish nurseries, construct the St. Lawrence waterway, improve inland navigation, and authorize the Boulder Canyon project (now called Hoover Dam). As president, he continued to actively encourage conservation policies, especially for flood control, waterway development, and oil conservation.

> As the first conservationist President since Theodore Roosevelt, Hoover had aroused expectations among conservation partisans. He failed to fulfill their high hopes. His primary contribution, achieved in spite of a severe economic depression, was to rekindle national interest in the orderly development of natural resources. . . . Hoover prepared the way for some of the dramatic conservation successes of Franklin Roosevelt by renewing the image of the President as a conservation leader.[30]

In the 1920s energy resources seemed limitless to most Americans. Pollution and a vanishing wilderness seemed small prices to pay for the benefits of the electric motor and the internal-combustion engine. Inexpensive, electrically powered consumer products, such as the radio and kitchen appliances, and, most important, an affordable automobile, abounded. These items are some of the most enduring symbols of American life. They were made possible by mass production and the optimistic belief that economic progress would continue indefinitely. Yet the damage inflicted on the environment and the long-term effects of depleting ever-greater amounts of resources were hardly recognized during the 1920s and 1930s. From 1920 to 1929 consumption of electricity rose from 57 million kilowatt-hours to 188 million kilowatt-hours. To maintain this energy flow, U.S. power plants consumed 42 million tons of coal, 10 million barrels of oil, and 112 million cubic feet of natural gas. The automobile incessantly devoured even more resources. U.S. oil refineries produced fewer than 50 million barrels of gasoline in 1916, but in 1929 they refined 435 million barrels, consuming more than a billion barrels of crude oil in the process.[31] Power plants, steel mills, and automobile engines pumped hundreds of thousands of tons of gaseous pollutants into the atmosphere.

The automobile revolutionized American life. Americans now could reach previously difficult and inaccessible regions for recreational purposes. A maze of asphalt roads and freeways crossed the land. Gas stations, billboards, restaurants, and tourist cabins quickly followed. During the 1920s tourists and their automobiles became increasingly common sights in national parks, and traffic entering Yosemite, for example, increased more than tenfold. However, human contact meant human pollution, and soon the wilderness was under siege by masses of Americans seeking enjoyment and peace. Tourism became a gauge of success, which transformed the focus of the national park system. Park administrators began to base their policies on strategies to increase the number of visitors.

> In Yellowstone, for example, the Park Service sought to increase the elk population as a showpiece to attract tourists and helped accomplish this by creating an open war on elk predators such as the mountain lion.[32]

There were protests. The Sierra Club and the **National Audubon Society**, established in 1905, continued to work for the preservation of the nation's wilderness and wildlife. The **Izaak Walton League**, organized in 1922 by sportsmen to protect wilderness areas, published *Outdoor America*, a magazine filled with articles by famous writers and personalities who spoke out for the protection of nature.

An important environmentalist of the time was **Aldo Leopold** (1886–1948), who fought for wilderness protection and against the damage done by unchecked technology. He developed a set of ethics in which all forms of life were imbued with the right to a healthy existence. This was a new concept and, as Roderick Nash explains, a unique contribution to the environmental movement.

> Prior to Aldo Leopold, American conservationists had justified their programs in terms of economics or democracy or, less frequently, aesthetics and religion. The emphasis, in each case, was on humanity's well being. . . . The environment, Leopold pointed out, did not "belong" to people, they shared it with everything alive. And because of their power, they bore the responsibility of maintaining it in the best interests of the life community.[33]

Leopold's work helped pioneer ecology, the study of the complex interrelationships between organisms and the environment.

Leopold graduated from the Yale Forestry School in 1909 and then joined the U.S. Forest Service. In 1917 he was promoted to assistant district forester for operations in the Southwestern District. He attracted other foresters' attention for his advocacy of wilderness preservation. He was largely responsible for the Gila Wilderness Area in New Mexico in 1924, the first national wilderness area established as part of a program to preserve forests of exceptional beauty and uniqueness.[34] In 1925 Leopold wrote, "For too long in the United States a stump was our symbol of progress." He added that Americans accustomed to a seemingly boundless wilderness "are unconscious of what the disappearance of wild places would mean." Wilderness preservation demanded not just sentimental pronouncements, Leopold stressed, but careful planning and political savvy. Yet few listened.

During the 1930s, as a professor at the University of Wisconsin, Leopold formulated ideas that are often espoused today by environmentalists. He advocated a land ethic based on scientific roots rather than on religious or sentimental ones.

> In short, a land ethic changes the role of Homo Sapiens from conqueror of the land-community to plain member and citizen of it. It implies respect for his fellow-members, and also respect for the community as such. . . .
>
> No important change in ethics was ever accomplished without an internal change in our intellectual emphasis, loyalties, affections, and convictions. The proof that conservation has not yet touched these foundations of conduct lies in the fact that philosophy and religion have not yet heard of it. In our attempt to make conservation easy, we have made it trivial. . . .
>
> It is inconceivable to me that an ethical relationship to land can exist without love, respect, and admiration for land, and a high regard for its value. By value, I of course mean something far broader than mere economic value; I mean value in the philosophical sense.
>
> Perhaps the most serious obstacle impeding the evolution of a land ethic is the fact that our educational and economic system is headed away from, rather than toward, an intense consciousness of land. Your true modern is separated from the land by many middle-men, and by innumerable physical gadgets. He has no vital relation to it; to him it is the space between cities on which crops grow. Turn him loose for a day on the land, and if the spot does not happen to be a golf links or a "scenic" area, he is bored stiff. If crops could be raised by hydroponics instead of farming, it would suit him very well. Synthetic substitutes for wood, leather, wool, and other natural land products suit him better than the originals. In short, land is something he has "outgrown."[35]

Aldo Leopold died in 1948, fittingly while fighting a brush fire along the Wisconsin River, but his writings remain one of the most important influences in today's environmental movement. Furthermore, his work coincided with a resurgence of the conservation movement under Franklin Roosevelt's presidency.

Conservation Policies under Roosevelt's New Deal

In 1933 President Franklin Delano Roosevelt took an aggressive political approach to the continuing Great Depression and transformed the nation with his New Deal, a doctrine in which the government assumed responsibility for ensuring economic prosperity and the well-being of all citizens. A stream of legislation poured out of Washington during President Roosevelt's tenure as he tried to solve the nation's ills. Among those that have remained influential are Social Security, the Wagner Act, and the Fair Labor Standards Act, which together define the basic outline of the modern activist welfare state. Although the successes of New Deal programs were sporadic and failed to completely solve the social and economic problems, Roosevelt's presidency (1932–1945) was a pivotal event in United States history. The New Deal extended presidential power so vastly that since that time the public has expected the president to initiate programs and to set the agenda for public debate. This forever altered the balance of power between the White House and Congress.

Proponents of the New Deal sought to solve practical problems of business stagnation, unemployment, and the maldistribution of economic resources. As Robert Gottlieb writes, Roosevelt was sympathetic to environmental issues but had to give priority to more pressing economic concerns.

> For conservationists and preservationists, the main order of business during the 1930s and 1940s continued to be the development of policies related to the management of resources or protection of the natural environment. . . . Both approaches, however, were largely subsumed under the economic development policies established to deal with the overriding question of unemployment and the depression.[36]

Still, Franklin Roosevelt was at heart a lover of nature and expressed this feeling both publicly and privately. He combined his support for conservation with the problem of tackling the economic depression.

> We seek to use our natural resources not as a thing apart but as something that is interwoven with industry, labor, finance, taxation, agriculture, homes, recreation, good citizenship. The results of this interweaving will have a greater influence on the future American standard of living than the rest of our economics put together.[37]

The fact that policies for one predicament could simultaneously solve the problems of another was a major contribution to American politics. As Anna Lou Riesch explains,

> The idea of "pump priming" through government expenditure during depression was itself in its infancy. But in addition political economy owes much to the Roosevelt Administration for the idea that this expenditure could be concentrated on conservation activities, of permanent benefit to

the nation with a minimum of interference in the private investment sector of the economy.[38]

There are many examples of this approach. For instance, the **Civilian Conservation Corps** was one of the New Deal's most successful agencies. It took young, unemployed men off the streets and paid them to plant trees and build trails, lookout towers, roads, and bridges, and complete numerous other projects essential to conservation.

Soil conservation is another example of how sound conservation principles could help solve economic problems. At the turn of the century the mean annual rainfall on the Great Plains averaged a feeble 20 inches, often inadequate for farming. By the late 1920s the rain had tapered off until drought plagued the region.[39] In 1933 there was no rain at all. The land, weakened by years of overuse and poor management, dried out, exposing the fragile top soil to the elements. The winds blew and the dirt swirled, creating the Great Dust Bowl of the 1930s. During the next ten years the soil turned to sand as thousands of square acres literally blew away. Roughly two hundred thousand people fled their farms and moved west in an effort to find relief.

In 1934 Congress passed the **Taylor Grazing Act** to prevent additional erosion on the Great Plains by limiting grazing to designated districts. The following year, it passed the **Soil Conservation Act**, establishing the Soil Conservation Service, to manage soil and water conservation throughout the nation. Under Hugh Bennett's leadership, the Soil Conservation Service built dams, straightened streams, regulated land use, and gave demonstrations to farmers on the benefits of land conservation.[40]

The Roosevelt administration also developed the multipurpose approach to resource development and conservation. With limited finances and resources, the administration chose projects that were both economically beneficial and conscious of environmental concerns. The fact that the president himself made some effort to achieve these often contradictory goals is a credit to Roosevelt's innovative style.

The **Tennessee Valley Authority** (TVA), established to develop an entire river valley, demonstrates this dual-purpose approach. The basis of the TVA began during World War I when the government constructed a hydroelectric plant on the Tennessee River at Muscle Shoals, Alabama, to serve a local nitrate plant. After the war, the electrical plant was expanded to serve the farmers of this extremely poor region. The Roosevelt administration decided to develop this concept even further, basing its approach on the proper-use philosophy of past conservationists like Gifford Pinchot. Through the TVA, the government planned to build a hydroelectric network that would supply cheap power, develop a flood-control system, construct recreational facilities, and establish a soil-conservation program. The TVA was extremely popular and, as Anna Lou Riesch describes, made a permanent contribution to government policy making.

The subsequent experience obtained in the practical implementation of this scheme, were critical steps toward the acceptance of multipurpose development as a characteristic feature of the American system.[41]

Less popular, among the general public, was the Roosevelt administration's attempt to regulate overproduction in farming. Farmers tried to compensate for low prices by increasing output, which unfortunately led to even lower prices. To discourage the resulting surplus, the government instituted the **Agricultural Adjustment** Act of May 1933, which paid farmers *not* to produce specific abundant crops or livestock, such as wheat, corn, hogs, and dairy products. The Agricultural Adjustment Agency (AAA) supervised this program and soon was paying subsidies to farmers who left fields fallow or slaughtered pigs. At a time when people were standing in lines for a bowl of soup, this program was met with vociferous criticism. The fact that the government restored farmers' purchasing power to that of the prosperous prewar period by passing the costs to the public in higher food prices further antagonized critics.

Despite the problems of struggling with an economic depression, Roosevelt's administration successfully instituted more traditional forms of conservation. **Harold L. Ickes,** FDR's secretary of the interior, was an old-style progressive conservationist who believed conservation should be a primary concern of the government. He argued that a Department of Conservation should supervise administration of federal lands and resources; many of today's environmentalists strongly support this, though it has yet to be achieved. Ickes, with Roosevelt's support, helped expand the national park system in the 1930s by establishing Olympic National Park in Washington, Shenandoah National Park in Virginia, and Kings Canyon National Park in California, as well as acquiring land in Wyoming that would become Grand Teton National Park in 1950. The need to preserve wildlife also gained ground. The administration outlawed killing predators in national parks in 1936, as it strove to create sanctuaries.[42] In 1940 the administration created the **U.S. Fish and Wildlife Service,** which established 160 new wildlife refuges by the next year.

Robert Marshall was an important champion of conservation issues during the 1930s. As chief of the Division of Recreation and Lands for the Forest Service in 1937, Marshall influenced the Forest Service's policies on recreation and preservation of wilderness areas. Like John Muir before him, Marshall believed that the wilderness should be protected for both aesthetic reasons and the mental and spiritual health of all Americans. He envisioned "the organization of spirited people who will fight for the freedom of the wilderness," and subsequently he and Aldo Leopold founded the **Wilderness Society** in 1935.[43] Marshall also promoted the socialization of the nation's commercial timberlands, which he outlined in the pamphlet *The Social Management of American Forests* (1930) and in the book *The People's Forests* (1933).[44]

Conservation during the Roosevelt years had many successes as the president strove to protect the environment while using the nation's resources as a way to end the Great Depression. President Roosevelt's programs, however, failed to address some areas, including air pollution, poisonous pesticides, overpopulation, and limited fossil fuels. Much of this can be attributed to a belief among the New Dealers, consistent with past governments, that economic growth should not be inhibited by overly restrictive policies. The hardships of the Great Depression also influenced Roosevelt's agenda and the activities of his administration.

Not everyone agreed with the government's policies. For example, preservationists criticized the effort to increase the number of park visitors. Generally, however, Roosevelt's efforts were made easier by a cooperative Congress and the sympathy and support of scientists, the press, and the average American citizen. This should not minimize the fact that as a practical conservationist, President Roosevelt's New Deal environmental record remains impressive.[45] If it were not for the ravages of the Great Depression, Roosevelt may have ranked among the most successful of environmental leaders in American history.

Conclusion

The environmental movement in the United States became a popular public consideration during the Progressive Era. Leading figures such as Theodore Roosevelt, Gifford Pinchot, and John Muir helped make conservation and preservation national issues. Although there may have been more rhetoric than achievement in the final analysis, during this period the conservation movement set in motion ideas that would shape future environmental policies.

The years of mass consumption and urban development during the 1920s left little room for environmental issues. It was the time of the radio, prohibition, gangsters, and most of all the automobile. The prevailing belief was that nature should be tapped for its riches. That this was happening encouraged public confidence. In the 1930s and 1940s the New Dealers also viewed consumption as a sign of progress and a healthy economy. Still, they took a much more active role than did the 1920s administrations in asserting the government's responsibility to protect and regulate the nation's natural resources. More practical than the progressives, the Franklin Roosevelt administration established the precedent for the government to act as the mediator among business interests, public access, and national use of the environment. Although the means were not yet fully established, much of the philosophy and most of the methods needed to construct an active environmental movement had been well formed during the first half of the twentieth century.

Chapter Notes

1. Roderick Nash, *The American Environment: Readings in the History of Conservation* (London: Addison-Wesley, 1968), 4.
2. Ibid., 97.
3. Samuel P. Hays, *Conservation and the Gospel of Efficiency: The Progressive Conservation Movement, 1890–1920* (Cambridge: Harvard University Press, 1959), 262.
4. Ibid., 267.
5. John Muir, *Our National Parks* (Boston: Houghton Mifflin, 1901), 2.
6. Hays, *Conservation and the Gospel of Efficiency*, 15.
7. Theodore Roosevelt, "Opening Address by the President," *Proceedings of Governors in the White House*, ed. Newton C. Blanchard (Washington, D.C.: Government Printing Office, 1909), 5.
8. Robert Gottlieb, *Forcing the Spring: The Transformation of the American Environmental Movement* (Washington, D.C.: Island Press, 1993), 23.
9. Ibid.
10. Philip Shabecoff, *A Fierce Green Fire: The American Environmental Movement* (New York: Hill and Wang, 1993), 68.
11. Hays, *Conservation and the Gospel of Efficiency*, 112.
12. *A Centennial Celebration 1892–1992* (San Francisco: Sierra Club, 1992), 4.
13. Shabecoff, *Fierce Green Fire*, 68.
14. Frank Graham, Jr., *Man's Dominion: The Story of Conservation in America* (New York: M. Evans, 1971), 135.
15. Henry Clepper, ed., *Leaders of American Conservation* (New York: Ronald Press, 1971), 278.
16. Nash, *American Environment*, 39.
17. Gifford Pinchot, *Breaking New Ground* (New York: Harcourt, Brace, & World, 1947), 5.
18. Graham, *Man's Dominion*, 109.
19. Hays, *Conservation and the Gospel of Efficiency*, 2.
20. Graham, *Man's Dominion*, 109.
21. Gottlieb, *Forcing the Spring*, 24.
22. Nash, *American Environment*, 64.
23. *Centennial Celebration 1892–1992*, 2.
24. John Muir, *The Yosemite* (New York: Century, 1912), 256.
25. David R. Long, "Pipe Dreams: Hetch Hetchy, the Urban West, and the Hydraulic Society Revisited," *Journal of the West*, July 1995, 22.
26. Rik Scarce, *Eco-Warriors: Understanding the Radical Environmental Movement* (Chicago: Noble Press, 1990), 17.
27. Gifford Pinchot, *The Fight for Conservation* (New York: Harcourt, Brace, 1910), 42.
28. Long, "Pipe Dreams," 23.
29. Hays, *Conservation and the Gospel of Efficiency*, 193.
30. Donald C. Swain, *Federal Conservation Policy, 1921–1933*, 76 (Berkeley: University of California Publications in History, 1963), 165.
31. Paul S. Boyer, *The Enduring Vision* (Lexington, Mass.: D. C. Heath, 1995), 812.
32. Gottlieb, *Forcing the Spring*, 32.

33. Nash, *American Environment*, 105.
34. Clepper, *Leaders of American Conservation*, 201.
35. Aldo Leopold, *A Sand County Almanac and Sketches Here and There* (New York: Oxford University Press, 1949), 209.
36. Gottlieb, *Forcing the Spring*, 35.
37. Nash, *American Environment*, 151.
38. Anna Lou Riesch, "Conservation under Franklin Roosevelt," in Nash, *American Environment,* 148.
39. John Steele Gordon, "The American Environment: The Big Picture Is More Heartening Than All the Little Ones," *American Heritage*, Oct. 1993, 43.
40. Graham, *Man's Dominion*, 267.
41. Riesch, "Conservation under Franklin Roosevelt," 148.
42. Donald Worster, *Nature's Economy: The Roots of Ecology* (San Francisco: Sierra Club Books, 1977), 277.
43. Robert Marshall, "The Problem of the Wilderness," *Scientific Monthly* 30, 1930, 148.
44. Clepper, *Leaders of American Conservation*, 219.
45. Riesch, "Conservation under Franklin Roosevelt," 150.

We have met the enemy and he is us.
—Pogo

6

The 1940s through the 1960s: Prelude to the Green Decade

The two decades after World War II were years of confusion and inconsistent activity for conservationists. Preoccupied by the traumas of "hot" and "cold" wars, public officials often lacked the drive of either Theodore or Franklin Roosevelt, or the determination of Gifford Pinchot for conservation. As victors in the world conflict, Americans thought they deserved improved living standards and material comforts. Conservationists struggled as the nation focused on these expectations rather than on environmental concerns. The public at large did not begin to comprehend the environmental damage caused by two hundred years of uncontrolled industrial expansion until the mid–1960s. At that point, historian Roderick Nash explains, Americans focused their attention on environmental issues, but with different priorities, as the proper-use concepts of the past were being replaced with a more altruistic view of nature.

> By the 1960s this concept challenged utilitarianism as the central purpose of conservation. Continued improvements in technology, for one thing, eased fears of overpopulation and resource exhaustion. More importantly, many Americans were coming to realize that an environment conducive to survival—even to affluence—was not enough. They demanded that the land had to do more than just keep people alive.[1]

Environmental Costs of Scientific Progress in the 1940s

Immediately following World War II, America entered a new age of scientific and technological achievements that made it the most powerful nation in the world. As the first atomic bomb exploded in the New Mexico desert on July 16, 1945, physicist J. Robert Oppenheimer recalled the words of Krishna from the *Bhagavad Gita*, "I am become Death, the destroyer of worlds."[2] Humanity had gained not only the ability to destroy all life on earth but also the confidence that science could control nature. As historian Donald Worster observes,

> The Age of Ecology began on the desert outside Alamogordo, New Mexico on July 16, 1945, with a dazzling fireball of lights and a swelling mushroom cloud of radioactive gases. One kind of fallout from the atomic bomb was the beginnings of widespread, popular ecological concern around the globe. It began, appropriately, in the United States, where the nuclear era was launched.[3]

Driven by the power to command nature, some scientists, government officials, and social leaders started to replace the early-nineteenth-century myth of superabundance with the myth of scientific supremacy, which rationalized that science would fix everything . . . tomorrow. Corporate America, land developers, and other users of natural resources eagerly justified short-term gains by minimizing the long-term losses. Because science could and would solve any future problems, "Present the repair bill to the next generation" became the unspoken slogan of those who exploited nature for short-term gains.

Despite America's confidence in the benefits of technology and science, alarming evidence soon appeared that these innovations came with a high price. In 1940, 130 million Americans had a spacious National Park system of 22 million acres; twenty years later, a more mobile population of 183 million inherited an overcrowded system that had been enlarged by only a few acres. Of 21,000 miles of ocean shoreline in the contiguous forty-eight states, only 7 percent was reserved for public recreation. In addition, the most eroded lands in the United States—the overused grasslands of the **western public domain**—were not restored to full fertility despite the new American awareness of the importance of soil conservation.[4] In October 1947 a deadly smog settled over the small steel-mill town of Donora, Pennsylvania, in the Monongahela River Valley. Before winds swept away the acrid air inversion, twenty people died and some six thousand fell ill.

Chemicals such as DDT, which reduce insect damage to agriculture, were hailed as miracles of modern science when they first became available in the post–World War II era. Their use spread rapidly. In 1947 the United States produced 124,259,000 pounds of chemical pesticides. Few people questioned the use of such deadly chemicals or their effect on the environment, and by 1960 the country was producing 637,666,000 pounds of DDT potent pesticides.

By 1949 air pollution damaged almost half a million dollars in crops in Los Angeles County. Leafy greens, such as lettuce and spinach, were most seriously affected. In 1959 industrial, private, and other sources of pollution emitted 24.9 million tons of soot into the air throughout the nation. In 1961 the estimate of crops lost in California to air pollution was $8 million.[5]

The Conservative 1950s

With the Cold War, McCarthyism, and the civil rights movement shaking the comfortable stability of the "good life" that Americans craved in the 1950s, conservation hardly made a ripple on public or political agendas. There were exceptions. In 1956 the Sierra Club, with the Wilderness Society and other groups, blocked the construction of the Echo Park Dam in Dinosaur National Monument on the Utah-Colorado border. Still, these types of victories were uncommon. In fact, President Dwight Eisenhower's secretary of the interior, Douglas McKay, tried but failed to block public power projects, turn energy resources over to the private sector, abolish a number of federal Fish and Wildlife Service areas, and transfer Nevada's big Desert Game Reserve to the state's fish and game department. McKay's constant efforts to get rid of federal property earned him the nickname "Giveaway McKay." But McKay was only one manifestation of the homage most Americans of that era were paying to the gods of unrestrained economic growth.[6]

During the postwar era of the 1950s and 1960s, Americans often took their parks and wilderness for granted. Irresponsible management and overuse steadily devastated the remaining unprotected wilderness areas. Americans became accustomed to outdoor recreation—hunting, fishing, hiking, and swimming—as a way of life and found the public areas increasingly overcrowded each year. As cities, and the population in general, continued to grow, city and state governments had little time to devise plans for the urban development. Litter started to accumulate as people carelessly dumped their garbage wherever they liked. Each year 5 million battered autos were dragged into junkyards. Industries produced an incredible array of boxes, bottles, cans, gadgets, and a thousand varieties of paper products. Litter threatened to become a permanent part of the landscape.[7]

In response, the conservation movement sought to associate the quality of the environment with human needs. Books such as William Vogt's *Road to Survival* (1948) and Fairfield Osborn's *Our Plundered Planet* (1948) and *The Limits of the Earth* (1953) grimly raised the old Malthusian specter that population was surpassing the world's productive ability. These writers contended that birth control, the prevention of needless waste, and new processes to provide food were essential for the survival of the human race. From this perspective, conservation was the way to maintain the physical basis of life. Osborn's *Our Plundered Planet* roused strong alarms because it warned that the leaps in food production from new scientific methods could not continue indefinitely. This was one of the first manifestations of the neo-**Malthusian theory**, which states that the natural resources humans need for survival cannot last forever because of society's penchant for overconsumption. This was a new, and unappealing, concept for Americans.[8]

Rather than investigate the environmental predicament of the 1950s and early 1960s, many Americans preferred to contemplate the romanticized naturalists of the past. John Muir's popularity surged, though academics continued to ignore him, in part because his family locked away his papers and personal records. The revival was spurred along by several publishing events: a biography of Muir won a Pulitzer Prize in 1945; a collection of nature photographs by **Ansel Adams** paired with Muir's quotations was published in 1948; and an anthology of Muir's essays was put out in 1954. In 1964, the fiftieth anniversary of Muir's death, the government issued a commemorative stamp and renamed a half million acres in the Sierra Mountains the John Muir Wilderness Area. The following year, *Time* commented that "the real father of conservation is considered to be John Muir, a California naturalist." (Several additional biographies appeared in the 1980s shortly after the Muir archives were opened to researchers.)[9]

As Muir's popularity grew, a new generation was about to shatter the complacency of the American conservation movement. Marine biologist **Rachel Carson** demonstrated an uncanny ability to convey the technical and complex problems of environmental issues in her book *The Sea Around Us*, published in 1952. From a very modest first printing, to everyone's astonishment, most of all hers, the book became a titanic bestseller, making its author famous across America.

Emerging Voices in the 1960s

Since the end of World War II, environmental values have reflected the search by increasingly affluent Americans for new, nonmaterial amenities—such as clean air and water, better health, open space, and recreation. By the 1960s many Americans, with their increased leisure time and security, demanded these amenities, which they considered consumer items. Public concern arose after numerous environmentalists clearly described the condition of these amenities.

Although some scientists had raised cautionary flags, most Americans were unaware of how synthetic chemicals poisoned the environment until the publication of Rachel Carson's *Silent Spring* in 1962. Carson, a former researcher for the Fish and Wildlife Service, discussed the problems created by the indiscriminate use of the insecticide DDT and its spread through the food chain. The "silent spring" of her title refers to the death of robins from DDT toxicity. As Roderick Nash says, Carson's work was both timely and effective.

Carson was less concerned about the "ethics" of pesticides, as Aldo Leopold might have been, and more about the possible consequences for man's health of unenlightened use of his ability to kill other forms of life. Keyed to react strongly to Miss Carson's message by the radioactive "fall-out" scare that occurred simultaneously, many Americans were horrified at her revelations.[10]

Carson warned that the speed of change in society was based not on natural factors but on the impetuous pace of human inventiveness. Atomic power, she wrote, had created an "unnatural" overabundance of radiation; the chemicals being poured into the nation's waters were "the synthetic creations of man's inventive mind, brewed in his laboratories, and having no counterparts in nature." These manufactured creations proliferated as people who were "largely or wholly ignorant of their potentials for harm" heralded their perceived benefits and often used them indiscriminately. As a result, an enormous number of people were unknowingly contaminated by the poisonous wastes of an unregulated industrial economy. Carson wrote,

> I contend, furthermore, that we have allowed these chemicals to be used with little or no advance investigation of their effect on soil, water, wildlife, and man himself. Future generations are unlikely to condone our lack of prudent concern for the integrity of the natural world that supports all life.[11]

Silent Spring clearly presented the widespread harm that pesticides caused birds and other wildlife, as well as the damage agricultural runoff did to waterways. Carson's pro-environmental work was effective and timely for an American public that had blindly accepted the comforts technology provided. The book's passionate warning about the inherent dangers in the excessive use of pesticides ignited the imaginations of an enormous and disparate audience. The realization that the new synthetic chemicals in agriculture and industry had potentially disastrous consequences captured the public's attention. Individual states gradually banned DDT use, and in 1972 the federal government followed suit.

The responses to Carson's best-selling book included not only a multitude of scientific and popular debates about the issues she raised, but also a groundswell of public support for increased controls over pollution. Yet some scientists and, of course, the chemical companies that manufactured pesticides, dismissed her fears as unfounded. Several industry representatives charged that *Silent Spring* was part of a communist plot to ruin U.S. agriculture; the president of a DDT manufacturer called Carson "a fanatic defender of the cult of the balance of nature."[12] John Maddox, a theoretical physicist, charged that Carson had played "a literary trick" on her readers.

> The most seriously misleading part of the narrative is the use of horror stories about the misuse of DDT to create an impression that there are no safe

uses worth consideration. Miss Carson's sin was the use of "calculated overdramatization."[13]

Maddox's own view was much more optimistic. He believed in humanity's ability to overcome future problems, unlike the disbelieving environmentalists, whom he called "prophets of doom." In conclusion he warned that "in the metaphor of spaceship earth, mere housekeeping needs courage. The most serious worry about the doomsday syndrome is that it will undermine our spirit."[14]

Other critics "sexualized their contempt" for Carson, charging her with "emotionalism."[15] A Federal Pest Control Review Board member said he "thought she was a spinster, [so] what's she so worried about genetics for?"[16] Yet Carson had awakened Americans to the pending catastrophe of unrestricted consumption and environmental decay.

Silent Spring was the most popular environmental book published in the early 1960s, and it heralded the beginning of the modern environmental movement. Other books from the time had less impact on the general public but nonetheless influenced the growing environmental movement. For example, in *Our Synthetic Environment* (1962), social ecologist Murray Bookchin contended that technological growth and the pollutants industry dumped into the environment caused ecological disasters and damaged human health. Bookchin accepted that technology was part of modern life, but believed machinery should be adapted in a more nature-friendly way,

> a reordering and redevelopment of technologies according to ecological sound principles . . . based on non-polluting energy sources such as solar and wind power, methane generators, and possibly liquid hydrogen that will harmonize with the natural world.[17]

Bookchin concluded that "there can be no sound environment without a sound, ecologically orientated social environment." To achieve this he recommended decentralizing society into compact, biologically rational spheres where economies would serve human needs rather than the appetites of industry. The relationship between humanity and nature was a public issue by the early 1960s, and its importance was reflected in the political arena.

The election of John F. Kennedy in 1960 brought a young, vital, popular leader to the presidency. The Kennedy administration was strongly aware of the public's concern for environmental issues. In 1962 President Kennedy hosted a White House Conference on Conservation, which was attended by politicians and conservationists. He then proposed the **Land and Water Conservation Fund**, which, with a 1968 congressional amendment, used federal revenues from offshore oil drilling to acquire land for national and state parks and recreation areas. Congress set up the fund in 1965. The Kennedy administration made additional advances in 1963. The **Clean Air Act** appropriated funds for a federal attack on air pollution, and the Bureau of Outdoor Recreation coordinated federal environmental efforts from within the Department of the Interior.

Stewart L. Udall was President Kennedy's secretary of the interior in 1961 and remained in office under President Lyndon B. Johnson. Udall believed that a society could not consider itself a success if, despite its material abundance, it permitted its land to become blighted and uninspiring. He wanted to bring about more responsible use of natural resources and also to institute a policy that would preserve nature for the future benefit of all Americans.

> We have reached the point in our history where it is absolutely essential that all resources, and all alternative plans for their use and development, be evaluated comprehensively by those who make the over-all decisions. As our land base shrinks, it is inevitable that incompatible plans involving factories, mines, fish, dams, parks, highways, and wildlife, and other uses and values will increasingly collide. Those who decide must consider immediate needs, compute the value of competing proposals, and keep distance in their eyes as well. . . .
>
> One of the paradoxes of American society is that while our economic standard of living has become the envy of the world, our environmental standard has steadily declined. We are better housed, better nourished, and better entertained, but we are not better prepared to inherit the earth or to carry on the pursuit of happiness.[18]

Secretary Udall's ideas represent the sentiment of the Kennedy administration, although not its action, and created a precedent for future administrations to recognize the environment as an important political issue.

After President Kennedy was assassinated in November 1963, Lyndon B. Johnson continued the government's efforts to respond to the public's concerns about environmental issues. Like the Kennedy administration, President Johnson's team provided a great deal of rhetoric and promises but also showed some real progress. In 1964 the **Wilderness Act** established the National Wilderness Preservation System to designate sections of forests as protected wilderness areas. The high point for the environmental movement during the Johnson administration was the White House Conference on Natural Beauty. On February 8, 1965, President Johnson sent a special message to Congress about the importance of natural beauty in the United States. His message became a landmark in defining the aims of the government's conservation policies in the post–World War II era, and stimulated action on local, state, and federal levels. The conference, held on May 24 and 25, 1965, was similar in many ways to Theodore Roosevelt's 1908 White House Conservation Conference; "again the power and prestige of the executive office was used to dramatize the most pressing conservation issue of the time."[19] However, Johnson's "new conservation" emphasized a concern for aesthetic rather than material issues.

To deal with these new problems will require a new conservation. We must not only protect the countryside and save it from destruction, we must restore what has been destroyed and salvage the beauty and charm of our cities. Our conservation must be not just the classic conservation of protection and development, but a creative conservation of restoration and innovation. Its concern is not with nature alone, but with the total relation between man and the world around him. Its object is not just man's welfare but the dignity of man's spirit.

In this conservation the protection and enhancement of man's opportunity to be in contact with beauty must play a major role.[20]

President Johnson advocated a new attitude toward nature along with an appreciation for its intrinsic beauty, as in the days of Thoreau. In a practical sense, Johnson's approach did more to define a problem than to enact specific methods of solving it. Still, the influence of the conservation movement had again reached the White House—and that was progress.

Despite this political action, some people failed to see the significance of the government's involvement. "Environmental science" was blasted in a 1966 *Science* magazine editorial as "one of the newest fads in Washington—and elsewhere." The writer feared that the government was about to take responsibility for all of man's surroundings "in the heavens, beneath the sea, and upon and under the dry land."[21] While the White House was becoming more aware of and responsive to conservation and environmental issues, other forces were also taking action to save land and wildlife.

The Environmental Movement Begins to Mobilize

The 1960s were a decade of social turbulence in the United States. Many people, especially the younger generation, supported such issues as the civil rights movement, sexual freedom, feminism, alternative lifestyles, and the anti-Vietnam War movement—all of which countered traditional American views. These activists rallied against the evils they perceived in American life. One of these evils was the uncontrolled exploitation of the environment. The mobilization of environmentalists reflects the mood of the times as people organized to promote their cause.

During the early 1960s the Sierra Club, led by nature photographer Ansel Adams and his colleague **David Brower**, became much more publicly visible and active. Brower, a prominent environmentalist of the time, was twice elected as a director of the Sierra Club (1941–1943 and 1946–1953) and then appointed its executive director in 1952, a position he held until 1969. He also narrated motion pictures about endangered wilderness areas and wrote many books about nature. Brower and the Sierra Club parted ways in 1969: the organization accused him of financial mismanagement, while he countered that he left because the group was too conservative. Brower soon formed **Friends of the Earth** (FOE), taking the name from the John Muir quotation, "The earth can do all right without friends, but men, if they are to survive, must learn to be friends of the earth."[22] Friends of the Earth took an aggressive stand on many environmental issues, attempting to publicize diverse issues, from forest conservation to whale hunting to air pollution. In the 1980s, after Brower's relationship with Friends of the Earth soured, he left to form another environmental group, **Earth Island Institute**, which publishes books on environmentalism and ecology and fights for the protection of wildlife and other natural resources.

In the 1960s television was used for the first time to bring public attention to an environmental issue. The National Advertising Council released a commercial that showed a Native American dressed in traditional garb staring at a littered landscape while a tear rolls slowly down his cheek. This powerful image helped raise the public's awareness of the problem of litter.

Since *Silent Spring*, a plethora of popular magazines, technical journals, organizational newsletters, and books devoted to environmental issues appeared. Books by Lewis Mumford, *Technics and Civilization* (1962), and Rene Dubos, *So Human an Animal* (1968), contended that nature was being permanently damaged by human activity.[23] Their basic concept was that ecosystems are interdependent and, unlike machines, cannot be easily manipulated by humans. **Ralph Nader** became famous for his book *Unsafe at Any Speed* (1965), which charged that defective mechanical design in the Corvair was the cause of accidents and injuries. His fight for consumer protection has continued and includes a strong emphasis on the dangers of pollution, in particular the problem of auto emissions. By 1967 auto emissions had become a serious issue for Americans, who owned half the world's 200 million motor vehicles and burned 80 billion gallons of fuel. Paul Ehrlich's *Population Bomb*, published in 1968, sounded an alarm about the dangers of overpopulation and became a best-seller.

Barry Commoner helped establish the modern environmental movement by writing popular and widely read books. His most famous were *Science and Survival* (1963) and *The Closing Circle* (1972), a best-seller. These books combined science and moral sensibility in an easy-to-read text. They called attention to the natural limits inherent in all resources, a central idea of the neo-Malthusian theory. Commoner was the most prominent scientist of the 1960s to highlight the problem of industry being a threat to the environment. He added nuclear fallout to his warnings about the environment. [24]

Activism was growing and continued to gain supporters as a barrage of ecological disasters befell the country at the end of the decade.

> the turning point, when people had had enough, came in 1969, a year that
> included the Santa Barbara oil spill, the seizure of eleven tons of coho

salmon in Wisconsin and Minnesota because of excessive DDT concentrations, application for permission to build a trans-Alaska pipeline, and the burning of the Cuyahoga River in Cleveland.[25]

On June 22, 1969, an oil-slicked, debris-choked section of the Cuyahoga River near Cleveland caught fire. Firefighters quickly doused the flames, but the incident acquired a notoriety that lingers. To many Americans, the blazing Cuyahoga—the absurdity of a river catching fire—symbolized the growing environmental problems in the country. But there were more serious signs of trouble.

Oil spills from offshore wells and grounded tankers were devastating beaches. Air pollution in some large cities occasionally forced residents indoors. For example, in July 1969, California radio and TV stations announced, "The children of Los Angeles are not allowed to run, skip, or jump inside or outside on smog alert days by order of the Los Angeles Board of Education and the County Medical Association."[26] The Florida Everglades were drying out. And the bald eagle, the very symbol of the United States, was near extinction, poisoned by decades of exposure to DDT and other agricultural pesticides.

The public was also outraged by their outdoor surroundings. Secretary of the Interior John C. Whitaker put it this way in 1969,

> As Americans traveled in their automobiles, which had doubled in number from 1950 to 1970, they saw garish road signs, fields of junked automobiles, choked and dying streams, overgrazed and eroded hills and valleys, and roadsides lined with endless miles of beer cans, pop bottles, and the tin foil from candy wrappers and cigarette packages. They could no longer move a few hundred miles West: the frontiers were gone.[27]

The generation that took on these environmental problems was the post–World War II "baby boomers," born between 1944 and 1964. Population growth during this period was dramatic. The fertility rate, births per thousand women, rose from 80 in 1940 to 106 in 1950 and 123 in 1957. The nation's population during the 1950s surged from 151 million to 180 million. Born when the United States was the richest nation in history, the baby boomers enjoyed many opportunities that had not been available to their parents. The gap between them was educational as well as generational. Only 13 percent of twenty- to twenty-four-year-olds attended college in 1960; by 1970 this number had jumped 10 percent.[28] The baby boomers' influence grew substantially in 1971 after passage of the Twenty-sixth Amendment to the Constitution, which lowered the voting age from twenty-one to eighteen, instantly created 11 million possible new voters. These voters became the activists who would energetically attack the country's traditional values and assumptions.

Older Americans also were active in the environmental movement, though their approach tended to follow traditional avenues through established organizations. However, their desire to improve the environment was no less than that of their younger compatriots. As historian Victor B. Scheffer explains, they were alarmed at the deterioration of America's natural surroundings.

> They had watched their surroundings worsen and had been forced to accept a declining standard of living. Many longed, naively, for a return to the pastoral America that Norman Rockwell used to paint for the covers of the *Saturday Evening Post.* Ecology, the miracle science, now promised to bring back the landscapes they remembered. Their contribution was not less than that of the young but less intense.[29]

In 1974 the well-established environmental organizations were substantially the same as those existing in 1950. These traditional groups remained a stable force in the environmental movement and often acted as an incubator for the younger generation.

The environmental movement, which erupted from the social changes of the 1960s, was not merely an expression of organized conservation groups but also a manifestation of growing anger among the public. There were daily reminders of the deteriorating condition of the environment, in both rural and urban areas, as well as alarming reports of humanity's wasteful behavior. As Victor B. Scheffer describes,

> It was the daily commuters who drove with smarting eyes through city smog, the mothers who learned that DDT was present in their breasts and that arsenic from smelter smoke was accumulating in the bodies of their children, the poultrymen who wondered why eggshells broke more easily then they used to, the fishermen who saw trout streams, once pure, now running brown, the farmers who wondered where all the bluebirds had gone, and why the water level in the wells had dropped and why the water tasted queer.[30]

Opinion polls results indicated a rapid rise in public concern about environmental issues in the United States. Surveys taken in 1965 and 1970 showed an increase from 17 to 53 percent in the number of respondents who rated "reducing pollution of air and water" as one of the three problems to which they wanted the government to pay more attention. President Richard M. Nixon, who had previously ignored the environmental issue, found it expedient to declare in his February 1970 State of the Union that the 1970s "absolutely must be the years when America pays its debt to the past by reclaiming the purity of its air, its waters. . . . It is literally now or never." His secretary of the interior, John C. Whitaker, later recalled,

> When President Nixon and his staff walked into the White House on January 20, 1969, we were totally unprepared for the tidal wave of public opinion in favor of cleaning up the environment that was about to engulf us.[31]

The increased attention to the environment culminated in the first Earth Day celebration on April 22, 1970. Some 20 million Americans took part. The event was the brainchild of Senator **Gaylord Nelson** of Wisconsin, a longtime advocate for clean water and a leader whom many conservationists regarded as one of the few voices of conscience on Capitol Hill. Nelson originally envisioned the event as The National Environmental Teach-In where participants could debate issues and share information, hoping to capture the spirit, if not the politics, of the "sit-ins" of the fractious 1960s. As the planning for the event progressed, however, Nelson and his followers (mainly campus activists) focused more on environmentalism. Earth Day spotlighted such problems as **thermal pollution** of the atmosphere, dying lakes, the profusion of solid waste, ruinous strip mining, catastrophic oil spills, and dwindling natural resources. The event emphasized that the obsession with industrial growth and consumerism was straining the environment to the breaking point, and introduced many Americans to the idea of "living lightly on the earth." Earth Day took place largely as a result of the efforts of these former antiwar and civil rights activists. Nelson recalled,

> No one could organize 20 million people, 10,000 grade schools and high schools, 2,500 colleges and 1,000 communities in three and a half months, even if he had $20 million. [Nelson had $190,000.] The key to the whole thing was the grass-roots response. And that has been true every year since.[32]

The older conservation groups—the Sierra Club, the National Audubon Society, the National Wildlife Federation, the Izaak Walton League, and others—played little or no role in Earth Day. They were, in fact, surprised by the surge of national emotion and tremors of activism. Still preoccupied by traditional land and wildlife preservation issues, most of the old guard in conservationism ignored the growing national anger over pollution and other environmental threats to human health. In a few years, the fissure between the traditional conservation groups and the pollution- and public health-oriented activist national organizations would narrow and largely close.

In the aftermath of Earth Day, new environmental institutions emerged that combined strong social sensibility with concern for the natural world. **Environmental Action,** formed in 1970 to coordinate Earth Day activities, became an aggressive lobbying and public information group that focused on issues such as solid waste and alerted voters to the "Dirty Dozen"—companies with the worst pollution records. Leaders of a number of national groups pooled resources in 1970 to create the **League of Conservation Voters.** The league tracked voting records and policy decisions of members of Congress and the executive branch, and endorsed and organized electoral support for environmentally minded politicians while attempting to maintain a bipartisan approach.[33] Such organizations exemplify the fact that by the 1970s, the environmental movement had matured and begun to effectively promote its cause.

Conclusion

The modern environmental movement in the United States was ushered in between the publication of *Silent Spring* in 1962 and the Earth Day celebration of 1970. In many ways the movement was a product of the times. The rabid consumerism and dependence on science of the immediate post–World War II years (late 1940s and 1950s) was contrasted by the ever-increasing decay and devastation of the environment. It was a condition that could not be ignored for long—particularly by a people whose traditional love for nature was well established. Environmentalism was an integral part of the social protest movements of the '60s generation. Rising from the cult of materialism in the 1950s and the turbulence of the 1960s, the environmental movement found its place in every part of American life—political, economic, generational, urban, and rural. The foundations of the environmental movement were well laid by the beginning of the 1970s—the **Green Decade**, though its greatest triumphs and challenges were yet to be faced.

Chapter Notes

1. Roderick Nash, *The American Environment: Readings in the History of Conservation* (London: Addison-Wesley, 1968), 155.
2. Paul Rauber, "An End to Evolution: The Extinction Lobby in Congress Is Now Deciding Which Species Will Live and Which Will Die," *Sierra* 80, Jan./Feb. 1996, 28.
3. Donald Worster, *Nature's Economy: The Roots of Ecology* (San Francisco: Sierra Club Books, 1977), 339.
4. Stewart L. Udall, *The Quiet Crisis* (New York: Holt, Rinehart and Winston, 1963), 175.
5. John Steele Gordon, "The American Environment: The Big Picture Is More Heartening Than All the Little Ones," *American Heritage*, Oct. 1993, 44–45.
6. Philip Shabecoff, *A Fierce Green Fire: The American Environmental Movement* (New York: Hill and Wang, 1993), 91.
7. Udall, *Quiet Crisis*, 176.
8. Shabecoff, *Fierce Green Fire*, 94–95.
9. Marcy Darnovsky, "Stories Less Told: Histories of U.S. Environmentalism," *Socialist Review*, Oct. 1, 1992, 20.
10. Nash, *American Environment*, 197.
11. Rachel Carson, *Silent Spring* (New York: Houghton Mifflin, 1962), 13.
12. Frank Graham, Jr., *Since Silent Spring* (Boston: Houghton Mifflin, 1970), 56.

13. Victor B. Scheffer, *The Shaping of Environmentalism in America* (Seattle: University of Washington Press, 1991), 11.
14. Ibid.
15. H. Patricia Hynes, *The Recurring Silent Spring* (New York: Pergamon Press, 1989), 116.
16. Ibid.
17. Shabecoff, *Fierce Green Fire*, 97.
18. Udall, *Quiet Crisis*, 188.
19. Nash, *American Environment*, 172.
20. Lyndon B. Johnson, "Natural Beauty—Message from the President of the United States," *Congressional Record*, Feb. 8, 1965, 89th Congress, 1st Session, vol. 111, pt. 2, 2087.
21. Scheffer, *Shaping of Environmentalism in America*, 9.
22. Shabecoff, *Fierce Green Fire*, 100–101.
23. Anna Bramwell, *Ecology in the 20th Century: A History* (New Haven: Yale University Press, 1989), 81, 211.
24. Robert Gottlieb, *Forcing the Spring: The Transformation of the American Environmental Movement* (Washington, D.C.: Island Press, 1993), 173.
25. Scheffer, *Shaping of Environmentalism in America*, 6.
26. Harrison Welford, "On How to Be a Constructive Nuisance," *The Environmental Handbook*, ed. Garrett De Bell (New York: Ballantine Books, 1970), 268.
27. Scheffer, *Shaping of Environmentalism in America*, 6.
28. Ibid., 7.
29. Ibid.
30. Ibid.
31. Gordon, "The American Environment," 45.
32. Mary H. Cooper, "Environmental Movement at 25," *CQ Researcher*, March 31, 1995, 275.
33. Gottlieb, *Forcing the Spring*, 146–47.

My job is to save the f—— wilderness.
I don't know anything else worth
saving. That's simple, right?
—EDWARD ABBEY, *The Monkey Wrench Gang*

7

The 1970s:
The Conservation
Movement Matures

T he decade following the Earth Day celebration witnessed an
unprecedented surge in environmental legislation as the public
responded to environmental disasters of the 1960s. Air and
water pollution, endangered wildlife, and the use of natural resources
became public concerns. As historian Donald Worster observes, Americans finally realized that humanity had obtained the power to disrupt
and destroy the "entire fabric of life on the planet" and that this power
must necessarily be controlled.[1] This newfound awareness and the influence of the 1960s protest movements helped create a more action-oriented approach to the environmental movement.

Buoyed by public enthusiasm, environmental groups expanded and
consolidated their efforts during the 1970s. Their work led to an ambitious array of legislative initiatives, regulations, and legal precedents. An
environmental government bureaucracy developed as environmentalists
attempted to correct the problems of urban and industrial growth
through political activism. The terms *conservationist* and *preservationist* became synonymous and characterized anyone active in environmentalism, which encompassed a broad spectrum of ecology issues. Yet the
progress of the environmental movement remained subject to economic
concerns—the dominant theme of American life and politics since the
colonial period.

Mainstream and Alternative Environmental Groups

Membership in environmental organizations increased dramatically after
Earth Day and overflowed into more than two hundred new national and

regional groups and three thousand local ones. While new organizations proliferated, environmentalists disagreed on the most effective methods to forward their cause and split into two general groups—mainstream and alternative. The **mainstream groups** focused on four arenas: legislation, administrative and regulatory action, the courts, and the electoral sphere. By the end of the decade, the mainstream groups' influence and participation in the political arena had increased, and they were actively influencing the development of environmental policies as well as the government agencies established to regulate them. In contrast, alternative groups took a more direct-action approach that used protest to publicize environmental issues.

Earth Day 1970 demonstrated the popularity of environmental issues among the general public. The traditional environmental groups had not played a major part in the event and were slow to take advantage of this new support. Their primary problem was that they were too narrowly focused on special issues, such as wilderness preservation, national parks, and so forth, while the public was often much broader in its approach and concerned about a variety of problems. Mainstream organizations, which include the National Audubon Society, the Wilderness Society, the National Wildlife Federation, the Sierra Club, and the Izaak Walton League, struggled to redefine themselves. The Audubon Society grew more rapidly than other traditional organizations shortly before and immediately after Earth Day. However, its growth leveled off in the late 1970s. In response, the group embraced broader environmental themes, though it still had difficulty increasing its membership.

The Wilderness Society was often caught up in its own history. Instead of trying to tap the energies of the contemporary environmental movement during the 1960s and 1970s, the organization's publications contained articles about its key founders and leaders, such as **Benton MacKaye**, Robert Marshall, and Aldo Leopold. During the 1970s the Wilderness Society further limited its appeal to the public by maintaining its narrow interest—primarily preserving wilderness areas. Fully absorbing itself with implementing the Wilderness Act (1964) and protecting the Alaskan wilderness reinforced the public's view that the organization remained a narrowly focused conservation group.

Another mainstream organization that had difficulty adapting was the **National Wildlife Federation.** Established in 1936 by sportsmen to protect the wilderness areas for hunting and fishing, the federation was one of the most conservative environmental groups. Its approach was similar to the right-use philosophy of the progressive conservation movement, in which protecting the wilderness was based on economic as well as environmental concerns. Its members worked closely with industry and government officials to achieve their goals. Accordingly, the federation often denounced the more alternative elements of the movement. By the 1970s the group switched to a more youth-oriented approach. Its "Cool

It" program, which supported such issues as recycling and global warming, was essentially a youth- and student-based effort.[2]

The **Environmental Defense Fund** (EDF), an early mainstream group, was formed in 1967 by a group from Long Island, New York, and soon became a major source of environmental expertise and policy action. Originally called the Brookhaven Town Natural Resources Coalition, a discussion group, the EDF included concerned local residents and scientists from the Brookhaven National Laboratory and the State University of New York at nearby Stony Brook. Similar to other antipollution or anti-development groups that sprang up in middle-class residential communities during the 1960s, the Long Island group, historian Robert Gottlieb notes, addressed a wide range of environmental issues.

> These included pollution from duck farms, dredging, sewage pollution, groundwater protection, dump sites, wildlife and habitat preservation, and the use of DDT. The DDT issue was of particular importance for the group, given the widespread use of the pesticide throughout Long Island's Suffolk County.[3]

Throughout the mid–1970s, the Environmental Defense Fund became a major litigator in campaigns that focused on eliminating lead toxicity, fighting against the supersonic transport, protecting sperm whales, and reducing pesticide hazards—the latter being the group's preeminent issue since its founding. Other lawyer-scientist–based organizations include the Natural Resources Defense Council and the Sierra Club Legal Defense Fund, both established in 1971.

While the mainstream environmental groups worked within the established political and economic systems, with professional staffs of lawyers, lobbyists, scientists, economists, organizers, fund-raisers, publicists, and political operatives, a small but growing alternative movement appeared. As the 1970s began, the environmental movement was influenced by the changing social values that had emerged during the '60s. Young people had experimented with alternative lifestyles and philosophies, and from this came the movements that besieged and toppled many of the established social norms. Alternative views of the human-nature relationship challenged the "nature must be dominated" philosophy of the past as social change influenced the development of environmentalism and vice versa. Such new ideas as eco-feminism, deep ecology, the Gaia hypothesis, and Green Party politics sought to link lifestyle with a new environmental consciousness.

As the women's movement energetically reappeared the 1960s, many feminists began to question and reevaluate the traditional arguments that linked biological determinism to male superiority. They argued that the doctrines of "man above nature" and the drive to exploit nature historically had been used to justify the inequality of women, that this need to control was essentially part of the male consciousness. A new egalitarian doctrine, which espoused the oneness of humanity and nature and thus equality among the genders, became an important part of the feminist agenda. The **eco-feminist movement** that evolved, particularly in Western culture, obtained its inspiration

> from tree-planting communities, alternative healing communities, organic food coops, performance art happenings, Witchcraft covens, and the retelling of ancient myths and tales to new forms of political resistance such as the Chipko (hugging) tree actions and women's peace camps. Through poetry, rituals, and social activism that connected the devastation of the Earth with the exploitation of women.[4]

Although the eco-feminist movement is still only a small part of the feminist movement, it nonetheless is an important one, which offers a positive alternative dichotomy for human interaction among the genders and with nature.

The Gaia hypothesis, first espoused in the writings of British biologist James Lovelock in 1969, is named for the Greek earth goddess Gaea. It argues that the earth should be regarded as a living organism that sustains and advances life through its many changes. Thus, the earth will maintain itself whatever damage might be done to it. Although many environmentalists criticized Lovelock's methods as being unscientific, his ideas gathered a popular following. Since then, he has modified his ideas along more accepted concepts of the maintenance of equilibrium in biological systems.

The idea of **deep ecology** was first used by Norwegian philosopher Arne Naess in the 1970s to illustrate the differences between those who sought to harmonize human activity with nature and those who viewed humans as the most important element in the human-nature relationship, deemed shallow ecology. Essentially, deep ecologists believe that nature has intrinsic value and should not be exploited for the needs of humanity. To do this, they argued that a new philosophy is needed that will alter social actions and reverse our technology-based industrial civilization.

Some activists took a more practical approach by applying an environmental philosophy to politics—called **green parties.** The central goal of green political activists is to link environmental issues with the broader social issues of democracy, peace, social justice, and the changing of social values and economic relationships. The general message is that society must alter its living habits and priorities to protect nature and in turn enable nature's resources to improve everyone's lives. The roots of the Green Party political movement began in Australia in April 1972 when the United Tasmania Group (UTG) went to the polls to attempt to halt the flooding of Lake Pedder. Having been unable to persuade the existing political parties to take up their cause, they had decided to go directly to the people. Although their efforts failed to gain them any political power, their example encouraged some of their neighbors in New

Zealand. One month later a green party, calling itself simply Values, entered the political arena in that country. The following year, the first European green party was established in Britain. Originally called People, it later changed its name to Ecology Party and finally to Green Party, and forwarded a platform warning of the earth's limited resources and the dangers of pollution. While the political clout of such parties was minimal in the beginning, their debate did influence the creation of the United Nations Environmental Program in 1972, which was established to promote international awareness of global environmental problems.

As the environmental movement grew in the 1970s so did political activism, especially in Europe, where Daniel Brélaz became the first Green Party candidate to be elected to a national parliament when he won a seat in the Swiss assembly in 1979. In 1981 four Greens were elected to the Belgian parliament, and in 1983 Die Grünen ("the Greens") won twenty-eight seats in the Bundestag, the lower house of the West German parliament. Since then, green parties have sprouted in many nations around the world with an estimated seventy on six continents. There continue to be success stories, particularly in industrialized nations, while in poorer nations green party issues have often taken a backseat to economic and social issues. The progress green parties have made, however, can be measured in many ways. Winning political office to promote and institute their cause is certainly an important achievement. Yet the green parties also have influenced in a rather indirect way: Many of their issues have been adopted by traditional parties who seek popular issues for their own platforms; although this draws voters away from green parties, it does insinuate their views into the general political debate.

Eco-feminsim, deep ecology, Gaia, green politics, were just some of the alternative views that emerged during the 1970s in an effort to change human perceptions of nature and alter the way we live. These philosophies became the foundation and products of the growth of alternative environmental groups.

Alternative groups took a more action-oriented approach than mainstream groups. These alternative groups used protest to publicize environmental issues and to directly influence legislators and political policy making. Often these groups supported civil disobedience and sometimes violence to promote their causes.[5] Novelist Edward Abbey romanticized this kind of eco-sabotage as "monkeywrenching." As Philip Shabecoff describes, members of alternative groups, such as Earth First! and Animal Liberation Front,

> [have placed] themselves in front of logging trucks, pulled up survey stakes for an oil exploration project, chained themselves to upper branches of centuries-old trees marked for the chain saw by timber companies, and driven iron stakes into trees to make it dangerous for loggers to cut into the wood.[6]

These groups, which represented a powerful current in contemporary environmentalism, focused on empowerment issues, environmental justice, political impartiality, and promoting alternative views to the mainstream groups. Their efforts were usually community based, as they attempted to enlist public support from all levels of society to promote the preservation rather than the management of nature.

An example of the alternative philosophy is the **Southwest Research and Information Center** (SRIC), created in 1971 in Albuquerque, New Mexico. Groups such as SRIC tried to create a framework that applied their professional expertise and organizational skills to a specific issue with strong community support, to help the local people be more effective. Robert Gottlieb explains that the philosophy of this organization reflected those of some leading environmental activists.

> In establishing this framework, such groups were influenced by a number of key analysts and advocates, including Ralph Nader, with his critique of corporate power and call for citizen action; Barry Commoner, with his critique of postwar technologies and production decisions; and Paul Connett and Peter Montague, with their critique of the use of expertise in policy development.[7]

Other alternative groups include the National Resources Defense Council, Friends of the Earth, the League of Conservation Voters, Greenpeace, Environmental Action, and Zero Population Growth.

When charismatic David Brower established Friends of the Earth (FOE) in 1969, he had wanted to create an organization that took part in the growing direct activism of the movement. Brower wanted his new San Francisco–based organization to pursue certain issues and strategies that the Sierra Club had not or would not address. These included "a greater emphasis on international issues, a more direct ideological role through an expanded publishing effort, and a more expansive agenda, including but not limited to traditional wilderness and resource policy themes."[8]

An important component of Friends of the Earth was the League of Conservation Voters, which began in 1970 with few resources and a small overhead. Housed in FOE's Washington, D.C., office, the league soon developed into a vibrant advocate for pro-environmental politicians and a center for electoral data collection. In 1972, after philosophical differences split FOE, most of its East Coast staff departed and created a new Washington, D.C.–based organization, the **Environmental Policy Center** (EPC, later called the Environmental Policy Institute). The EPC became an advocacy group composed of experts who support lobbyists and researchers interested in water conservation. They emphasize cost-benefit techniques as a more powerful and conservative way to limit government water control projects, such as the Bureau of Reclamation's Central Utah Project and the Army Corps's Tennessee-Tombigbee project.

One of the most well-known citizen action groups is **Greenpeace.** Today, Greenpeace has offices in twenty-seven countries, more than 5 million members worldwide, and an annual budget of $130 million. Its members currently run thirty-seven different campaigns around the world. This international organization is a far cry from "the motley crew of 12 men" who set out on September 15, 1971, in an antiquated halibut seiner called the *Phyllis Cormack* to stop a U.S. underground nuclear bomb test on Alaska's Amchitka Island. The protest voyage's organizers were James Bohlen, Irving Stowe, and Paul Cote, three Vancouver environmentalists who had quit the San Francisco–based Sierra Club because it refused to take a stand against nuclear weapons testing. Before leaving Vancouver on their maiden voyage, they emblazoned the bridge of the boat with "Greenpeace," which combined their concern for the planet and their opposition to nuclear arms.[9] Because of bad weather, the *Phyllis Cormack* never reached the testing site. But when it returned to port six weeks later, the publicity its crew had generated helped to persuade the federal government to halt future tests. One year later, the fledging group's name became known around the world when a Vancouver-born yachtsman and developer-turned-environmentalist named David McTaggart skippered a Greenpeace ship to a French nuclear test site in the South Pacific. There, the Greenpeace vessel was rammed by a French warship, but failed to stop the test.

In the early 1970s Greenpeace launched campaigns from its Vancouver headquarters to save the whales and to stop the killing of Newfoundland harp seal pups. By 1977 the entire operation seemed on the verge of collapse because of shaky finances and bickering within Greenpeace. In addition, dozens of unconnected groups in North America used the Greenpeace name, which caused more problems. The Canadian, American, and European groups eventually agreed to form an umbrella body, Greenpeace International, based in Amsterdam. When Paul Watson, an active Greenpeace member, led other members to adopt an aggressive eye-for-an-eye approach, such as blowing up whaling ships, they were forced to leave; in 1977 they formed a new group called the **Sea Shepherd Conservation Society,** which continues to actively pursue a direct-action strategy.

The problem of nuclear energy was one of the earliest issues to attract alternative environmentalists. In the early 1970s concerned citizens began to question the safety and necessity of such energy sources, and to protest in earnest against the construction of nuclear power plants. The Clamshell Alliance organized protests at the proposed Seabrook nuclear plant in New Hampshire in August 1976, which symbolized the public's apprehension. Such protests encouraged similar **direct-action groups,** such as the Abalone Alliance in California, to organize their own protests. The Abalone Alliance was a community organization formed in the late 1970s to protest the proposed Diablo Canyon nuclear power plant on California's central coast. Mothers for Peace, based in San Luis Obispo, California, which was earlier active in the anti-Vietnam War movement, joined the Abalone Alliance. Together, they consolidated opposition with the discovery of an earthquake fault near the plant. Mobilization for Survival, another important alternative organization formed in 1977, joined other action groups protesting nuclear weapons, installations, and research facilities, such as the Hanford complex in Washington State and the University of California's Lawrence National Laboratory.[10]

Real and fictional examples of nuclear power's potential dangers encouraged public support for the antinuclear movement. On March 28, 1979, a cooling-system valve failed to close in Unit II at the **Three Mile Island** nuclear power plant near Harrisburg, Pennsylvania. This set in motion the worst commercial atomic power accident in U.S. history. Around the same time, the film *The China Syndrome* was released. The movie portrayed a fictional accident at a nuclear power plant that eerily approximated the Three Mile Island disaster, which enabled protesters to attract a great deal of attention to the issue.

By the late 1970s critics of the environmental movement frequently pointed out that environmental organizations amassed members mostly from the upper socioeconomic classes. The poor, urban minorities, and blue-collar workers, critics argued, were more concerned with the nation's economic and social inequalities. Defending the wilderness, wildlife, and numerous eco-issues mostly benefited those who could enjoy these amenities. Critics also pointed out that environmental policies ignored the problems of urban America, which bore much of the burden of environmental pollution and degradation and instead concentrated on a natural world that most Americans did not have the luxury of enjoying. Thus, the concerns of minorities and the urban poor, people without the financial means or free time to enjoy nature, were usually not priorities of the various environmental groups.[11]

The environmental movement by the end of the decade was often considered just another of the many "special interest" groups, which included women, gay men and lesbians, seniors, and various ethnic cultures, lobbying for attention. There was also the opposition of "hard" scientists and engineers such as industrial chemists, oil geologists, physicists, and others working outside the "life" sciences who argued that humanity's ingenuity and perseverance would enable it to overcome whatever obstacles nature may put in the way of progress. Added to this was criticism from individuals on the Christian Right who charged that the views of environmentalists were against biblical teachings. Some church leaders went so far as to argue that because environmental issues attempted to praise nature above humanity, they were un-American, antihuman, and anti-Christian. The influence of religious critics permeated society. One incident, described by historian Victor B. Scheffer, exemplifies just how emotional this issue had become for some people.

Once, after writer Joseph Wood Krutch had spoken from a Tucson radio station, an irate woman phoned in to denounce him for blasphemy. "Only man," she said, "was valuable in God's sight. Whereas Krutch had put himself on the devil's side when he had confessed that he should not like to see even such 'noxious' creatures as the tarantula and the scorpion totally exterminated." Krutch retorted by pointing out that the God of the Bible had carefully provided, through the agency of Noah, for the preservation of all species.[12]

Although critics of the environmental movement appeared in many forms, the momentum for environmental regulation was increasing and was particularly evident in the political arena.

New Environmental Legislation

The environmental movement benefited from the public's initial enthusiasm for its cause after Earth Day and enjoyed the support of both Congress and the president. The federal government rapidly passed environmental legislation in response to the nation's concerns.

Perhaps the most significant environmental legislation of the Nixon era was the **National Environmental Policy Act,** which President Nixon signed three months before Earth Day. It required environmental-impact statements for federally funded construction projects and established the **Environmental Protection Agency (EPA)** to enforce new statutes. The EPA became an amalgamation of programs that included the Federal Water Quality Administration, all the Department of Interior's pesticide programs, the National Air Pollution Control Administration's pesticide research, the Bureau of Water Hygiene, and parts of the Bureau of Radiological Health from the Department of Health, Education, and Welfare. It also inherited the Department of Agriculture's pesticide activities and both the Atomic Energy Commission's and Federal Radiation Council's radiation and standards programs. Lastly, the newly created Council on Environmental Quality sent its ecological research to the burgeoning EPA.

Nixon chose William D. Ruckelshaus, formerly of the U.S. attorney general's office, as the EPA's first administrator. Ruckelshaus found himself directing a brand-new staff of nearly six thousand people and administering a budget of $1.3 billion. He later recalled that it "was like trying to perform an appendectomy while running the 100-yard dash."[13] An EPA review of his administration concluded,

> Ruckelshaus inherited an agency with no clearly defined mission, no set of priorities, and no organizational structure. When he left EPA on April 30, 1973, to become acting director of the Federal Bureau of Investigation, he left a legacy of standard-setting and strong enforcement of federal anti-pollution laws—command and control as it has come to be called. And he left an organizational structure little changed today.[14]

Ruckelshaus had helped to establish a well-running EPA, which soon oversaw many new environmental laws.

Since the beginning of the twentieth century, air pollution had blackened the skies of midwestern industrial cities. The ensuing environmental and health hazards galvanized public opinion, and the first of the new major environmental legislation was to improve air quality. The revised Clean Air Act of 1970 identified 189 pollutants that caused smog and established standards to regulate their emissions. The act stipulated that factories and power plants must install special smokestack filters, known as scrubbers, to prevent the discharge of ash and other pollutants into the air. They were also required to install antipollution equipment or use alternate fuels in order to limit the release of sulfur dioxide. Sulfur dioxide is produced when coal or oil burns and is linked to **acid rain**. The act also identified the automobile as a major pollutant; its provisions forced automakers to equip their cars with catalytic converters to reduce exhaust fumes and required oil companies to remove lead from gasoline.

The Clean Air Act was followed in 1972 by the **Clean Water Act**, which regulated the release of pollutants into waterways, storm sewers, and reservoirs while mandating steps to restore polluted waters for recreational use. Although the ultimate goal of the law was zero discharge of pollutants, Congress quickly realized that this was unrealistic for the near future. Instead, it set attainable interim goals to ensure that polluted waters would be "fishable" and "swimmable" within a few years. For example, Congress established national limits on industrial and municipal discharges and set up a permit system based on these limits. It also created a public works program, supported by an $18 billion grants program, to build wastewater treatment plants across the country. Two years later, the Safe Drinking Water Act required the EPA to set and enforce standards that protected the nation's drinking-water supply from contaminants.

A series of environmental laws designed to protect nature and the public from the hazards of industrial growth were also passed. These included the Marine Mammal Protection Act, the Toxic Substances Control Act, and many other federal and state statutes. To these, President Nixon added his Commission on Population Growth and the American Future, which promoted zero population growth—the idea that the nation's birthrate should not exceed its death rate. He also signed the Environmental Education Act, which attempted to educate the general public about the problems of environmental decay and ecological issues. Unfortunately, this act failed to attract sufficient financial support from Congress and soon disappeared.[15]

The momentum for environmental reform continued to grow during the first years of the decade. The use of the pesticide DDT was finally banned in 1972, while the **Ocean Dumping Act** regulated the intentional disposal of material into the ocean and authorized related research. In

1973 Congress passed the **Endangered Species Act** (ESA), which allowed species to be listed as threatened or endangered without considering the economic consequences of those decisions, such as ensuing unemployment. "For the first time in history, the government undertook a concrete, systematic effort to save wildlife from the destructive behavior of humans."[16] The ESA mandated that federal agencies use the most current scientific evidence to list all species in danger of extinction as either "threatened" or "endangered" and to develop and carry out plans for their recovery.

The support for such environmental policies continued to grow among the public, who were being constantly reminded that their existence was often threatened by irresponsible human interaction with nature. In 1973 more than ten thousand Michigan farm residents were exposed to polybrominated biphenyls (PBBs), a group of fat-soluble, biologically persistent compounds similar to polychlorinated biphenyls (PCBs), which are used as flame retardants. The crisis had occurred when several hundred pounds of PBB were accidentally substituted for magnesium oxide, which is used in animal feed. Cattle exposed to the chemical suffered numerous ailments, including birth defects, and humans who drank the milk and ate the meat from these animals exhibited symptoms of PBB poisoning. It may be years before the long-term health effects of this incident are known.

The domestic environmental movement was beginning to have an effect on the international scene. Environmentalists were able to point to numerous U.S. laws supporting their cause at the 1972 United Nations–sponsored Conference on Human Environment, known as the Stockholm Conference.

> This conference which was action-oriented (or at least was supposed to be), supported broadly by NGOs (nongovernmental organizations), and well managed (before and after the conference), recognized four broad areas of concern: balance or conflict between development and environment, human settlement, natural resources, and pollution. The two principal results of the Stockholm Conference were an official recognition of the international concern for the environment, and the establishment of the United Nations Environment Programme (UNEP) to "institutionalize" the environment.[17]

Despite the plethora of new environmental legislation, public support for environmental issues began to decline after the first flush of enthusiasm. The troubles that befell the Environmental Protection Agency demonstrate this. With strong congressional support, the EPA "rode the crest of the environmental wave of the late 60s and early 70s, right into the first oil shock in 1973." The OPEC (Organization of Petroleum Exporting Countries) oil embargo hit the United States hard. The country imported one-third of its oil from OPEC, and the escalating costs of gasoline, heating oil, and assorted petroleum-based products intensified inflation. It was then that Russel E. Train took over the EPA from Ruckelshaus. Train was a lawyer turned conservationist who had been the first director of the president's Council on Environmental Quality. The oil crisis, Train recalled, "left little support for new environmental initiatives and much pressure for rolling back environmental standards like sulfur oxide emissions." Train spent much of the late 1970s struggling to retain the gains from the initial surge for environmental causes and to ensure that "there was no significant roll-back in environmental protection."[18]

The oil crisis eroded much of the public's enthusiasm for environmental regulations. Industries buckled under the sudden rise of energy prices and the public's demand for affordable gasoline and heating oil. The business community was also against much of the environmental legislation. They complained that environmental standards were too expensive, hampered their ability to compete with foreign competitors, reduced employment, and hurt profits.

One example of the concerted backlash against environmentalists began in 1974. That year the first fuel-economy standards, which required that automakers produce energy-efficient cars to save fuel and reduce harmful emissions, legally took effect. The ensuing conflict pitted environmentalists, who supported the law, against the auto industry, which loudly denounced the law as a threat to the survival of a key industry that employed hundreds of thousands of Americans. Many Americans worried that an overzealous environmental agenda was supplanting economic priorities.

Faced with such pressure, President Nixon retreated from his initial support of pro-environment legislation and tried to slow its progress. However, Congress usually countered his efforts by passing pro-environmental legislation and generally ignored corporate leaders. As a result of the Watergate scandal, President Nixon resigned in 1974 and Gerald R. Ford stepped in to finish the term. The environmental movement stalled during President Ford's brief tenure. Ford's response to the energy crisis was conservative, like him, and reflected the concerns of many Americans who thought improving the economy should be the top priority of any administration. As Ford explained in 1975,

> I pursue the goal of clean air and pure water, but I must also pursue the objective of maximum jobs and continued economic progress. Unemployment is as real and sickening a blight as any pollutant that threatens the nation.[19]

Still, even an economic crisis and the Ford administration's conservatism could not erase the need for environmental protection to regulate new environmental disasters. In 1976 the dumping of the hazardous chemical ketone in the James River in Hopewell, Virginia, PCB contamination of the Hudson River, and the accidental PBB chemical poisoning of cows in Michigan increased public concern about toxic substances. Public outrage again led to political action. In 1976 Congress passed the **Resource Conservation and Recovery Act (RCRA)**, which regulated the disposal and treatment of solid and hazardous waste from "cradle to grave." Congress also enacted the **Toxic Substances Control Act**, which required that all chemicals produced or imported into the country be tested, regulated, and screened. It also required schools to inspect for and remove asbestos hazards, and the EPA to study radioactive **radon gas** levels in schools and to regularly inform the public of health risks associated with radon exposure.

Jimmy Carter and the Envirocrats

As a result of the nation's economic problems, which stemmed primarily from the OPEC oil embargoes, Ford's 1976 presidential campaign floundered. Jimmy Carter, a little-known Democratic governor from Georgia, presented himself as an anti-Washington candidate who would bring a higher moral approach to government. The public elected him president in 1976, but the same poor economy that had hampered his predecessors plagued Carter. Throughout his term President Carter struggled to control a recession in which inflation rose rapidly, mostly as a result of the energy crisis that began during the Ford administration. Consumer prices had jumped 12 percent in 1974, rose 11 percent in 1975, and continued to rise 13 percent in both 1979 and 1980. Unemployment reached nearly 11 percent in 1975 as business stagnated and the federal deficit climbed to unprecedented levels. To make things worse, a second major oil crisis hit in 1979. This time OPEC raised oil prices to $30 a barrel, which forced a shocked American public to pay nearly $1 per gallon to put gas into their tanks—more than three times the previous price. In 1979 Americans paid an additional $16.4 billion because of oil price increases.[20] Faced with an angry public and continued oil price hikes, President Carter tried to institute voluntary programs that would curtail energy consumption. However, he failed to significantly curb inflation or the demand for oil.

As the economic crisis worsened, Carter decided that America's use of natural resources—and oil in particular—had to change.

> The nation's wasteful approach to dwindling fossil-fuel resources must give way to a new ethic of conservation. [President Carter] recognized that two key factors underlying a generation of U.S. economic growth—cheap, unlimited energy and the lack of foreign competition—could no longer be counted on. Americans, he concluded, must learn to survive in a "zero-sum society" that could no longer anticipate endless future expansion.[21]

Determined to promote a more frugal energy use policy, Carter tried to limit waste and consumption across the board. With congressional support, he set fuel efficiency standards for automobiles in 1975 and established a national speed limit of 55 miles per hour. In 1977 he created a cabinet department, the **Department of Energy**, to record and regulate energy use. He also tried to institute a series of tax reforms that would limit oil and gasoline consumption as well as reward industries that practiced conservation. These reforms generally failed.

While Carter struggled with economic problems, environmental issues continued to attract public and political attention. In 1978 residents living near **Love Canal** in upstate New York were evacuated after it was discovered that their homes were built atop a chemical waste dump. In the same year, a hundred thousand hazardous-waste-leaking barrels were found at the **Valley of Drums**, in West Point, Kentucky. The problem of abandoned hazardous waste sites, often referred to as "ticking time bombs," was thrust into the nation's consciousness.

Although the public had become more aware of environmental issues, and even supported government regulation as a means of controlling the use of nature, its concerns did not result in the development of a political party that would champion this cause. Barry Commoner was the New Citizens Party presidential candidate in 1980. This green party failed to attract the attention of Americans the way similar political efforts, such as the Die Grünen in West Germany and the Ecology Party in England, had Europeans. The lack of a strong green party in the United States even today can be attributed to a number of factors. In a nation dominated by a two-party system, many Americans seem not to want to "waste" their vote on a fringe group. Also, many people believe that environmental lobbyists have achieved a great deal for specific issues and that established politicians, particularly within the Democratic Party, have adopted basic environmental causes. As historian Anna Bramwell states, "More probably, it was the surprising success of the environmental lobby in the USA that vitiated the need for party political activity."[22] Considering the array of environmental legislation since 1970, the lack of a viable green party in the United States has not perceptibly hampered environmentalists' efforts or their influence in Washington.

However, public concern did generate political action in other forms. In 1980 Congress passed the **Comprehensive Environmental Response, Compensation, and Liability Act**, better known as Superfund. The law earned its nickname, Superfund, from the five-year, $1.6 billion trust fund set up by the statute. The fund was to be financed primarily by a tax on industrial feedstock chemicals. Although controversial, Superfund enabled the EPA to respond to emergencies caused by abandoned hazardous waste dumps. Superfund also helped the EPA sue to recover cleanup costs if it could locate the liable parties. Such legislation enabled the EPA to establish a strong bureaucratic structure for protecting the environment.

The head of the EPA, Douglas M. Costle, who took office in 1977, believed tremendous environmental progress occurred during the late

1970s. He explained that with the EPA's infrastructure in place, the agency was "focused much better on what it was we could do and how to get it done." There were dramatic breakthroughs in compliance, he said, because "industry in general finally came to grips with the fact that these issues were here to stay" and that its relationship with EPA "had to evolve into a cooperative mode as opposed to a constant confrontational mode."

> I'd like to think that part of what we did during my time was to stabilize relationships between government and industry in terms of getting every-body harnessed and pulling in the same direction. We tried to give indus-try clearer signals of what would be expected of them as best as we could given the legislation we were working with.[23]

As concerns for public health increased, the EPA began to work with industry to limit pollution and became less involved with broader ecologi-cal issues.

As the EPA more clearly defined its goals, environmentalists found increased influence in the White House. The Carter administration seemed to welcome them and their cause. As a result, mainstream envi-ronmental groups became more involved in politics and the policy-mak-ing process.

> These groups inherited the label "environmentalist," a term employed by the press to designate both the largest of the Washington-based main-stream groups (often excluding other locally based or direct-action move-ments and groups) as well as the environmental bureaucracies with which the groups were associated. Growing in terms of staff and financial resources, the mainstream organizations were increasingly absorbed by the operation and maintenance of the policy system itself. A revolving door between staff positions in the mainstream groups and government and industry positions especially in terms of crucial lobbying and litigation functions, became more and more centered on keeping the system intact.[24]

These new "envirocrats" helped to formulate policies and influence the direction of the mainstream environmental movement. Their ranks included such notables as Joseph Browder of the Environmental Policy Center; Katherine Fletcher, Harris Sherman, and Gerald Meral of the Environmental Defense Fund; and Gus Speth and John Bryson, cofounders of the Natural Resources Defense Council. All managed to secure positions either with the Carter administration or at state resource agencies.[25]

However, President Carter found himself embroiled in a fight, as cor-porate opposition warned that environmental restrictions would further damage the economy. His administration, despite its stated aims, also failed to adequately incorporate local citizen groups into the Washington decision-making process. As Robert Gottlieb explains, the advocacy work, despite the spirited and creative efforts of certain staff members within these groups, never became linked to the possibility of creating a new kind of social movement. . . . There was little effort to mobilize at the local level, despite a proliferation of local environmental groups throughout the 1970s.[26]

As a result, business coalitions, such as the Business Roundtable, attacked regulations established by the EPA and the Occupational Safety and Health Act (OSHA), declaring that they cost too much, caused inefficiency, and hurt business morale. On the defensive, Jimmy Carter began to retreat. Ambitious environmental programs were put on hold, or weakened. The Energy Bill of 1978 was intended to embody a wide array of energy-saving programs, but faced with a reeling economy, corporate detractors, and a reluctant Congress, its final form reflected more intention than enforcement.

Conclusion

The 1970s witnessed the rise of the environmental movement in the United States, as both a political and a public issue. Numerous governmental organizations and private-citizen groups formed to promote proenvironmental causes and to actively protect nature. The result was an assortment of legislation that created a bulwark of environmental laws and agencies designed to incorporate environmentalism into the political arena. Public support blossomed throughout society, as mainstream and alternative organizations formed to tackle environmental causes. However, the activists' successes caused a significant backlash. The initial enthusiasm for environmental causes was tempered by economic concerns and a growing criticism that environmentalists were more concerned about narrow ecological themes than human needs. By the end of the decade domestic problems undermined the movement and weakened its momentum. The heyday of the environmental movement was over. The 1980s would be a time of transition, with environmentalists struggling to maintain their gains while alternative elements took a more active role.

Chapter Notes

1. Donald Worster, *Nature's Economy: The Roots of Ecology* (San Francisco: Sierra Club Books, 1977), 339.
2. Robert Gottlieb, *Forcing the Spring: The Transformation of the American Environmental Movement* (Washington, D.C.: Island Press, 1993), 311.
3. Ibid., 136.
4. Irene Diamond and Gloria Orenstein, "Two Feminists Discuss the Emergence of Ecofeminism," ed. Carolyn Merchant, *Major Problems in*

American Environmental History (Lexington, Mass.: D. C. Heath, 1993), 546.

5. For more information, see Rik Scarce, *Eco-Warriors: Understanding the Alternative Environmental Movement* (Chicago: Noble Press, 1990).

6. Philip Shabecoff, *A Fierce Green Fire: The American Environmental Movement* (New York: Hill and Wang, 1993), 123.

7. Gottlieb, *Forcing the Spring*, 170.

8. Ibid., 144–145.

9. John DeMont, with William Lowther, "A Bigger, More Influential Greenpeace Begins Its Third Decade," *Maclean's*, Dec. 16, 1991, 46.

10. Gottlieb, *Forcing the Spring*, 178–183.

11. Garrett De Bell, "The Recovery of the Cities," *The Environmental Handbook* (New York: Ballantine Books, 1970), 234.

12. Victor B. Scheffer, *The Shaping of Environmentalism in America* (Seattle: University of Washington Press, 1991), 9–14.

13. Lois R. Ember, "EPA Administrators Deem Agency's First 25 Years Bumpy But Successful," *C&EN*, Oct. 30, 1995, 19.

14. Ibid.

15. Shabecoff, *A Fierce Green Fire*, 137.

16. Paul Rauber, "An End to Evolution: The Extinction Lobby in Congress Is Now Deciding Which Species Will Live and Which Will Die," *Sierra* 80, Jan./Feb. 1996, 31.

17. George L. De Feis, "Sustainable Development Issues: Industry, Environment, Regulation and Competition," *Journal of Professional Issues in Engineering Education and Practice* 120, no. 2, April 1994, 178.

18. Ember, "Agency's First 25 Years Bumpy But Successful," 19.

19. Mary H. Cooper, "Environmental Movement at 25," *CQ Researcher*, March 31, 1995, 418.

20. Paul S. Boyer, *The Enduring Vision* (Lexington, Mass.: D. C. Heath, 1995), 1077.

21. Ibid.

22. Anna Bramwell, *Ecology in the 20th Century* (New Haven: Yale University Press, 1989), 56.

23. Ember, "Agency's First 25 Years Bumpy But Successful," 20.

24. Gottlieb, *Forcing the Spring*, 130.

25. Ibid.

26. Ibid., 131.

Intentionally forbidding proper access
to needed resources limits this nation,
dooms us to shortages and damages our
right as a people to dream heroic dreams.
—JAMES WATT

8

The 1980s:
A Conservative Backlash

The 1980s marked a reversal in the move toward environmental protection. The energy crisis of the mid–1970s and the Reagan revolution of the 1980s demonstrated that environmental issues, though important, were subordinate in the public mind to material living standards and economic security. Bolstered by widespread support from business people and landowners, President Ronald Reagan dismantled many existing environmental regulations. As Reagan put it, "Government is not the solution to our problems: government is the problem."[1] His administration cut the budgets of government regulatory agencies, rolled back and tried to repeal environmental legislation, and appointed notoriously antienvironmentalist individuals, such as James Watt and Ann Gorsuch Burford, to key environmental positions.

Deregulation was moderated during Reagan's second term when Congress passed several new measures, including funding to clean up hazardous wastes and impose tighter controls over water purity, preserve endangered species, and reduce pesticides. Although no major new environmental statutes were enacted during President Reagan's second term, many of the existing laws were renewed and strengthened.

Ronald Reagan's Environmental Deregulation

In the 1980 presidential election Ronald Reagan defeated Jimmy Carter. President Reagan, a conservative Republican governor from California, made it clear right from the start that the White House was no longer sympathetic to environmentalists. When Reagan moved into the White House, he immediately removed the rooftop solar panels Carter had installed.

As Reagan began his first term in 1981, a significant congressional environmental achievement occurred: the Superfund program to clean up hazardous chemical dumps took effect. Also, the United States supported a global moratorium on commercial whaling, enacted by the International Whaling Commission in 1983. Such activities reflected the popularity of environmental issues. The following year, pollster Louis Harris reported to Congress that 69 percent of the public favored making the Clean Air Act more stringent.

However, these were exceptions. Although many people sympathized with the need to protect the environment, there was a backlash against the perceived liberal agenda of the 1970s. Government and public support for environmental issues waned in the glare of the emerging conservative beliefs of the 1980s: individual ambition, opposition to big government, and belief that the increasingly unpopular liberals supported environmental issues. For example, in 1982 actor Robert Redford, a renowned supporter of liberal causes, offered Washington State University and the University of Idaho $400,000 to open an Institute for Resource Management, where graduate students would study earthkeeping (how to institute policy, analyze relevant information, and work to maintain and protect the environment). In the planning stage, the institute drew fire from Idaho reactionaries who feared that "it could thrust Idaho into a role of environmental advocacy."[2]

Reagan's environmental views oscillated in a narrow band between indifference and hostility. His appointments often reflected this hostility and his desire to deregulate environmental agencies. He hired Donald Hodel as energy secretary. Hodel became notorious for suggesting that the way to deal with ozone depletion is to apply stronger suntan lotion.

Reagan's secretary of the interior, James Watt, shared Reagan's visceral dislike for government regulation and began dismantling environmental protection programs with fanatical zeal. Watt became the darling of the **Sagebrush Rebellion**, a movement led by western loggers, miners, and ranchers to sell public land to private interests, when he publicly supported their views. Environmentalists, appalled by Watt's excesses, called for his removal. Members of Congress from both parties joined the fight. GOP defeats in the 1982 election did much to build that bipartisan support. A "Dump Watt" petition drive gathered upward of a million signatures from the eager public. This outpouring and Watt's unrelenting churlishness forced him to resign in 1983.[3]

President Reagan chose Ann Gorsuch Burford to head the Environmental Protection Agency. She seemed more determined to dismantle the EPA than administer it. Burford made President Reagan's goal of cutting government expenses and regulations her own. She reduced the EPA's budget, excluding the Superfund, by $200 million, and the staff by 23 percent. As seasoned professionals departed, the remaining EPA personnel quickly became demoralized.

In the political atmosphere of the conservative 1980s, the EPA had lost much of the popularity and support that it had enjoyed in the 1970s among politicians and the general public. Public and congressional trust was at its lowest, and their distrust of the agency lingered. So in May 1983, Reagan brought back the EPA's first director, William D. Ruckelshaus, to appease congressional and environmental critics. Instead of the enthusiastic optimism that had characterized his first tenure, Ruckelshaus encountered anxiety among his staff. The issues he faced—toxic chemicals and risk assessment, hazardous wastes, acid rain, climate change, and dioxin—were more complicated and had a thinner science base than those in 1970. To regain public support, Ruckelshaus stressed enforcement and strengthened the EPA's Science Advisory Board, which would build up the science base. Ruckelshaus recalled,

> by the time I got back, the agency was in such a state of turmoil that the main thing that needed to be done was to calm it down and put it back to work. I think I accomplished that—almost by just coming back.[4]

Ruckelshaus regretted not being able to get "started on the process of rationalizing our environmental policy . . . our regulatory system" because of the way President Reagan handled regulatory reform early in his first term. The EPA's approach to regulation had "become so politicized." He concluded that the Reagan administration undermined the EPA because it erroneously believed that the popularity of environmentalism had declined.

> When the Reagan Administration came in, the public was willing to give it a good deal of leeway on the means to achieve our environmental goals because it was by then clear that some of the approaches we were taking were not going to work or were causing distortions. I don't think the public was ready to abandon—nor do I think it is now—its commitment to a clean environment.[5]

Ruckelshaus left the EPA in 1985 at the end of President Reagan's first term, and Reagan replaced him with Lee M. Thomas. Thomas was a career government official—having served in the Federal Emergency Management Agency before moving to the EPA. His tenure saw few major advancements for the EPA. He did manage to get Congress to renew the Superfund in 1986. Although passage of the Superfund was heavily debated because environmental legislation attracts controversy especially when it includes large amounts of money, and the Superfund barely made the renewal deadline, Congress hiked the trust fivefold, from $1.6 billion over five years to $8.5 billion. Thomas believed the Superfund was fundamentally flawed in how its regulations were applied. He preferred delegating "the majority of responsibility to the states, and putting most of the money out at the state level." This would disengage the EPA from the Superfund, he said, without a loss of environmental protection and very probably with a gain in efficiency. Not surprisingly, Thomas regretted that he was unable "to do a better job in restructuring" the Superfund.[6] Transferring environmental protection to the states was a unique idea in the wake of the regulatory bonanza of the 1970s and, although not instituted, it remained popular with many conservatives.

Environmental legislation regained its momentum during President Reagan's second term, as the lame-duck president faced a more courageous Democratic Congress. In 1986 Congress reauthorized the Safe Drinking Water Act. The **Emergency Planning and Community Right-to-Know** Act of 1986 required industries to report toxic releases and encouraged local communities to plan their responses to chemical emergencies. Congress also dropped consideration of any legislation that would open the Arctic National Wildlife Refuge in Alaska to oil and gas drilling, which environmentalists had heatedly contested. Sharon Newscome, the National Wildlife Federation's legislative affairs director, declared, "Conservationists were successful in getting Congress to focus on energy needs and to question whether oil from the Arctic refuge is really essential."[7] Their success encouraged many environmentalists to believe that they could influence the federal government.

Such successes continued, though not with the unbridled enthusiasm of the past. In 1987 the National Wildlife Federation lauded the $65 million earmarked for the Forest Service and Wildlife programs—a healthy increase over the $45 million Reagan requested. Congress also appropriated $64 million for additional land acquisition and $16 million for recreation trails, even though the administration had requested no money for these purposes. The budget also provided funds to inventory old-growth forests on the Pacific Coast and to study the feasibility of transferring ownership of some private forest lands in the Northwest to the public.

Congress tempered its pro-environmental actions with less favorable appropriations. It shaved $20 million from the administration's forest roads budget rather than the $106 million decrease recommended by the National Wildlife Federation, although the $175.5 million appropriated was still $4 million more than in 1986. The legislation also entitled the Forest Service to sell 11.5 billion board-feet of timber from the national forests, 1.5 billion more than National Wildlife Federation had recommended. The Federation achieved a symbolic victory when, at the group's urging, Congress passed a law recognizing the 100th anniversary of Aldo Leopold's birth.[8]

George Bush as the Environmental President

As Reagan's vice president for two terms, George Bush had supported deregulation and business development. But during the 1988 presidential campaign, he promised to usher in a new era of environmental concern and to be an "environmental president." After his election, Bush signaled his commitment by appointing William K. Reilly, a respected environmentalist, to head the EPA. But President Bush often fell short of his environmental promises as he struggled to balance economic and environmental concerns in his policies. As the economy slid into recession—unemployment surpassed 7 percent that year—public support for strong environmental legislation characteristically weakened. Still, environmental disasters continued to demand the public's attention.

Two major environmental problems arose in the 1980s that theoretically threatened the safety of the world—depletion of the **ozone layer** and **global warming**. Such a widespread danger, precipitated by the activities of industrialized nations, helped to publicize environmental issues and to promote a public call for government regulation of pollutants.

In the 1980s scientists had postulated that chlorofluorocarbon (CFC) gases rising into the stratosphere were depleting the earth's protective ozone layer. Although other experts questioned this theory, all doubt evaporated in 1986 when scientists discovered a hole in the ozone over the Antarctic. Studies linked the hole to excessive amounts of chlorine in the atmosphere, much of it carried there by CFC molecules.

Then, in 1988 scientists from the National Aeronautics and Space Administration (NASA) warned that rising carbon dioxide levels from petroleum use were causing a potentially catastrophic global-warming trend by trapping the sun's radiation close to earth, a phenomenon they dubbed the "**greenhouse effect**." The EPA went even further, concluding that rising sea levels could inundate 30 to 80 percent of U.S. coastal wetlands by the year 2100 if emissions of carbon dioxide and other "greenhouse" gases continued at the current rate.[9] Adherents of the global warming theory argue that higher earth temperatures will cause extreme climatic changes and flooding and will disrupt agriculture around the world. Reports of global warming have been based on computer models, which skeptics contend are flawed and overstated.[10]

Faced with these official findings, the industrial nations were forced to take action. In 1987 the United States and twenty-three other countries signed the **Montreal Protocol**, pledging that they would phase out production and use of CFCs by 1999.

Arguably, the nation's greatest ecological disaster of the 1980s occurred in March 1989 when a 987-foot oil tanker, the *Exxon Valdez*, ran aground off the coast of Alaska's Prince William Sound. Some 11 million gallons of crude oil spilled into the water, fouling 600 acres of coastal and marine habitats, killing thousands of sea otters and shore birds, and jeopardizing vital salmon and herring industries. The nation was outraged by the disaster. President Bush publicly described the spill as a "major tragedy," but he continued to support offshore oil exploration and drilling.[11]

Just as the *Exxon Valdez* crisis was disappearing from the headlines, the EPA reported that air pollution had exceeded federal standards in

106 *First Along the River*

more than a hundred cities during the summer of 1989. In Louisiana alone, industry pumped 2 million pounds of pollutants into the air every day.

The EPA's warnings did little to stem the problem of air pollution. In 1990 the nation's 23,638 largest industrial chemical users released some 4.8 billion pounds of 320 toxic chemicals or chemical groups into the air, water, or land, or transferred these chemicals to treatment and disposal facilities. This represented only a fraction of the seventy thousand chemicals used commercially. Additionally, more than two hundred thousand manufacturing plants, ranging from mom-and-pop operations to large companies, made or used chemicals in the United States, exposing thousands of workers to risk. Tens of thousands of nonmanufacturing facilities, such as waste treatment plants, farms, public utilities, photo finishers, dry-cleaning operations, and other small businesses, also used toxic chemicals and discharged chemical waste.

In the face of federal apathy, many states applied their own solutions to the environmental troubles that plagued them. In 1989 New York, New Jersey, and the six New England states agreed to adopt California's strict vehicle emissions standards for nitrous oxides and hydrocarbons, the chief ingredients of urban smog, which were tougher than the clean air proposals the Bush administration recommended. The plan also required auto manufacturers to extend warranties on mandated pollution control equipment from 50,000 to 100,000 miles. Governor Mario Cuomo of New York said, "We will do what we must to protect the health of our people. But it's still true that it would be better for the nation if Washington would recognize its special responsibility."[12] In 1990 a CBS News/*New York Times* survey found that 74 percent of respondents supported protecting the environment regardless of the cost, up nearly 30 percent from 1981.

This public pressure influenced President Bush and the Congress to take stronger action on environmental fronts. In 1990 the Republican White House and the Democratic Congress worked to together to pass amendments to the Clean Air Act that called for stricter standards. They also began a multibillion-dollar cleanup of nuclear weapons facilities and power plants, by disposing of radioactive wastes that had been contaminating soil and ground water for years.

However, despite such legislation, the Bush administration was not eager to support environmental concerns and was even likely to dismiss those that were not immediate problems or appeared questionable. For example, the federal government did almost nothing about the legal sale of endangered or protected wildlife, which totaled $1.5 billion a year, or about 30 percent of total wildlife sales worldwide. The administration also scuttled international treaties on global warming and mining in Antarctica, recommended oil exploration in the Alaskan wilderness, and proposed opening vast tracts of protected wetlands to development.

Public concern about the environment stayed high during the 1990s, though the practical results remained mixed. Despite popular support of recycling programs, the United States remained the world's leading consumer society and the leading throwaway society. At the end of 1990, each American was producing 4.3 pounds of trash each day, up from 2.7 pounds in 1960.

By 1990 after twenty years of legislation enacted by the Clean Air Act, there was evidence that air quality in the United States had improved. The emission of pollutants in the atmosphere had dropped from nearly 25 million tons per year to less than 10 million. Restrictions on the use of leaded fuel had decreased lead emissions (identified as a major contributor to retardation in children) more than 200,000 tons a year to less than 10,000. Yet serious problems associated with air pollution remained. Smog, which is related to vehicle emissions and industrial wastes, continued to plague congested cities.[13] Then, in 1991 the EPA reported that pollutants were depleting the ozone shield, the stratospheric layer that protects humans from cancer-causing solar radiation, over the United States at twice the rate that scientists had predicted in 1986.

The government's response was moderate, reflecting the public's desire to protect jobs and the economy. On November 15, 1990, President Bush signed amendments to the Clean Air Act to place stricter limits on the emissions of toxic air pollutants. These amendments called for a significant reduction in the emissions that cause acid rain and smog, airborn toxic chemicals, and substances that deplete stratospheric ozone. In an effort to protect industry and jobs, the law relied heavily on market incentives such as voluntary compliance credits and performance standards. The **Pollution Prevention Act** of the same year sought to prevent pollution by encouraging companies to reduce the germination of pollutants through cost-effective changes in production, operation, and raw material use.

Employment versus the Environment

As President Bush entered his last year in office, he struggled to balance environmental policy with economic rights. Yet the economy remained the predominant issue for most Americans in 1992. In May the Labor Department announced that by the year 2005 job opportunities would decline in thirty occupations, with more than half being manufacturing jobs. In January 1992 President Bush had instituted a ninety-day moratorium on new regulations, including those that affected the environment, purportedly to save American businesses money and protect employment. On April 29, 1992, still nervous about the nation's poor economy, he extended the moratorium.[14]

The problem of job losses versus environmental interests erupted with the conflict over the northern spotted owl. In January 1987 the Fish and Wildlife Service received the first petition to list the owl as threatened under the Endangered Species Act. In December that year the agency determined that the listing was not warranted, which several environmental organizations immediately challenged. In June 1990, as a result of their efforts, the owl was finally listed as threatened under the Endangered Species Act, which activated measures to protect its habitat, the ancient forests of the Pacific Northwest.

Actually, these old-growth forests were the main reason environmentalists sought protection for the northern spotted owl in the first place. The timber industry protested that protecting the forests would cause widespread unemployment among loggers and other workers in the region who depended on the timber industry. They estimated that logging operations would drop 2 percent in the next fifteen years, eliminating 106,000 logging jobs.[15]

Robert E. Jenkins, Jr., vice president for science at the Nature Conservancy, a conservation organization based in Arlington, Virginia, said,

> It's quite clear that timber employment in the Pacific Northwest is going down anyway. . . . Even if the timber interests up there were allowed to cut every last tree that they would like to—which would probably be every last tree—it would still only stave off their day of reckoning for a few years.

A study by the Wilderness Society in Washington, D.C., found that the Northwest's timber industry already had lost nearly fourteen thousand jobs in the past decade because of automation and a shift in timber exports from milled products to raw logs. In Jenkins's view, however, automation accounted for only part of the decline.

> They are running out of timber, and it's just a question of whether you stop before you cut down the last tree or whether you stop some time before that.[16]

The timber industry disputed some of the Wilderness Society's findings. Denny Scott of the carpenters union, for example, called the study "basically flawed" because it downplayed the role of regulations.

> As long as the environmental community tries to make this false case that old-growth preservation does not impact negatively on unemployment, we're not going to get very far.[17]

The profitability of the logging industry remained a serious point of contention. In the Tongass National Forest of southeast Alaska, **clear-cutting** ancient forests was profitable only because the government gave loggers massive subsidies. Whereas those who supported clear-cutting argued that it was necessary and that it was followed by the planting of seedlings for the renewal of the forests, environmentalists argued that in most of America's national forests, logging was an economically unsound activity and such methods were unnecessary because logging would wither away without continual federal handouts.

Similarly, public funds sustained most of the environmentally destructive water projects in the West, including most of the irrigation. The same was true of the massive overgrazing of almost all the federal government's rangelands. State subsidies and other governmentally mandated economic distortions often stimulated tropical deforestation in such states as Florida and Louisiana. As one critic of antienvironmental efforts wrote,

> The fact that many self-proclaimed conservatives consistently support such subsidies may indicate that they care less about achieving economic efficiency than about making sure key constituents can remain at the public trough.[18]

Environmental Groups Actions and Reactions

Activists had continued their efforts during President Reagan's second term. In 1986 Kirkpatrick Sale wrote in *Mother Jones* magazine of "the passion of a new and growing movement that has become disenchanted with the environmental establishment and has in recent years mounted a serious and sweeping attack on it—style, substance, systems, sensibilities and all."[19]

Most of the large environmental groups continued to grow throughout the 1980s. In 1965 the ten largest mainstream groups combined had fewer than five hundred thousand members and a less than $10 million annual budget; by 1985 those numbers jumped to 3.3 million members and $218 million, and by 1990 to 7.2 million members and $514 million.[20] By 1992 the largest environmental groups, including the Sierra Club and the League of Conservation Voters, had doubled their combined spending to $1 billion. The Environmental Defense Fund's annual revenue increased nearly sixfold from $3.4 million to $20.2 million between 1985 and 1992. The National Wildlife Federation, with 5.3 million members and supporters, had an annual budget larger than that of the United Nations' Environmental Programme. Other organizations, such as the World Resources Institute, Worldwatch Institute, Rocky Mountain Institute, and the Environmental and Energy Study Institute, also saw their financial strength, membership, and influence grow. By the end of 1992 there were estimated to be as many as ten thousand environmental organizations in the country.[21] Much of this increase can be attributed to the perceived threats to environmental protection during the Reagan-Bush years. Earth Day 1990, the first nationally organized celebration since 1970, had a far less confrontational tone than the original. The event triggered a frenzy of corporate **green marketing** and was heralded as the beginning of another green decade.[22] However, for many environmentalists the movement had become diluted by its own popularity, becoming trendy and corporate rather than aggressive, as it had been in the proactive days of the 1970s.

Unhappy with setbacks of the 1980s, many activists began taking a more violent approach to promote their causes. The **Animal Liberation Front** (ALF) led a series of attacks against animal experiments. Members raided Oregon State University's mink research farm and burned a barn. They vandalized offices at Washington State University and freed a number of animals. On February 28, 1992, ALF members broke into a hall at Michigan State University and set fire to the office of Richard Aulerich, who used minks as experimental animals in his toxicology and nutrition research. The attack caused about $75,000 worth of damage. **People for the Ethical Treatment of Animals,** which acted as a spokesgroup for ALF, stated that Aulerich "has killed thousands of minks in painful and scientifically worthless experiments." Aulerich countered that his "animals are not allowed to suffer" and were euthanized when necessary to avoid pain. He explained that minks are ideal subjects for toxicology research because they are susceptible to various environmental chemicals. Barbara Rich of the National Association for Biomedical Research deplored such attacks and lamented that, because of limits in the states' investigation capacities and their jurisdiction, the eighty or so break-ins and other illegal episodes involving animal activists during the past decade had resulted in only "three little bitty convictions."[23]

Environmental activists remained direct-action oriented, even at the risk of their own lives. In 1985 French government agents sank the Greenpeace flagship *Rainbow Warrior,* which was campaigning against nuclear testing in Auckland, New Zealand. A Greenpeace photographer died as a result. Auckland police arrested two of the French agents, and in 1986 the French government agreed to pay New Zealand $8.5 million in compensation.

Greenpeace continued its efforts and in 1985, six years after Greenpeace activists in rubber rafts began putting themselves between whales and hunters' harpoons, the International Whaling Commission enacted a global moratorium on commercial whaling. Japan alone refused to renounce whaling.[24] Pressure by Greenpeace and other groups also led to a 1989 United Nations ban on the use of drift nets by industrial-sized fishing ships. Drift nets kill dolphins and other marine life along with tuna. International interest in the environmental movement was increasing and would continue to grow in the 1990s.

International Environmental Concern

In the 1990s environmental issues started to garner concern and support worldwide. In 1991 President Bush supported signing a treaty that banned development on the Antarctic continent for fifty years. The next year, he joined delegates from 170 countries at the **Earth Summit** (also called the Rio Conference), in Rio de Janeiro, Brazil, June 3–14, 1992.The Earth Summit was the first international meeting of national leaders to address the problems of environmental decay in industrial states and global environmental issues common to all people. Neither gained Bush much credit from environmentalists.

The Earth Summit, held in a country responsible for the well-publicized burning of millions of square acres of Amazon rainforest, accomplished little and added to President Bush's opportunist reputation. The summit had the potential to establish a global approach to environmental problems and to make the United States the world leader on this issue. However, Bush's lackluster performance and his adherence to economic priorities portrayed the United States as a "cranky Uncle Scrooge." At the summit President Bush said, "To sustain development, we must protect the environment, and to protect the environment, we must sustain development." He said the summit treaties would harm U.S. economic growth and business interests and would cost too much. He offered an unspecified amount to help poorer nations inventory their lands to find out what species exist before they become extinct. He also pledged an underwhelming $25 million to help countries analyze and find ways to reduce their greenhouse-gas emissions and $150 million to help protect the world's forests. Then he called for an international conference to discuss progress.

At a press conference just before he left Rio, President Bush defended his record, saying, "Policy is not going to be dominated by the extremes." Yet as the conference chair, Tommy Koh of Singapore, put it, Bush "totally missed the point that the axis of world affairs has shifted from East-West to North-South."[25] Koh was referring to the idea that the world was now divided between the industrialized prosperous nations of the Northern Hemisphere and the poorer agrarian nations of the Southern Hemisphere, rather than between a U.S.-led Western Hemisphere and a Soviet-led Eastern Hemisphere. The people of the Southern Hemisphere suffered poverty, overpopulation, disease, political instability, and yet, because their countries were underdeveloped, they retained many of their natural resources. In the future, the richer nations would greatly depend on these poorer nations for their resources. Helping these people to build stable societies was considered essential to the interests of both hemispheres. Bush's unenthusiastic support of treaties that gave economic assistance to financially poor but resource rich nations appeared to damage efforts to nurture a closer North-South relationship.

A key to improving relations between prosperous and poorer nations was the Biodiversity Treaty proposed at the Earth Summit. The **Biodiversity Treaty** obligated signer nations to protect species within their borders: plants that act as the planet's lungs, bugs that eat oil and toxic chemicals and that contain substances used to treat cancer, microbes that support the soil that feeds the world's 5.4 billion people. Signer nations also agreed to share profits derived from the use of protected resources. As one observer put it,

While few delegates know a fungus from a mold, they do know the most important thing about biodiversity: the rich North needs it, the poor South has it. The North wants the South to develop in a way which protects species vital to life on earth (some 90 to 100 species become extinct every day). The South, however, often needs to chop its forests to fuel immediate development and feed a growing population. The South wants royalties and property rights in return for supplying pharmaceutical companies with the genetic treasures of their forests. So the pact would require a company that developed a drug from say, snake venom—as Bristol-Myers Squibb did—to share profits with the nation that saved the snake by preserving its habitat. This demand derailed the treaty.

The United States opposed paying nations to save their forests and wildlife because, as David McIntosh, the executive director of the Council on Competitiveness (a U.S. government organization chaired by Bush's vice president, Dan Quayle, that acts as a liaison between the White House and corporate leaders), said, the Biodiversity Treaty would "facilitate access to genetic material for environmentally sound uses, and promote fair and equitable sharing of . . . benefits arising from the use of genetic materials."[26] Essentially, McIntosh feared that U.S. companies would have to share their discoveries and lose their competitive edge. Nonetheless, 160 nations at Rio endorsed the treaty.

Japan and Britain initially squirmed over the financing provisions, but seemed willing to sign the treaty, as were Germany, France, Canada, and India. The United States alone refused to agree to the treaty. Britain's environment secretary, David Maclean, made it clear that U.S. influence on such international matters was ineffective, stating, "We'll sign and leave the U.S. on its own." Nations such as Germany and Japan seized the initiative on the environmental issue by showing a willingness to financially support the environmental programs of poorer nations, an issue that Senator Al Gore, a Democrat from Tennessee, called the "single organizing principle of the planet."[27] The United States had potentially become a follower in one of the future's most important global movements. But Bush said "the fact that we didn't sign that one treaty does not diminish in my view the U.S. leadership role. Sometimes leadership is not going along with everybody else."

Despite U.S. frugality in pledging only $25 million in aid, other nations pledged an impressive amount. Japan increased its aid for such "**sustainable development**" from about $800 million to $1.4 billion a year through 1996. The European Economic Community (EEC) pledged $4 billion. In addition, Germany (its east and west sectors newly unified into one nation) met the Third World's long-standing demand that rich nations contribute 0.7 percent of their gross national product (GNP) to foreign assistance. Bonn, the German capital, promised to send more than $6.3 billion a year in an effort to ease the poverty that drives nations to savage their environment. Eventually, 178 nations agreed to an 800-page blue-print for environmentally benign development in poor countries. They established a nonbinding declaration of eco-principles and mustered enough signatures to pass pacts into international law that preserve the planet's species and stave off global warming. For the first time in history, nations vowed to consider global environmental concerns when making internal economic decisions. Still, the refusal by the United States to agree to tougher measures led the organizer to conclude that the treaty was an "agreement without sufficient commitment."[28]

In the end President Bush got what he wanted. The final agreement at the Rio Conference contained no deadlines for curbing carbon dioxide emissions, weakening efforts to halt global warming. In addition, President Bush protected the U.S. biotechnology industry by refusing to sign the Biodiversity Treaty.

Why would the "environmental president" take such a stance? With a presidential election looming, he probably was looking at polls. In 1992 nearly 80 percent polled said the economy had worsened over the previous year, up from one-third who felt that way in 1990. By comparison, 40 percent thought the nation's environment had worsened—down 13 percent. These polls indicated the economy, not the environment, was more important to people. What better place to show a resolve to deal with the economic problems than at the highly publicized conference where Bush could stand against the world to protect U.S. jobs and businesses? But to many Americans, President Bush was failing to fulfill his campaign promises, which damaged his credibility as much as reneging on his "Read my lips, no new taxes!" campaign pledge.

Bush offered the American public the choice of a strong economy or environmental protection. In fact, a survey by Cambridge Energy Research Association (CERA) showed that most Americans believed the nation could have both.[29] Two-thirds of the respondents said that most pollution in America could be cleaned with little or no harm to the economy. The pollsters also questioned how people felt about a political candidate who "favors policies that encourage industrial growth and new jobs, even if it risks harming the environment." Surprisingly, 63 percent said that they would be less likely to support a candidate who favored the economy over the environment. Cleaning up the environment was a concern for all Americans—whether Democrat, Republican, conservative, liberal, rich, or poor. In an October 1992 *Time* poll, 62 percent of those who replied said the quality of the environment was not getting better, while 60 percent agreed that Bush's statement that he would be the "environmental president" was a lie.[30] As a reviewer of the CERA survey stated, "It was foolish for Bush to ask people to choose between economic growth and environmental protection. On the issue of principle, most Americans are not where the President is."

Conclusion

By the end of the decade the environmental movement in the United States had survived the backlash of the twelve-year Reagan-Bush era. Despite their efforts to deregulate the government and dismantle environmental agencies such as the EPA, a strong legal foundation to promote environmental issues remained. In 1989 John Adams, a former assistant U.S. attorney who was the director of the Natural Resources Defense Council, noted,

> In 1970 there were no environmental laws. There were zoning laws, public health laws, but no real environmental laws. Now we have forty or fifty federal statutes. Today we have laws across the United States—every county, every town, every city. And even though we've had ups and downs in environmental awareness between 1970 and now, the fabric gets built up each day—more people, more environmental analysts, more enforcers, more this, more that.[31]

J. William Futrell, president of the Environmental Law Institute, estimated in 1989 that there were some twenty thousand environmental lawyers—more than practice labor law. By that year Futrell estimated that federal courts had handed down at least three thousand decisions on environmental cases. By the end of the 1980s environmentalism had become a permanent part of the consciousness of the American public.

The environmental movement had remained largely an American phenomenon from 1960 to the early 1980s. But in the late 1980s, environmentalism became a global movement that culminated in the Earth Summit of 1992. Powerful green political parties began to appear in Germany and other European countries. Environmentalism was an issue in which people of all nations could find common ground.

Chapter Notes

1. Paul S. Boyer, *The Enduring Vision* (Lexington, Mass.: D. C. Heath, 1995), 709.
2. Victor B. Scheffer, *The Shaping of Environmentalism in America* (Seattle: University of Washington Press, 1991), 10.
3. *A Centennial Celebration 1892–1992* (San Francisco: Sierra Club Books, 1992), 21.
4. Lois R. Ember, "EPA Administrators Deem Agency's First 25 Years Bumpy But Successful," *C&EN*, Oct. 30, 1995, 21.
5. Ibid.
6. Ibid.
7. *Wildlife Digest*, "Trends, Issues, Views and News," Nov. 1988, 25.
8. Ibid., 27.
9. Ibid., 25.

10. Margaret E. Kriz, "Warm-Button Issue," *National Journal*, Feb. 8, 1992, 320.
11. Boyer, *Enduring Vision*, 730.
12. *Wildlife Digest*, "Trends, Issues, Views and News," Nov. 1989, 25.
13. Mary H. Cooper, "Environmental Movement at 25," *CQ Researcher*, March 31, 1995, 280.
14. Mary H. Cooper, "Jobs vs. Environment," *CQ Researcher*, May 15, 1992, 419.
15. Cooper, "Jobs vs. Environment," 421.
16. Ibid.
17. Ibid.
18. Martin W. Lewis, "The Green Threat To Nature," *Harper's Magazine*, Nov. 1992, 32.
19. Marcy Darnovsky, "Stories Less Told: Histories of U.S. Environmentalism," *Socialist Review*, Oct. 1, 1992, 43.
20. Ibid., 41.
21. Brad Knickerbocker, "Environmentalism Extends Its Reach," *Christian Science Monitor*, Jan. 1993, 9.
22. Darnovsky, "Stories Less Told," 44.
23. Constance Holden, "Animal Rightists Trash MSU Lab," *Science*, March 13, 1992, 1349.
24. Rik Scarce, *Eco-Warriors: Understanding the Radical Environmental Movement* (Chicago: Noble Press, 1990), 50.
25. Sharon Begley, "And Now, the Road from Rio," *Newsweek*, June 22, 1992, 46.
26. Sharon Begley, "The Grinch of Rio," *Newsweek*, June 15, 1992, 31.
27. Begley, "And Now, the Road From Rio," 46.
28. William Schneider, "A Firm Stand on Wrong Issue in Rio?" *National Journal*, June 20, 1992, 1494.
29. Ibid.
30. Eugene Linden, "The Green Factor," *Time*, Oct. 12, 1992, 58.
31. Philip Shabecoff, *A Fierce Green Fire: The American Environmental Movement* (New York: Hill and Wang, 1993), 133.

Our policies must protect our environment,
promote economic growth, and provide
millions of new high-skill, high-wage jobs.
—PRESIDENT BILL CLINTON

9

The Early 1990s: Government Retrenchment and Public Apathy

The environmental movement in the United States during the early 1990s suffered from government retrenchment and public apathy. The economy and human needs were the paramount issues. A conservative backlash portrayed environmentalists as eco-terrorists and the environmental movement as a vast array of bewildering issues espoused by fanatical groups committed to a "nature before humanity" philosophy, whatever the consequences.

Although a majority of Americans did not share this extreme interpretation of the environmental movement, it influenced many people who viewed the mammoth government agencies that regulate the use of nature as a hindrance to their development and ambition. In response to their concerns, the Clinton administration limited environmental regulations. The environmental movement continued, though it was tempered by practical considerations for human welfare and needs. It was a more balanced and conscientious approach.

Environmental Optimism under Bill Clinton

The environmental movement took heart in January 1993 when Bill Clinton became the first Democrat to occupy the White House in twelve years and, after Jimmy Carter, only the second Democrat there since Lyndon Johnson left office in January 1969. President Clinton promised to reverse his Republican predecessors' weak record on environmental protection. He publicly differed with George Bush on most environmental issues. Clinton's energy strategy favored conservation and efficiency over production. He committed to protecting forests and wetlands and supporting the controversial Endangered Species Act. Additionally, environmentalists praised his appointments of Carol Browner at the EPA and Bruce Babbitt at the Department of Interior.

Particularly encouraging to environmentalists was Clinton's choice of Senator Al Gore as his running mate. Gore is an outspoken environmentalist and the author of the 1992 best-seller *Earth in the Balance*, an unequivocal call for tougher environmental laws. Gore's book blends environmental wisdom, political leadership, and economic pragmatism, drawing fire from both extremes of the environmental movement. A reviewer noted that "It proposed an innovative way forward by borrowing the best from each side without accepting either's zero-sum conclusions."[1]

On April 21, 1993, President Clinton celebrated Earth Day by declaring his support for environmental issues.

> If there is one commitment that defines our people, it is our devotion to the rich and expansive land we have inherited. From the first Americans to the present day, our people have lived in awe of the power, the majesty, and the beauty of the forest, the rivers, and the streams of America. That love of the land, which flows like a mighty current through this land and through our character, burst into service on the first Earth Day in 1970.[2]

Clinton then announced that he would sign two treaties that President Bush had turned down at the Rio Conference in 1992: the Biodiversity Treaty and a pledge to lower emission of greenhouse gases to 1990 levels by the year 2000.

President Clinton's support for environmental causes extended to the federal government. He committed to purchasing ozone-friendly products, energy-conserving computers, fuel-efficient vehicles, and recycled products. He ordered all agencies with facilities that released toxic pollutants, such as military bases and research laboratories, to develop a plan to cut their toxic output in half by 1999; he also required the agencies to report their pollution levels to the public, just as private companies already do.[3] But he was less willing to accede to environmentalists' wishes on the question of federal regulation.

President Clinton made it clear from the outset that his central goal was to "grow the economy"; he placed employment and business opportunities at the top of his agenda. Although less than optimistic about voluntary restrictions for industry, Clinton seemed convinced that cleaner technologies could and should be applied, without damaging profits or jobs. He was also concerned that complex regulations had discouraged the business community and therefore he was receptive to using market forces—for example, tax incentives to encourage energy efficiency or taxes imposed to cover hidden environmental costs—to encourage industry to clean up its act. Clinton attempted to balance the need for environmental protection with the desire to make such social and technological benefits at least equal to the costs.[4]

A Growing Countermovement

With a new president in office who seemed to support environmental causes, the controversy over the direction of environmental policy and activism was revitalized. Private citizens organized and lobbied for their personal causes during the early 1990s. In particular, they focused on their neighborhoods and local environmental problems. They most fiercely opposed any proposed landfills or hazardous waste dumps near their homes. Even when scientific studies showed that a site was environmentally safe, these protesters were prone to point to examples like Love Canal, where such reassurances later proved disastrously incorrect. Critics of these groups depicted them as narrow-minded and characterized their protests as "NIMBYism" (for Not In My Back Yard).[5]

A more significant conflict was the belief among proponents of environmental justice that industrialists, government officials, and environmentalists have generally ignored the plight of urban minorities and low-income neighborhoods. They argued that environmental racism has caused these communities to become disproportionately polluted by hazardous toxins in the air and water, congestion, and as the dumping sites for the nation's industrial waste. The terms racism, civil rights, and class struggle have been used to describe the basis of the **environmental justice movement**, which believes that those with little access to power have been ignored and often suffer the worst of the nation's pollution problems. Many of those who live in polluted urban neighborhoods criticize what they consider to be white-dominated environmental organizations that fight to save the forests, whales, wilderness areas and so on while ignoring the deteriorating city environments. They argue that most low-income city dwellers will never have access to the natural beauties that environmentalists deem so important. They also see government and business interests teaming together to exploit their lack of power and use their low-income neighborhoods as dumping grounds.

The genesis of the environmental justice movement can be traced to 1985 when Warren County, North Carolina, a rural area populated by mostly African-Americans, was selected for a PCB (polychlorinated biphenyl) landfill. The community marched in protest, resulting in over five hundred arrests—including District of Columbia Delegate Walter Fauntroy (chairman of the Congressional Black Caucus), the Reverend Benjamin Chavis, Jr. (Commission for Racial Justice), and the Reverend Joseph Lowery (Southern Christian Leadership Conference). Despite the protestors' failure to halt the establishment of the landfill, their efforts were significant. In fact, they made environmental racism a national issue and challenged the popular assumption, often made by pro- and antienvironmentalists alike, that minorities were not interested in environmental issues. A precedent was set, which, as stated in the *Directory of the People of Color Environmental Groups 1994–95,* became the basis of the multifaceted environmental justice movement.

> Grassroots groups, after decades of struggle, have grown to become the core of the multi-issue, multi-racial, and multi-regional environmental justice movement. Diverse community-based groups have begun to organize and link their struggles to issues of civil and human rights, land rights and sovereignty, cultural survival, racial and social justice, and sustainable development. The impetus for getting environmental justice on the nation's agenda has come from an alliance of grassroots activists, civil rights leaders, and a few academicians who questioned the foundation of the current environmental protection paradigm—where communities of color receive unequal protection. Whether urban ghettos and barrios, rural "poverty pockets," Native American reservations, or communities in the Third World, grassroots groups are demanding an end to unjust and non-sustainable environmental and development policies.

The environmental groups made some effort to promote participation of minority groups within their organizations including the creation of an **Environmental Consortium for Minority Outreach.** Still, by the time Bill Clinton took office in 1993, no African-American or Hispanic individual held a leadership position in any of the major environmental organizations. President Clinton's Executive Order of 1994, which stated that "each Federal agency shall make achieving environmental justice part of its mission," was a triumph for the environmental justice movement. However, little practical progress was made and most efforts have mirrored the failure of the Warren County protestors.[6]

More dangerous to the environmental movement was the **wise-use movement,** a growing countermovement that advocated numerous causes aimed at dismantling government restrictions. For instance, it argued that the government should only lightly regulate resource extraction and any other economic activity.

The movement began during the 1970s Sagebrush Rebellion as a grass-roots movement. By the early 1990s it had become much more widespread, more sophisticated in strategy and tactics, and more effective. For example, the Oregon Lands Coalition, first established as an advocate for timber workers in spotted owl country, now oversaw the activities of sixty-one grass-roots organizations and grew to a membership of 81,000.

Similar wise-use groups include the Multiple-Use Land Alliance and the League of Private Property Voters. A small number of people who own private land within national parks founded these groups to oppose government restrictions and regulations that affected personal use of their property. The wise-use movement quickly grew into a network of four hundred local groups, which

included businesses that extracted natural resources, commodity producers, recreationalists, and landowners who had been increasingly impacted
by state and local growth-management plans, wetlands restrictions, and
endangered-species-protection measures. These umbrella organizations
operated a nationwide electronic network called "Multa-Net."[7]

Copying a tactic that environmentalists favor, these groups issue a regular
"Private Property Vote Index," which records how members of Congress
vote. The index identifies who, in their view, supported or opposed private property rights legislation.

The growing popularity of this countermovement alarmed environmentalists and elicited calls for a renewal of their efforts. Ron Tipton, a
leader of the Wilderness Society, argued that "One of the results of the
[1992] election is that the wise-use movement is going to be bigger and
meaner and better financed. Now that they have a bogeyman in the
White House." The Sierra Club felt even more threatened, sending its
members a letter that warned

> We are confronted by a super-financed, anti-environment juggernaut that
> is craftily masquerading behind a totally deceitful public relations "wise
> use" blitz to conceal their profit-driven designs. . . . They will stop at noth-
> ing to destroy us and the entire environmental movement.[8]

The letter urged recipients to send an "emergency contribution" right
away.

A Green Revival

In contrast to the intensifying conflict between environmentalists and
wise-users, 1993 saw a rebirth of green products and packaging, which
consumers buy specifically because they are marketed as having environmental benefits. According to *Advertising Age* magazine,

> After an initial burst of environmental claims in the late 1980s, major mar-
> keters pulled back when environmental groups and state governments
> claimed that consumers were being misled. But now marketers are moving
> forward with green products and packaging developments, this time with
> new more focused strategies.

This revival coincided with an improving economy, the Clinton administration's pro-environmental views, and the public's increasing concern
about the environment. Industrial analysts predicted that people were
receptive to responsible products and packaging and prepared to pay for
them. Numerous companies began to experiment with new green products. In Florida, for example, Procter & Gamble tested Tide Refill—a refill
carton that slips into the powder detergent's original box, cutting waste in
half. In its mid-Atlantic markets, Church & Dwight tested a 98 percent
phosphate-free Arm & Hammer automatic dishwashing detergent. In

Midwest cities Scott Paper tested its Scotties Recycles—a facial tissue made entirely from recycled paper. And 3M introduced Scotch-Brite Never Rust wool soap pads made from recycled plastic fiber. The green consumer products market totaled $110.1 billion in 1992 and was expected to grow to $121.5 billion in 1993 and to $154 billion by 1997.⁹

While the business community saw an upswing in the green market, President Clinton struggled to placate political forces on both sides of the environmental debate. In his Earth Day speech in April 1993, Clinton announced the creation of a new national biological survey within the Department of Interior. The survey would have an annual budget of $180 million, with more than $100 million coming from the U.S. Fish and Wildlife Service, and would draw sixteen hundred employees from the Department of Interior. Its duties would include inventorying and monitoring biological resources as well as providing government officials with independent scientific advice on ecological science. The scientists reassigned to the survey were experts in areas such as population dynamics, physiology, animal behavior, habitats, and biodiversity.

President Clinton's reticence, in the face of the growing wise-use movement, was evident in a speech he gave at the National Botanical Gardens in Washington, D.C., in April 1993. He made only passing reference to his efforts to elevate the Environmental Protection Agency to a cabinet-level Department of the Environment, weakly indicating that he hoped it would happen "soon, by the grace of Congress."¹⁰ Congress's "grace" however, was not forthcoming and the idea was soon forgotten.

In 1993 demands grew by both Congress and business leaders for the administration to curtail the expense of environmental regulation. Clinton's commitment to the environment remained important, but subordinate to his primary concerns of health care and economic issues. He pledged, early in the year, to change the style of government management by emphasizing pollution avoidance and solving problems before they occurred, over the more expensive methods of pollution control and cleanup. Although Clinton proclaimed that he would work more closely with business to achieve these goals, critics argued that he had done little to alleviate the burden of government regulation. They pointed to the EPA, which required states, communities, and businesses to comply with costly and underfunded regulations. Furthermore, they argued that this "command-and-control" approach to environmental protection had often been applied without looking at how difficult it was to comply.

The U.S. Conference of Mayors reported that compliance with the EPA and nine other environmental mandates cost the 1,050 American cities with populations above thirty thousand an estimated $6.4 billion in 1993—nearly 12 percent of all local tax revenues. Dallas Mayor Steve Bartlett explained,

> If we are to have a shot at increasing local taxpayer support for additional investment in environmental facilities and services, we must begin to

realign the partnership to reflect local decision-making and local needs. We must find a way to give local governments the opportunity to exercise more control and authority in shaping the agenda.[11]

To mollify such complaints, EPA Director Carol Browner proposed in her 1994 "Common Sense Initiative" that the government work more closely with industry in forming environmental policy to achieve

> a fundamentally different way of doing business that takes use beyond the pollutant-by-pollutant, crisis-by-crisis approach of the past to an industry-by-industry approach for the future. . . . [W]e are bringing together leaders of business, state and local government, the community, labor, and the environmental movement—to sit down and examine environmental protection.[12]

The Clinton administration introduced greater flexibility into the regulatory framework, which enabled businesses and communities to devise the most cost-effective means to achieve federal environmental goals.

Clinton's awareness of the importance of environmental issues and the priority he had given to economic issues was evident in the debate concerning the North American Free Trade Agreement (NAFTA), signed by the United States, Canada, and Mexico in 1992. Environmentalists argued that, because of Mexico's less stringent environmental laws, the proposed free trade zone along the U.S.-Mexico border would create a high concentration of export manufacturing plants that would exacerbate the preexisting environmental and public health problems. Clinton seemed to agree that there was a danger, but countered that NAFTA would

> relieve pressure on the border region by extending trade benefits to Mexico's interior, thus reducing the incentive for U.S. industrial firms to locate along the border." Indeed, the Administration went so far as to claim that without NAFTA, the growth of the maquiladora sector would cause an environmentally devastating spiral of industrial and population growth and resulting air and water pollution. [13]

The Clinton administration pushed hard for the agreement, with significant Republican support, and achieved its passage in 1993. However, in NAFTA's first five years the U.S.-Mexico border witnessed extensive economic growth adding to preexisting environmental and health problems. Furthermore, the administration's promise to regulate and protect the environment has yet to be fulfilled while corporations have attempted to achieve their goals by using the NAFTA investor's right-to-sue-governments provision to avoid environmental regulations. Whatever Clinton may have believed, NAFTA has proved to be a detriment to the environment but a boon for business.

President Clinton's attempts to cooperate more closely with business were evident in his efforts to find a compromise for the continued controversy between the northern spotted owl and the Pacific Northwest logging industry. In July 1993 he presented an initiative that promised to supply $1.2 billion of federal money to develop alternate industries for the region while also protecting much of the ancient forests that the owls needed to survive. He went further in February 1995 when he suggested that the restrictions that limited the logging of timber on private lands the owl inhabited should be rescinded.

Business interests generally welcomed these compromises, yet Clinton was less successful in his attempts to achieve a more cost-effective environmental policy. Ranchers had grazed livestock on 280 million acres of federal land at below-market fees ever since the government granted them the right in 1885. Environmentalists believe this has seriously damaged fragile grassland ecosystems. Historian Mary H. Cooper explains,

> In an effort to curb degradation of grasslands through overgrazing while reducing taxpayers' subsidies to the livestock industry, Interior Secretary Babbitt, in 1993, proposed raising the below-market fees some 27,000 ranchers paid to graze cattle and sheep on public lands. Faced with an outcry by the industry, Babbitt abandoned the fee hike in December 1995.[14]

By 1993 the Clinton administration was caught between wanting to support environmental regulations and placate those who criticized the cost of such legislation. Not surprisingly, the results were often mixed. In 1993 the estimated annual cost to comply with federally mandated pollution control and cleanup programs was $115 billion. This figure had been roughly $26 billion in 1972. The escalating outcry against the cost of federally supported environmental programs influenced the proposed federal budget for 1994. For example, global change programs (which study natural and human influences on the environment) that would be well funded included NASA's Mission to Planet Earth, which was allocated more than $1 billion, and the Department of Energy's energy efficiency and new technology programs. However, there were examples of a growing trend toward limiting or cutting the cost of environmental programs. The EPA and the National Oceanic and Atmospheric Administration budgets, except for the global change programs, were substantially cut; for instance, the Sea Grant program was reduced 10 percent. The EPA's budget was reduced to $6.4 billion, a loss of $540 million. As a result, the EPA planned to cut nearly $90 million from the Superfund. Cuts to R&D programs included those for coal (more than $45 million) and nuclear power research (a program for advanced reactors dropped from $45 million to $15 million).[15]

As the government debated the allocation of funds for environmental protection programs, public opinion polarized, pitting action-oriented environmentalists against wise-use advocates. The controversy over **Cove Mallard**, 76,000 acres of federal timberland in the Nez Perce National Forest just outside Dixie, Idaho, exemplifies this situation. In September 1993 the U.S. Forest Service approved this area for logging.

They designated about 6,328 acres of trees to be felled—some by the controversial clear-cutting method—and proposed building 145 miles of access roads to the forest. This meant an influx of money and much-needed jobs for the local community, but according to Earth First! the deforestation of 76,000 acres would desecrate 5 million acres of pristine wilderness. The activists argued that the deforestation would destroy the largest roadless wilderness in the lower forty-eight states, threaten endangered species, and interfere with proposals to return wolves and grizzly bears back to the land they once roamed. The Forest Service called this a "classic Earth First! overreaction" and pointed out that several Congresses had left the Cove Mallard area open for logging, despite giving wilderness protection to the surrounding land.[16]

Earth First! set up a base camp of tents, teepees, and two aging school buses, occupied by forty eco-warriors, while sixty others camped in satellite posts around the Nez Perce National Forest. For the most part, the Earth First! campaign followed the nonviolent principles of Henry David Thoreau, Mahatma Gandhi, and Martin Luther King, Jr., of peaceful civil disobedience and many arrests. Their activities led to charges of trespassing, delaying officers in their duty, perching in trees to keep them from being cut down, and creating barricades of human bodies to block roads. However, the townsfolk of Dixie, Idaho, saw themselves as persecuted. The actions of Earth First! directly threatened their livelihood, they claimed. A cardboard sign propped against a roadside gas pump warned, "Earth First! Don't Stop," and a notice taped to a window of the Lodgepole Pine Inn warned: "We reserve the right to refuse service to all Earth Firsters and their associates." A poster at one end of town bore a crude drawing of a stringy-haired Earth First! activist with a bullet hole in his forehead.

In public view, the protests remained symbolic, relatively peaceful, and civil, but behind the scenes some demonstrators took more violent action. There was evidence, denied by Earth First!, of traditional monkey-wrenching tactics. In June someone put sand in a D-8 Caterpillar tractor's fuel tank, smashed its gauges, and cut its fuel and hydraulic lines. Trees were "spiked" by driving metal rods or nails into their trunks so that a saw blade might explode like a hand grenade when it hit the hidden metal. There were also signs that the locals were taking out their frustrations in more hostile ways. One afternoon a gang of drunken men ambushed one activist on a lonely road and beat him bloody. He was not hospitalized, but it was the worst case of physical violence between the two sides.

During the summer the Forest Service, along with local law enforcement agencies, made more than fifty arrests, issued over a hundred citations, and conducted an early-morning raid of the Earth First! camp seeking evidence to connect the group to the vandalism of logging and road-building equipment. No specific evidence was found, but the tension between the groups continued. Eventually the road was built, but the enmity between the two groups signified an escalation in the debate between pro- and antienvironmentalists. Meanwhile, the battle was heating up within the Clinton administration.

A Conservative Resurgence

By 1994 Bill Clinton's second year in office, his poll ratings were at a historical low, as confusing policy decisions and the slow pace of economic expansion and job creation influenced the public's view. Clinton's troubles had begun with his failed attempt to permit gay and lesbian soldiers to serve in the military without facing automatic expulsion. Then, Congress refused to allow his $30 billion in spending initiatives to "jump-start" the economy.[17] Furthermore, Clinton's efforts to reform health care, initially very popular, collapsed in part as the public balked at the complexity and potential costs of a government-run national health-care program in which all Americans would be guaranteed "health care that can never be taken away, health care that is always there."

The administration's inability to achieve its environmental goals was glaringly evident in 1994. Among President Clinton's environmental proposals were measures to overhaul laws governing mining on federal lands, to elevate the EPA administrator to the Cabinet, and to revamp the Superfund, the Clean Water Act, and the Safe Drinking Water Act. None won congressional approval in the climate of conservative resurgence. The 103d Congress passed only one major new environmental bill—the **California Desert Protection Act**, which set aside millions of acres as protected wilderness in the rapidly developing state.[18] Congress shelved or rejected nine major environmental bills, including those related to mining, the Superfund, safe drinking water, clean water, and toxic waste.

Worse was yet to come. The Clinton administration's faltering environmental agenda faced even dimmer prospects with the 104th Congress in 1995. After winning majorities in both houses of Congress for the first time in forty years, Republican lawmakers tried to gain hasty passage of their **Contract With America**, a document that espoused family values, individual freedom, government deregulation, and tax relief for the general public. This Congress intently sponsored legislation that would curtail the federal government's ability to impose regulations. This was particularly true of environmental policy.

In 1995 the House proposed legislation to deregulate the government, such as the Job Creation and Wage Enhancement Act, which included a bill called the Risk Assessment and Cost-Benefit Act.[19] At first glance, these bills seemed to focus on lowering the capital gains rate and otherwise reducing investors' tax burden. However, the bills contained a set of proposals that, depending on one's point of view, offered welcome relief from costly federal regulations or declared war on the nation's environmental laws. Proponents denied that the bill gave polluters license to flout existing laws, arguing that it instead forced the government to impose new environmental regulations much more selectively.

The bill required the EPA and a host of other federal agencies to shoulder for the first time a substantial share of the costs of regulation, which state and local governments and private enterprise bore at the time. According to the EPA, business and industry spent $150 billion a year to comply with federal antipollution laws. The National Association of Counties estimated that local governments would pay more than $30 billion over the next four years to comply with federal laws governing sewage treatment, toxic waste disposal, wastewater runoff, air pollution, and dozens of other environmental hazards.

Besides making it prohibitively expensive in many instances for the federal government to order local cleanups, the bill required complex risk assessment procedures that gave affected industries the chance to block any proposed new government regulation. In particular, critics were alarmed by a provision that created peer review panels open to members of regulated industries, with the power to block new regulations. Gary Bass of OMB Watch, a nonprofit environmental advocacy group, declared, "This is really the corporate veto-act."[20] Such opposition apparently had its effect as the act failed to pass the Senate in July 1995.

Another Republican effort to reduce government regulation was embodied in a "private property rights" bill, which proposed a change to the Fifth Amendment clause "nor shall private property be taken for public use without just compensation." In the past, "compensation" occurred only when the government physically occupied private land. The Republicans' bill included a "taking clause" that interpreted the amendment to mean any case in which the Endangered Species Act or other federal laws restricted use of private property. The new interpretation corresponded with Congress's efforts to deregulate government and fulfill the promises they had made in the 1993 congressional elections.

Representative Don Ritter, R-Pennsylvania, chair of the National Environmental Policy Institute, explained that the Republican victory in the 1994 congressional elections was the result of a public demand to make government less intrusive in people's private lives, and particularly in environmental policies.

> Part of the election message was the fact that big government bureaucracies don't work anymore. The command-and-control nature of environmental law is not the optimal system of the '90s, let alone the 21st century.[21]

The House of Representatives tried to live up to this message. On March 3, 1995, the House passed a measure that allowed property owners to demand compensation for environmental regulations that reduced the value of their land by as little as 20 percent of its fair market value. It also forced the federal government to compensate industry and landowners when the cost to comply with a regulation exceeded 10 percent of their property or business value. This meant the government could pay millions of dollars to real estate developers prohibited from building on fragile wetlands. It also meant the government could reimburse a small family farm for livestock killed by a grizzly bear or some other federally protected predator.

Supporters of the legislation contended that this reform directly resulted from a grass-roots movement of landowners who had suffered from government regulations that restricted the use of their land without considering the "economic impact." Representative W. J. "Billy" Tauzin, D-Louisiana, a longtime property rights advocate, concluded that this legislation reflected the public's anger with the Clinton administration's disdain for individual rights.

> I believe the fabric of the relationship between those who created this government and this government has been ripped apart for one word more than any other. That word is "arrogance."[22]

Despite the House's support, a comprehensive private property rights bill did not pass the Senate and has yet to become law. Still, there have been numerous efforts to redefine such legislation as the Endangered Species Act and the private property owners movement has continued to grow. In May 1999 Congress was yet again grappling with legislation, the Landowners Equal Treatment Act of 1999, which would increase the rights of private property owners.

In the face of both Republican and Democratic opposition, EPA Director Carol Browner could only say that while such congressional measures went too far, bipartisan agreement was needed to reform environmental regulation.

> We are absolutely committed to continue our efforts to bring people to the table, to build consensus. It is absolutely the best way to provide environmental protection to all the people of the country.[23]

In an effort to moderate the more radical congressional regulatory reforms, President Clinton proposed a "landmark package" of twenty-five environmental reforms. The general theme was that the government was prepared to be more flexible in its management of environmental policies. For instance, Clinton expanded a program that enabled companies to sell "credits" they had obtained for achieving lower than required air and water pollution standards to less successful businesses. Also, in response to House Republicans' charges that federal regulations were excessively burdensome, Clinton proposed

> a 25% reduction in reporting and record-keeping requirements for small businesses and governments, and a pilot program to allow companies to use "one-stop" emissions reports for all releases to the environment.[24]

Essentially, Clinton was attempting to moderate existing programs and appear to be offering compromises to the Republican's efforts to pass legislation that would weaken environmental restrictions. However, although the bureaucracy might be loosened, Clinton could not create legislation and many of his ideas were either too little or already part of the Republican agenda.

Simplifying and streamlining reports was intended to improve relations between business and the EPA and alleviate bureaucratic red tape. But the administration's attempt to neutralize the House Republicans' deregulation campaign failed to stem the tide of new legislation. In March 1995, shortly after Clinton proposed his reforms, the House rewrote the 1972 Clean Water Act. The new version eased pollution controls on cities and industry by abolishing requirements for treating contaminated water and by limiting restrictions on pollution caused by farms and street storm sewers. Environmentalists charged that this deregulation could endanger the Great Lakes and open half the nation's valuable wetlands to developers. However, supporters of the reforms argued that "excessive federal regulation . . . has caused undue hardship for industry, state and local governments, and individuals."[25] As if to echo such sentiments, in the same month a federal judge dismissed a huge government lawsuit against chemical companies that dumped millions of pounds of the pesticide DDT into the ocean off Palos Verdes Peninsula in California, sending shock waves through U.S. environmental agencies.[26]

The more extreme antienvironmental faction of Congress also worried environmentalists. For example, in the Republican sweep of 1994, Representative Helen Chenoweth, R-Idaho, upset incumbent Democrat Larry LaRocco. During her campaign Chenoweth had held an "endangered salmon bake" and proclaimed "white men are an endangered species." Her interpretation of the environmental movement expressed the feelings of many Americans who believed that environmentalists were too eager to sacrifice human needs for those of the northern spotted owl and other nature issues.

Despite these beliefs, or maybe because of them, House Speaker Newt Gingrich appointed Chenoweth to the Endangered Species Act task force. Idaho environmentalists warned that right-wingers such as Chenoweth threatened the state's 4 million legislated acres of wilderness but had few solutions to offer. Rick Johnson, director of the Idaho Conservation League, lamented, "She's the best grassroots organizer this state ever had. The more she talks, the more people laugh, but the more her base loves her." The fact was that Chenoweth and her constituents were in agreement.[27]

While Congress and radical antienvironmentalists gained the high ground in the debate over environmental regulation, President Clinton at least strove to appear to remain true to his promises. In June 1995 *Audubon* magazine reported,

Each presidential administration leaves its own mark on the White House. Martin Van Buren brought in central heating. The Kennedys replaced tacky furniture with fine antiques. Nancy Reagan bought new china. Bill and Hillary Clinton have installed the Golden Carrot. . . . It is intended as the Clinton's lasting legacy in one of the country's most famous buildings.[28]

The Golden Carrot—a Whirlpool refrigerator—at the time was the most energy-efficient, chlorofluorocarbon-free model in the country.

Another example, only slightly less symbolic, occurred near the end of the year, when President Clinton and Vice President Gore denounced Congress's attacks on environmental policies. In November 1995 Clinton declared that "Under the cover of balancing the budget, the Republican Congress is going after the essential environmental protections that have guaranteed the health and safety of all Americans for a long time now, and I am determined to stop them."[29] He further charged that Republican leaders had enlisted a "small army of lobbyists for polluters" to write environmental legislation and lead an assault on established environmental and health protections. Gore's rhetoric was even more condemnatory: "The Republican leadership is conducting a jihad against the environment in the most right-wing, extremist agenda we have seen in America in this century."[30] In regard to proposed cuts for the EPA, Gore exclaimed, "This is the most insidious part of their agenda—to take away the ability of the EPA and others to enforce environmental laws, by destroying the ability of the government to monitor pollution and to enforce the laws." Cutting EPA funds was only one issue in the budget debate of 1995, a debate that would become one of the most contentious in U.S. history. It would result in two government shutdowns, thirteen stopgap spending measures, and one threat of default and would not be settled until April 1996. In the end both sides could claim victories. For the EPA there was a modest increase of $727 million dollars, a little more than it had lost in the budget of 1994.

Yet the contrast between the administration's rhetoric for environmentalism and its apparent willingness to compromise with congressional policies began to damage its reputation among environmental groups. For example, the head of the Sierra Club charged President Clinton with "betraying" the environmental movement by supporting a Republican environmental rider to a bill in the summer of 1995 that opened much of Western federal land to "salvage" logging.[31] However, Clinton cannot be blamed as the sole cause of the public's eroding support for environmental issues.

The environmental activists and their message were not necessarily in tune with the views of many Americans. In April 1995 the *Wall Street Journal* reported that the public's support of the environmental movement "begins to fray in the face of the hard choices before Congress." The article concluded that

The political culture of environmental activism is that of contemporary upper-income liberalism. And the activists' heightened sense of ecological danger reflects this perspective, rather than mainstream opinion or, for that matter, any special expertise.[32]

This conclusion was drawn from a survey the Center for Media and Public Affairs conducted of 100 environmental leaders drawn randomly from senior staff members and boards of directors at such groups as the Sierra Club, Environmental Defense Fund, and Natural Resources Defense Council. The general public then answered identical questions about environmental and other social issues. The researchers discovered a distinct gap between the views and values of the two groups. For instance, the activists were more willing to back the green agenda with greenbacks: three out of four activists said they would increase taxes to protect the environment, compared with only one-third of the general public. Similarly, 59 percent of the activists favored saving all endangered species regardless of cost, while only 38 percent of the public felt the same way.

This was as much an economic gap as a philosophical one. Some 40 percent of activists' families had incomes above $75,000, about four times the proportion of the overall populace. Although this disparity may account for part of the difference in opinion, activists seemed prepared to pay for their convictions. Only one in five environmental leaders was prepared to compensate owners when the value of their land was reduced to protect endangered species. In other words, they would willingly accept financial loss if environmental regulations restricted use of their own property. In contrast, most of the public would provide compensation to property owners.

This last point of the *Wall Street Journal* article was demonstrated by comparing the activists' opinions on environmental health risks with those of scientific experts, who addressed the same issues in previous national surveys. Environmental leaders consistently perceived graver dangers to the environment than the experts. For example, only one in four activists regarded nuclear power plants as safe, compared with two out of three energy scientists. Two out of three activists believed that scientific evidence demonstrated a human-made greenhouse effect, compared with only two out of five climate experts. Finally, the activists were twice as likely as cancer experts to blame industry for rising cancer rates, and three times as likely to support the Delaney Clause (a stringent standard for regulating chemicals and food additives).

Furthermore, the activists placed less faith in private industry and more faith in government regulation than did the average American. Despite widespread suspicion of big business, the general public was nearly twice as likely as activists to view corporations as serving the public interest (40 percent versus 19 percent), and more than ten times as likely to regard government regulation of business as harmful (61 percent versus 6 percent). In general, the views of most environmental leaders tilted strongly to the left; 93 percent of those surveyed during the 1992 presidential campaign supported Bill Clinton.

Conclusion

During President Bill Clinton's first term in office, congressional cutbacks of federal programs continued while the rise of wise-users, radical antienvironmentalists, and numerous other opponents of the environmental movement proliferated and sought to undermine the movement's influence. The backlash against environmental activism indicated a very real belief that human needs were subordinated to the cause of nature.

Perhaps the environmental movement had been too successful. A majority of environmentalists were described as **Lite Greens**—people who like the idea of protecting the environment but not at the cost of lowering their standard of living. This was the conclusion proposed by Karlyn H. Bowman, a resident fellow at the American Enterprise Institute for Public Policy Research, and Everett Carll Ladd, the director of the Institute for Social Inquiry at the University of Connecticut (Storrs) in their study *Attitudes Toward the Environment.* They found that Americans suffered from complacency because "the urgency has been removed, and the battle to protect the environment is being waged satisfactorily." American no longer feared that they were on the precipice of ecological disaster and despite or perhaps because of activists' continual warnings, they were less willing to sacrifice for the cause. This does not mean that the fervor of the 1970s had disappeared completely. Frank Luntz, Republican pollster and an architect of the Republican Party's Contract With America, believes that the sentiment for environmental issues remained strong, if less strident.

> The public may not like or admire regulations, may not think more are necessary, but puts environmental protection as a higher priority than cutting regulations.[33]

Chapter Notes

1. Craig Collins, "The Green Knight," *Mother Jones,* Jan./Feb. 1993, 60.
2. "Presidential Earth Day Address," *EPA Journal,* April/June 1993, 2.
3. Ibid.
4. "Bill Clinton, Environmentalist?" *New York Times,* Jan. 5, 1993, A14.
5. George L. De Feis, "Sustainable Development Issues: Industry, Environment, Regulation and Competition," *Journal of Professional Issues in Engineering Education and Practice* 120, no. 2, April 1994, 179.
6. Philip Shabecoff, *A Fierce Green Fire: The American Environmental Movement* (New York: Hill and Wang, 1993), 264.

7. Brad Knickerbocker, "Environmentalism Extends Its Reach," *Christian Science Monitor,* Jan. 1993, 11.
8. Ibid.
9. Jennifer Lawrence, "Green Products Sprouting Again," *Advertising Age,* May 10, 1993, 12.
10. Tony Reichhardt, "Clinton Announces Package of Environmental Reforms," *Nature,* April 29, 1993, 779.
11. Mary H. Cooper, "Environmental Movement at 25," *CQ Researcher,* March 3l, 1995, 280.
12. Carol M. Browner, "The Earth Is in Your Hands," *EPA Journal,* winter 1995, 4.
13. "NAFTA Agreement," *Public Citizen Global Trade Watch*, Dec. 1998, http://www.citizen.org/pctrade/nafta/reports/5years.htm#environment.
14. Cooper, "Environmental Movement at 25," 290.
15. Alan Newman, "Clinton's Budget for the Environment," *Environmental Science and Technology,* 1993, 1000.
16. Vaughn Roche, "At Loggerheads in the Wilderness," *Washington Post,* Sept. 4, 1993, Fl.
17. Melissa Healy, "Partisan Politics Swamps Environmentalists," *Los Angeles Times,* Oct. 17, 1994, A5.
18. Ibid.
19. Frank Clifford, "Bill Would Limit Federal Power Over Environment," *Los Angeles Times,* Dec. 28, 1994, Al.
20. Ibid.
21. Margaret Kriz, "A New Shade of Green," *National Journal*, March 18, 1995, 661.
22. Bob Benenson, "House Passes Property Rights Bill," *Congressional Quarterly Weekly Report,* March 4, 1995, 680.
23. John H. Cushman, Jr., "Congress Forgoes Its Bid To Hasten Cleanup Of Dumps," *New York Times,* Oct. 17, 1994, Al.
24. Jeff Johnson, "Clinton Offers Regulatory Reforms as Congress Hammers Out Bills," *Environmental Science and Technology,* 29, no.5, May 1995, 204A.
25. Bob Benenson, "Water Bill Wins House Passage, May Not Survive in Senate," *Congressional Quarterly Weekly Report,* May 20, 1995, 1413.
26. Marla Cone, "Federal Suit Over DDT Dumping Is Dismissed," *Los Angeles Times,* March 23, 1995, Al.
27. Paul Rauber, "Eco-Thug: Helen Chenoweth," *Sierra,* 81, May/June 1996, 28.
28. Maryanne Vollers, "Greening the White House," *Audubon,* May/June 1995, 18.
29. Jeff Johnson, "Environment Emerges as Key Issue in 1996 Election," *Environmental Science and Technology,* 29, no. 12, Dec. 1995, 541A.
30. Margaret Kriz, "The Vice President Gores the Opposition," *National Journal,* Oct. 14, 1995, 2538.
31. Johnson, "Environment Emerges as Key Issue in l996 Election."
32. S. Robert Lichter, "Liberal Greens, Mainstream Camouflage," *Wall Street Journal,* April 21, 1995, A10.
33. Margaret Kriz, "Drawing a Green Line in the Sand," *National Journal,* Aug. 12, 1995, 2076.

10

The Late 1990s:
The Institutionalization of the
Environmental Movement

By the end of the twentieth century the environmental movement and its issues have become a major role in the lives of most U.S. residents. They recycle, join environmental groups, protest, buy eco-friendly products, and include the environment as part of their criteria for voting for candidates. A national debate has developed that pits opponents from every conceivable angle with only one thing in common—they all claim to be environmentalists. They may be eco-terrorists or wise-use proponents, but very few public figures or organizations are publicly antienvironment. It is on the degree, costs, and methods of preserving the environment that they differ. The American psyche has become so saturated by this issue that it seems every presidential candidate is declared to be the next "environmental president." There are government agencies, national and local organizations, international conferences, business roundtables, academic institutes, and even cartoons (Captain Planet) espousing environmental arguments and solutions to environmental crises. The debate continues to rage and solutions brought forth; some work, some don't. But perhaps it is the very existence of this process in the late 1990s that will preserve the environment of the twenty-first century.

Clinton's Moderate Environmental Approach

Although the Sierra Club had endorsed Clinton in the 1992 presidential election, the organization, as well as many other environmentalists, had expressed disappointment with his first term. The enthusiasm Clinton and Gore had expressed about environmental issues during the 1992 election had convinced many environmentalists that they would vigorously pursue a pro-environmental agenda. Yet Clinton had made few dramatic efforts during his first term and some, such as the so-called salvage logging rider, which increased timber cutting in national forests, angered many environmentalists. However, in the year preceding the 1996 election, Clinton returned to the pro-environment policies he stood for earlier in his administration, when he signed the Colorado Wilderness and California Desert Protection Acts into law. He earned widespread praise for vetoing budget bills that would have allowed oil drilling in Alaska's Arctic National Wildlife Refuge and clear-cutting in Tongass National Forest; weakened protection for California's Mojave National Preserve; slashed the Environmental Protection Agency's budget; cut funding for international family planning; and blocked enforcement of wetlands protections. In August 1996 dangers to Yellowstone National Park were averted when the administration negotiated an agreement with the firm that held gold-mining rights nearby. One month later, Clinton established the Grand Staircase-Escalante National Monument in southern Utah, effectively ending the threat of massive coal mining there. Such efforts recovered much of his support among environmentalists, including the Sierra Club. Its board of directors endorsed the president in September 1996, just days after Clinton moved to protect 1.7 million acres of Utah wilderness by executive action. Sierra Club president Adam Werbach said, "Bill Clinton has redeemed our faith in his administration . . . the President has earned our support in his own right."[1]

The Clinton-Gore victory in 1996 promised to keep a pro-environmental president and vice president in office. Yet once back in office the Clinton administration returned to a moderate, even uninterested approach to environmental issues. For instance, the Clinton administration did not initiate any major domestic environmental policies in 1997, although they did participate in international environmental events.

The most dominating international environmental event of 1997 was the Climate-Change Conference held in Kyoto, Japan, in November. Of the many issues to be discussed by the international conference, the cutting of emissions of heat-tapping greenhouse gases was the most important. As a forerunner to the conference the Clinton administration in October 1997 proposed a **Joint Implementation Plan** that would link business investments with greenhouse gas emissions.

> Joint Implementation (JI) is an innovative, market-based approach for addressing global climate change that uses international partnerships to achieve low-cost reductions in greenhouse gas emissions. Under JI, a company in the United States invests in a project which reduces emissions in another country and uses those reductions as a less expensive means of meeting its own target. The U.S. has proposed that a formal regime that gives credit for JI projects be part of a new climate change agreement.[2]

Pilot programs were set up during the same month that the plan was proposed. Under the U.S. program, twenty-eight projects had been approved in twelve countries, including Costa Rica, Bolivia, the Czech Republic, and Russia. These projects spanned a range of technologies, including solar, geothermal, and wind power; fuel switching for district heating; biomass energy; and reforestation. It was clearly an attempt to link environmentalism with commerce and give it a profit factor to motivate environmental protection.

Of the many issues discussed during the Kyoto Conference, one of the most contentious and emotional was that of the Third World and how much of a burden it should carry for reducing greenhouse emissions. The poorer nations insisted that because the rich countries had gotten rich largely by burning the coal and oil that produced the heat-trapping carbon dioxide, and because the rich countries were still responsible for most present-day emissions, it was only right that the wealthy be the first to take legally binding steps to reduce them. They pointed out that the Third World countries stood to be hurt worst by whatever climate changes resulted from the rich countries' emissions and were hard-pressed enough to assure a decent existence for millions of their people.

The Clinton administration, allied with the Republican-led Senate, opposed this view, arguing that because the warming of the atmosphere by greenhouse gases was a global concern, all countries must share in the solution. This was particularly so, they argued, because Third World countries' emissions were expected to surpass those of the rich countries in twenty or thirty years. Similar debates had taken place during the Rio De Janeiro Conference in 1992 and continued to highlight the growing divisions between developed countries and those nations that were often rich in raw materials but suffered from low standards of living. Dr. Mark Mwandosya of Tanzania, chairman of the developing-country caucus in the talks, argued,

> Very many of us are struggling to attain a decent standard of living for our peoples and yet we are constantly told that we must share in the effort to reduce emissions so that industrialized countries can continue to enjoy the benefits of their wasteful life style.[3]

On December 11, 1997, the Kyoto Conference reached an agreement, known as the Kyoto Protocol, that set legally binding limits on the man-made emissions of greenhouse gases from thirty-eight industrialized countries. These industrialized nations were required to reduce their greenhouse gas emissions from 1990 levels between 2008 and 2012. The European Union would reduce them by 8 percent, the United States by 7 percent, and Japan by 6 percent. As a group, the nations would cut emissions by just over 5 percent. However, global carbon emissions would continue to increase under the agreement because it exempted developing countries—including China, India, Mexico, Brazil, and 130 others—from any commitments to limit their rapidly growing emissions. Continued growth in energy demand, and thus greenhouse gas emissions, by developing countries would more than offset the reductions made by developed countries. President Clinton agreed to sign the Kyoto Protocol, but he would not submit the agreement to the Senate for its constitutional role of advice and consent until key developing countries agreed to "participate meaningfully" in the effort.[4] He would eventually fulfill this promise by signing the agreement on November 13, 1998. However, by the end of 1999 the Senate had yet to pass it. As with the Rio de Janeiro agreements of 1992, the Kyoto Protocol may prove to be long on promises but short on actual commitment.

Significant among the domestic environmental issues in 1997 was the continued growth of the environmental justice movement. This was remarkable considering the political, social, and business interests that opposed it. The fact that the environmental justice movement continued to be active, and could claim any victories at all, was encouraging. One example in California in 1997 demonstrated the grass-roots nature of the movement and how, on a small scale, it could be successful. The mostly Spanish-speaking residents of Huntington Park's Cottage Street began a grass-roots effort in 1993 to clean up a "huge mountain of concrete" they dubbed "la montana." It was in that year that Aggregate Recycling Systems (ARS) obtained a permit to recycle the enormous quantities of pavement unearthed during the construction of the Alameda Corridor project, an underground rail line from downtown to the harbor. It meant the tearing up of a corridor of concrete and debris 21 miles in length, 100 feet wide, and 32 feet deep. The recycling of this waste would mean millions of dollars for the ARS. It also meant that soon "la montana" would appear to tower over this quiet working-class community. The 1994 Northridge earthquake added to the problem as tons of broken Santa Monica freeway were added to the growing pile. Those living nearby felt the effects almost immediately.

> The mountain has been "a malevolent presence" for Linda Marquez, a neighborhood activist who lives directly across the street. Her family and others describe the taste of grit between their teeth when they first wake up—the concrete dust which makes children cough while they play or study after school. They've worried since 1993 about the long-term health effects of the blanket of microscopic concrete particles which has covered their neighborhood.[5]

The neighborhood soon organized and assailed the city council with protests to remove the hazard. For four years they fought city hall, the ARS, and local businesses that supported the project. By making it a political issue linked to environmental racism, they were able to obtain the assistance of environmental groups and mount a campaign against the city council members who supported the ARS. Finally their efforts were rewarded in April 1997 when Huntington Park's city government went into Superior Court, filing a seventeen-count indictment against the owner of the ARS, to hold him personally responsible for removing it. The success of this grass-roots environmental justice protest was significant. Carlos Porras, director of Communities for a Better Environment, one of the neighborhood's allies, stated

> This is the worst toxic environment in the country and the battle against la montana means a lot. A group of working-class residents, not highly-educated and with few resources, taught the politicians and the bureaucrats to be afraid. If they can do it, so can others.[6]

However, there is yet to be a comprehensive political policy to deal with the decay and pollution of the urban environment and, considering the lack of power these communities wield, it may be some time before there is one. Of course, it is this social dichotomy that makes the movement what it is and until the fate of poor urban communities ranks with that of recognized environmental issues—wilderness, endangered species, air and water pollution, and so on—ecojustice will probably remain a contentious but minor issue.

The Clinton administration's policy of connecting environmental protection with economic priorities allowed the president the luxury of professing concern for traditionally liberal ideals yet preserved his position regarding that the state of the U.S. economy, which he realized was the key to maintaining his popularity. In 1998, Clinton further pressed this strategy for both foreign and domestic environmental issues. In March he addressed a meeting of the World Trade Organization and called for new efforts by trading nations to shape rules that promoted open markets while allowing for a high level of environmental protection. Clinton urged delegates to use this special opportunity to shape an international consensus behind policies that promoted free trade and open markets while protecting the global environment.

The practical result of this rhetoric became evident in October when Congress passed the final federal budget agreement. During the debate over the budget Vice President Gore had declared,

> We are putting the Congress on notice. We will not tolerate stealth attacks that do unacceptable harm to our environment or threaten public health.

This was a reference to the administration's fear that the Republicans would attach environmentally damaging legislation to the budget as a way of sneaking them past the administration. The reality was that, as in all budgets, compromises were made on most fronts, including the environment. The administration declared a victory for winning an additional $476 million for favored programs involving climate change, water quality, and conservation lands. At the same time, the Republican Congress could claim its own victories, including provisions to spend millions more on items that included logging and transportation projects in Alaska. In the end, the increase in spending for environmental issues enabled Clinton to declare, "We honored our obligations to the next generation by strongly protecting the environment." Yet the compromises he had had to make were galling to many environmentalists. Gene Karpinski, the head of U.S. PIRG, the Washington lobbying office for state Public Interest Research Groups, argued,

> This bill deserves to be vetoed, not celebrated. It contains far too many unacceptable anti-environmental provisions that will weaken public health provisions and plunder public resources.[7]

Growing Public Concern

April 1998 had seemed to be a high point for environmental issues in the public and political arena. The focus on environmental spending had apparently shifted during the month as polls showed that voters were happy about economic growth but angered by the resulting traffic jams, air pollution, and disappearing countryside. The fact that land conservation had become such a significant political issue reflected the public's growing concern for environmental decay. The deterioration of the land, both nationally and globally, became one of the most publicized environmental issues. Human activity was not only damaging the wilderness but also destroying it in ways that were at best an inconvenience and at worst a potential threat to human existence. It was a problem that Americans could experience while visiting their favorite vacation spots, driving in the country, or listening to news reports.

Examples within the borders of the United States were plentiful. One of the most popular vacation spots in the country is Lake Tahoe, bordering on California and Nevada. Mark Twain had described this mountain-fringed lake as "so singularly clear that the boat seemed to be floating in air." The air itself, he wrote, was "very pure and fine, bracing and delicious . . . the same the angels breathe." However, by the late 1990s the fresh air, pine trees, boat-friendly lake, and casinos set seductively on the Nevada side were attracting 20 million tourists a year. As result, soil runoff and boat-based pollution had severely damaged the lake and its pristine surroundings. It had taken only a few decades for visibility in the lake to drop from 100 feet to 70 feet, and smog was not an uncommon sight during summer months. The forests were also suffering. Much of it had been cut in the late 1800s to supply Nevada's silver mines and, although reforested, was suffering from eight years of drought and subsequent insect invasions. One in six of the area's lodgepole pine, white fir, and jeffrey pine trees was dead or dying. The prognosis for the future was not optimistic as Don Lane, U.S. Forest Service forester, noted: Lake Tahoe "is an aging resort that's attempting to reinvent itself. . . . And the immense pressures it faces are only going to accelerate."[8]

In August 1998 the *New York Times* reported that "Alaska is thaw-ing, and much of northern Russia and Canada with it, and many scien-tists say that the warming of these cold regions is one of the most telling signals that the planet's climate is changing."[9] Using laser instruments, scientists had found evidence that many of Alaska's hundreds of gla-ciers were shrinking. The cause was determined to be a warmer atmos-phere in which higher moisture content produced more snow, but longer warmer summers often melted the glaciers faster than the heav-ier snows could rebuild them. The consequences rippled out through-out the state, causing erosion and destruction. Permafrost, ground that is perpetually frozen, was thawing in the interior along with under-ground ice trapped in the frost. As ice and snow turned to water, large sections of forest covering thousands of miles were drowning, turning gray as ground sank under them and swamp water flooded them. Deep holes were appearing throughout the state as pockets of ice melted, causing utility poles to tilt and trees to slump in angles—a phenomenon called "drunken forest." During the summer months, maintenance crews are kept busy repairing roads broken and cracked by the sinking and shifting land.

Scientists had warned that for years that the first region to show signs of global warming would be these northern regions. Apparently, their pre-dictions were proving correct. Over the century the world's temperature had risen by about 1 degree Fahrenheit but, according to scientists at the University of Alaska, for the last thirty years Alaska, Siberia, and north-western Canada had seen a temperature increase of 5 degrees. The debate was not so much about whether global temperatures were increas-ing but to what extent global warming was the culprit.

Although the human contribution to global warming continued to be a matter of debate, the destruction of the nation's wildlife by pollution, urban sprawl, and assorted other threats had been generally recognized since 1973 with the passage of the Endangered Species Act. During the 1970s and 1980s the act had been used to halt development and protect the habitats of species near extinction. However, the economic costs in lost profits and jobs had created a whirlwind of controversy, epitomized by the spotted owl conflict, causing politicians and government officials to seek a more creative path. By 1998 the government had decided to widen its interpretation of the act so that the emphasis would be on pro-tecting healthy and biologically diverse habitats rather than focusing on one endangered species at a time while simultaneously allowing develop-ment of private land to occur. If this could be done then it was hoped that environmentalists and private landowners could both be satisfied. This new approach became known as **habitat conservation plans** (HCPs), binding, voluntary agreements in which a landowner adopted conserva-tion measures, sometimes going beyond what the law strictly required, in exchange for permission to develop some property even if endangered wildlife and habitat were hurt in the process. Under the plan, landowners might agree to leave some forest untouched to protect wetlands from sediment and stream banks from erosion and to preserve natural corridors for animals. Otherwise, homes could be built, sewers trenched, and driveways paved. Congress had authorized HCPs back in 1982, but until 1994 only about twenty such agreements had been established. By the beginning of 1998 there were over two hundred active HCPs, the size of each being anywhere from a thousand to hundreds of thousands of acres with the tens of millions of acres coming under the policy in total.[10]

Supporters argued that this arrangement would not only protect threatened species and their environments but also the rights of property owners. The Clinton administration, struggling to maintain its environmental ideals with economic priorities, hailed the HCPs as a compromise that would satisfy all but the most extreme environmental or private property advocates. It credited HCPs with the recovery of hundreds of species, including the red-cockaded woodpeckers in rural Southeastern pine lands and the gnatcatcher songbirds in the heavily populated coastal-scrub ecosystems around San Diego. But such reassurances did not dissuade critics, particularly environmentalists, who argued that such arrangements were merely short-term solutions, pandering to economic interests, with long-term risks. A report by the Defenders of Wildlife argued,

> Under many HCPs, development is permitted and habitat is destroyed despite great uncertainty about whether the landowners have provided enough mitigation to sustain species in the long run.[11]

There has yet to be a clear solution to this problem or to the concerns of environmentalists, but clearly the Endangered Species Act is being transformed as Americans debate the price they are willing to pay for protecting nature.

Toxic wastes emitted by industry had been a major environmental issue since the 1960s when air and water pollution came to the general public's attention. In the early 1970s the Environmental Protection Agency made toxic waste one of its major priorities and maintained a constant surveillance of industrial pollution. The EPA began to make these findings public in 1988 as part of its "Community Right-To-Know" information under the Toxics Release Inventory (TRI). The TRI is an annual measure of toxic chemical releases, transfers, and waste generated by manufacturing facilities in communities throughout the United States. The 1997 findings, released in 1998, showed that about twenty-one thousand companies reported the quantities of 644 chemicals that their manufacturing facilities released annually into the air, water, and land. Facilities are also required to report on pollution prevention activities and chemical recycling. The data for 1997 showed that since 1988, total releases had decreased by almost 43 percent. In 1997 toxic air emissions continued to decline. However, in 1997 overall releases were up slightly for the first time with an increase of 2.2 percent.

The industries covered by the annual reporting requirement said that in 1997 they put 2.58 billion pounds of toxic waste into the air and water and onto land, including wastes injected deep into the earth. That compared with 2.52 billion pounds in 1996. The EPA said air pollution accounted for nearly 52 percent of the waste releases, or 1.3 billion pounds, a decline of 127 million pounds from 1996. About 30 percent of the total, or 785 million pounds, was disposed of on land, including landfills, on-site disposal, and transfers to waste brokers. An additional 218 million pounds, or 8.5 percent, were released into lakes and streams, an increase of 41 million pounds. Nearly 233 million pounds, or 9 percent, were injected deep into the ground. Texas had the largest amount of releases, 268 million pounds; followed by Ohio, 213 million pounds; Louisiana, 188 million pounds; Illinois, 134 million pounds; and Pennsylvania, 133 million pounds. The chemical industry accounted for the largest volume of toxic releases, followed by primary metals, and the pulp and paper industries.[12]

New Activism

By the late 1990s the United States had experienced nearly thirty years of the environmental debate. The enthusiasm of the 1970s had become the conservatism of the 1980s as environmental issues became both a recognized national priority and a target for those who saw it as an example of governmental regulation run amok. By end of the 1990s all sides had become well organized and fought in both the national and local arenas for their particular interpretation of the issues.

Finding new ways to promote the causes of environmental protection or conservatism might seem difficult, considering how many methods had already been used since the 1960s, but by the late 1990s the computer age added a new wrinkle to the environmental movement. E-mail and the Internet had transformed the environmental debate into a cyberspace war. It is certainly cheaper to ship electrons than paper, and for environmentalists e-mail has the added advantage of being a paper-free form of communication. As Paul Hughes, executive director of Forests Forever, in San Francisco, stated, the World Wide Web is "a marvelous tool for educating and organizing the world to save the last of the planet's intact forest ecosystem."[13] Most environmental groups had by the end of the decade logged on to the Web with their own sites. Web sites, such as **Econet** and **Greenwire**, provide current environmental news and a way to maintain constant communication. The Environmental Defense Fund went online in 1995 and by 1998 boasted 1 million annual visitors who read 20 million pages of environmental documents on numerous topics, a free e-mail newsletter subscription, an interactive Electricity Label Generator that showed how much pollution is generated by the electricity a person actually uses, and an Activists Alert program to enable members to send alerts to elected officials and companies about the issues they are most concerned about.

Grass-roots groups also were online. Mothers & Others for a Livable Planet publishes "The Green Guide," which informs readers of actions they can take to improve their personal health and the environment. Another group, Green Seal, awards a "Green Seal of Approval" to products it deems environmentally responsible and encourages its subscribers to buy those products. In fact, consumerism on the Web is one of the nation's fastest-growing industries and the environmental movement has been quick to exploit this avenue. On sites, such as EcoMall, consumers can buy environmentally friendly products and participate in a chat area that covers such topics as alternative transportation and hemp products. In May 1999 ENERGYguide.com, a one-stop information and e-commerce site for energy and energy-related shopping, hosted a Father's Day contest to promote the environmental benefits of energy efficiency. Web site visitors could register to win an environmentally friendly, energy-efficient Black & Decker cordless electric lawnmower for their father. The United States government's environmental policies are presented on the Web at the EPA's site, which includes a browsable database with late-breaking news and information on more than fifty topics, ranging from acid rain to wetlands. Visitors can also use the site to comment on proposed environmental regulations.[14]

The egalitarian nature of the Web means that environmental opposition groups also only need access to a server to present their views to a global audience. Such corporate giants as Weyerhaeuser and Monsanto, which harvest wood products, have Web sites that feature their corporate environmental policies. Lumber workers can promote their message of preserving jobs and managing forests to the public on the Web. On the Paperworkers Maine chapter Web site, the message reads, "We are people dedicated to preserving the environment while taking into account the economic stability of the workforce and surrounding community."[15] Cyberspace is growing and so is the battlefield for the environmental debate.

Although the Web has become a dominant site of debate, the environmental movement has not lost its propensity to take direct action. Actively promoting environmental issues continues to be an effective means of getting the environmental message out to the public. This method can range from encouraging people to enjoy the nature around them to destroying targets more radical environmentalists deem to be ecological threats. Nowhere is the need to get back to nature more compelling than in the sprawling cities of the nation. Yet in each urban community there are groups who seek out and find nature despite the growth of concrete and asphalt. For example, various groups organize white-water rafting in Washington, D.C., horseback riding in Los Angeles, and bird-watching in New York. In San Francisco, the Angling & Casting Club practices fishing skills in Golden Gate Park, the Audubon Society sponsors bird-watching tours of McLaren Park, and the Friends of Recreation and Parks leads park walking tours. These are modest but effective efforts to reconnect urbanites with nature.

However, peaceful promotion of the cause doesn't catch the headlines as easily as confrontation does, and the more radical activists are aware of this fact. They continue to protest the destruction and pollution of the environment through direct activism, which often attracts immediate media attention and even more so when lives are endangered and property destroyed. In September 1998 national attention was drawn to the battle over logging in the redwood groves in California's Humboldt County. For years the loggers and members of Earth First! had fought over the felling of the trees, which activists claimed destroyed the habitat of endangered seabirds. Earth First! activists sometimes took refuge in trees to prevent their being cut down. David (Gypsy) Chain was such an activist who sought to protect a redwood by daring the Pacific Lumber Company to cut it down while he was still in it. They did and he fell to the earth, crushing his skull and dying soon afterward. Chain's death has not dissuaded other activists from using such tactics. Julia Hill, known as Butterfly, who had climbed a 200-foot redwood near Eel River in November 1997 to save it from loggers, was still up there after Chain's death despite clear-cutting of surrounding trees and storm winds that often approached 90 mph.[16]

There are those who call such activists as Chain and Butterfly heroes, but few would condone the destruction in the name of environmentalism that took place in November 1998. A small group called Earth Liberation Front (ELF) claimed responsibility for history's costliest eco-terrorist attack when it set fire to Vail Mountain, destroying a restaurant, a patrol building, and a picnic shelter and damaging several ski lifts, in total worth $12 million. In a message to the press, ELF argued that the resort had endangered the ecology of the area and "For your safety and convenience, we strongly advise skiers to choose other destinations."[17] Although the act gained headlines and some sympathy from environmentalists, most pro-environment activists, aware of the criticism expressed throughout the nation, condemned it as counterproductive.

Perhaps a more constructive means of environmental activism was displayed in May 1999, when a student campaign, supported by more than fifty faculty and five hundred students, at the University of Washington, sought to induce the Board of Regents to divest the university's investments in eight companies "most responsible for inhibiting common sense solutions to global warming." The companies targeted were Allegheny Energy, Chevron, Exxon, Ford Motor, General Motors, Mobil, Southern, and Texaco. They were the top contributors to the Global

Climate Coalition (GCC), a lobbyist group that wants to delay any action until scientific certainty is achieved on the cause of global warming before initiating any remedies. David Roberts, the University of Washington student senator who launched the divestiture movement, explained,

> We are Generation Exxon. We have grown up witnessing the environmental disasters created by oil, auto and energy companies. We need the University of Washington to protect our environment and our future. The consequences of unchecked greenhouse gases, which trap heat in the atmosphere, and ozone depletion are significant and global. Weather pattern disturbances, including flooding, drought, and hurricanes, are just some of the early signs of global warming.[18]

Campus activism was not new to the environmental movement, although it has diminished greatly in the last two decades as students, consistent with the rest of the nation, seem more concerned with their economic future. Still, as Roberts argued, "The university is an excellent arena for activism." Other universities, including Harvard and Stanford, had also initiated such divestment campaigns. Still, it is a form of activism that often proves temporary, considering the transient nature of student life, but one that has made important contributions to changing American values in the past.

Congressional Action and Inaction

As domestic and global environmental issues and actions were debated, the public responded in the 1998 November elections by approving local and state ballot initiatives that called for spending more than $4 billion on urban parks and setting aside farmland and open spaces. Brent Blackwelder, president of Friends of the Earth, argued that land conservation was essentially a traditional American issue,

> There's not a significant constituency that's opposed to this. In this case, we're dealing with something that's motherhood and apple pie.[19]

Subsequently, both Republicans and Democrats declared their support for preserving wilderness, protecting wildlife, and cleaning up America. One congressional plan proposed the spending of $2.6 billion a year for land conservation. But the details were very much in dispute. Environmentalists and their Democratic allies wanted the bulk of funds to go for new parkland, suburban green spaces, and wildlife protection. Most Republicans backed a proposal to funnel money into coastal states with offshore oil drilling.

Mired in the Monica Lewinsky sex scandal and consequently his possible impeachment by the Senate, Clinton spent little time on environmental issues in 1999. This left Vice President Gore to champion the cause of environmentalism. In the past he had been a vociferous supporter of environmental causes and, with his eye on the presidential election of 2000, he once again positioned himself firmly in the environmentalists' camp. He started off the year by going to Iowa to announce that the administration was proposing a new financing tool that would aid farmers and generate $9.5 billion in bond authority for investments by state and local governments in a cleaner environment and open space. He also unveiled a plan that would grant $8.3 billion to ease traffic congestion and improve public transit. In the same month he hosted a national jobs summit where he unveiled a $60 million administration plan, plus a variety of tax breaks, to better educate needed high-skilled workers. He also declared that the administration would ask Congress for an additional $1.6 billion in grants to help pump new life and development into twenty selected poor urban and rural areas.

Critics argued that Gore's sudden reinvigorated interest in such issues was a self-serving and dishonest political maneuver. Senator Orrin Hatch, R-Utah, declared that Gore was "blatantly going around the country, at taxpayers' expense, campaigning and taking credit for things he shouldn't be taking credit for." In particular, Hatch was upset that Gore had claimed credit for the financial support given to farmers in Iowa, the state that coincidently would hold the first caucus of the 2000 presidential election, but that had been approved in 1998 by the Republican-led Congress. Concern was also evident among business leaders. Lonnie Taylor, chief lobbyist for the U.S. Chamber of Commerce, was more diplomatic in her observations of Gore's actions, stating, "Al Gore is making overtures to different groups, and that's what you do when you run for president." Yet Taylor warned that "There is a general concern that Gore would bring tougher environmental regulation as president."[20]

In fact, in the beginning of 1999 there were signs that both political parties were eager to show voters that they were environmentally friendly. First, the Clinton administration proposed doubling conservation spending to $1.1 billion, including $642 million for federal and state land purchases under a program that for years had been largely ignored. Then, Senators Mary Landrieu, D-Louisiana, and Frank Murkowski, R-Alaska, proposed spending $2.1 billion, including $620 million to buy new land for conservation. In the House, Representatives Don Young, R-Alaska and John Dingell, D-Michigan, came up with a $2.59 billion package, with $756 million for federal and state land purchases. Both of these bills would allocate about half of the total spending for "impact assistance" from offshore oil drilling. Under Young's bill, Louisiana alone would get $360 million, nearly the total earmarked for federal land purchases. In April the House approved legislation that would set national standards for beach water quality and require monitoring and notification to the public when the water is contaminated. The legislation required the Environmental Protection

Agency to establish criteria for pathogens and microorganisms in beach water. State and local governments would be required to establish standards as well as monitoring and notification programs. The bill also authorized $150 million over five years to help pay for the monitoring and notification programs. Only eight states have comprehensive monitoring of their beach water and notification to the public of health risks. One of the key sponsors, Representative Brian Bilbray, R-California, argued, "The public has a right to know what they're swimming in."[21]

Environmental issues had caught the public's and, therefore, the politicians', attention, but the problems were much easier to agree on than the solutions. For example, in March 1999 officials of the National Marine Fisheries Service formally declared that nine wild salmon species in the Pacific Northwest were threatened with extinction. It was the first listing under the twenty-six-year-old Endangered Species Act that affected an entire urban region. Although there was little criticism of the listing of the salmon, a recognized and cherished symbol of the region, the real question quickly became that of economics. Halting the decline of the salmon runs would be costly to everyone in the region. Higher taxes would be necessary to acquire land around waterways and to buy out floodplains so rivers could reclaim areas where salmon once spawned. Voluntary restrictions on the use of fertilizers and pesticides had already been encouraged, but they could become mandatory and there would certainly be limits on building near streams and other waterways. Yet some action was necessary because the Endangered Species Act stipulated that unless steps were taken to protect the affected species, governments and private citizens could face criminal penalties. Added to this was the quick mobilization of opposition groups prepared to confront any solution that did not satisfy their causes. Environmentalists were already arguing that the most likely solutions would not do enough to protect the salmon, whereas homebuilders and farmers were threatening lawsuits and calling state officials "jack-booted Nazis."[22] Perhaps the question is moot. With the Seattle metropolitan area projected to add as many as 1 million people in the next twenty-five years, the loss of the salmon may be a foregone conclusion.

By the summer of 1999 the destruction of America's wilderness continued at an alarming rate. In June, the Wilderness Society listed the nation's fifteen most endangered wildlands, blaming overlogging, oil and gas development, off-road vehicle use, various forms of noise pollution, and other ills for their demise. William H. Meadows, president of the Wilderness Society, encouraged the public to get involved to save these areas,

> All of us need to become familiar with the wild lands in our local areas and how they are being managed. Additionally, citizens should support crucial legislation to protect these special lands. With concerted action, the battle to protect these areas can be won.[23]

Meadows and his organization might be accused of using these lists as a way to alarm the public, gain support for their cause, and encourage public support for environmental issues. However, the deteriorating condition of wildlife and their habitats is unquestionably a serious problem. In March 1999, there were 1,180 species protected by the Endangered Species Act. Of those, 924 were endangered (357 animals, 567 plants) and 256 were threatened (121 animals, 135 plants). Fifty-eight species on the list had been added by the Fish and Wildlife Service from March 1998 to March 1999. There was little sign that the numbers of species on the list would decrease in the near future.[24]

Across the nation other signs of environmental destruction were alarmingly apparent. In April 1999 the environmental group American Rivers announced that the most endangered river in the United States was the Snake River in Washington. Specifically they blamed four dams— Ice Harbor, Lower Monumental, Little Goose, and Lower Granite—for bringing salmon runs to the brink of extinction on the river. In addition, the group blamed urban sprawl for much of the damage being done and as a major cause for the inclusion of many of the rivers on the list. For instance, Atlanta was growing so rapidly that water managers had proposed building and modifying dams on the Coosa and Tallapoosa Rivers, which threaten marine life in the rivers. Growth in Sierra Vista, Arizona, was partly to blame for taking water from an aquifer faster than it could be replenished in the San Pedro River. The Cedar River near Seattle was listed because urban sprawl threatened to destroy fish runs. And wasteful water practices in Salt Lake City were reducing flows in the Bear River and damaging a bird refuge. The fastest-growing county in California, Monterey County, was threatening wildlife and habitat by increasingly taking water from the Carmel River to serve the population growth.[25]

Industry remained a primary target for environmentalists as the largest source of pollution in the United States. During the late 1990s the strategy of most politicians and moderate environmentalists was to convince such industries that being environmentally friendly could also be profitable. It was hoped that such an appeal would both diminish pollutants and appeal to business leader's fixation with their bottom line. However, business was reluctant to accept this theory, despite growing supportive evidence.

For example, the auto industry continually resisted the message that being environmentally friendly could make wise business sense. The Ford Motor Company was attacked for introducing the largest sport utility vehicle (SUV) ever built: The Excursion, which came with a 44-gallon tank and would get only ten to eighteen miles per gallon. Most of Ford's profits came from the sale of trucks, and William Clay Ford, Jr., Ford Motor Company chairman, said that his company was only giving the people what they wanted. He defended his company's environmental record, arguing that the company's factories were the cleanest in the industry and that Ford has added equipment on many of its light trucks to qualify them as low-emission vehicles. However, because the market determined the products produced, it made little sense to build cars that would not sell.

> We could make all 80 miles-per-gallon small cars. . . . But if customers aren't buying them, if they're all sitting unsold on dealer lots, they're not doing the environment any good and Ford is not going to be in business very long.[26]

This argument might have some credibility, in a practical business sense, if not for the fact that Ford had the lowest overall fleet efficiency level in the industry. Furthermore, Ford's retort included an irrelevant attempt to blame the problem of carbon dioxide and other gases on developing countries, which he said must be forced to adopt new environmental policies.

America's love affair with the automobile had long been identified as a major source of pollution in the United States. By the late 1990s Americans owned over 200 million motor vehicles, four times that of the 1950s, and the mileage of the nation's highways doubled since the late 1970s. Studies showed that increasing the number and capacity of highways only encouraged more driving and thus more congestion. One theory, the Braess's paradox, stated that "by adding capacity to a crowded (highway) network you could actually slow things down."[27] Americans love to drive, and most federal highway officials predict that congestion will quadruple in the next twenty years. This trend is supported by data that shows that from 1970 to 1990, vehicle miles increased 90 percent and the registrations of those who drove them by more than 70 percent. In 1999, there were nearly two motor vehicles for every household in the United States, and the auto industry encouraged people to use them. The American auto industry spends $40 billion a year to promote the car with General Motors alone spending $1 billion. Yet despite the fact that Americans consistently claimed that air pollution was a major national concern, they got in their cars, turned on the engines, spouted pollutants into the atmosphere, and drove two blocks to the corner store for a gallon of milk.

However, despite the public's awareness of these problems and the apparent enthusiasm for environmental protection displayed among politicians, when it came to actually spending money the old antagonisms reappeared. In May it was announced that the House Appropriations Committee, controlled by Republicans, was planning bills that would cut spending for the environment, education, and other traditional Democratic priorities by billions of dollars in the federal budget of 2000. Constrained by the spending limits imposed by the 1997 balanced-budget pact, the committee was responsible for dividing $538 billion among thirteen bills covering all government agencies. That amount was nearly a third of the entire federal budget, including everything except automatic payments such as Medicare benefits and interest to bond holders. The amount they had available was $20 billion less than in 1999, leading to conflict over where the cuts would be made to reach this reduction. Under a plan proposed by the committee, many of the cuts would be made in programs closely associated with President Clinton's agenda. In particular, it would slash spending for social programs and the environment. The plan proposed cutting labor, health, and social services programs by nearly $10 billion and housing, veterans, and environmental programs nearly $7 billion, but boosted spending for defense, which already was getting an increase in a $15 billion emergency spending bill.

To most observers, the Republicans were setting a tough standard from which negotiations could begin. Clinton would surely veto the existing proposal even if it managed to pass through Congress. Sylvia Mathews, the White House deputy budget director, argued,

> The early reports about the Republican plan suggest their 2000 budget is simply not tenable. The level of cuts it would require would do enormous harm to critical areas that Americans care deeply about.

Representative John Edward Porter, R-Illinois, chair of the Appropriations subcommittee which oversaw Labor, admitted that some concessions might be made eventually. "We think of this as a placeholder, and hopefully we'll get more money later." This was not atypical of such a situation, a Democratic president and a Republican-controlled Congress, using the budget to forward their particular agendas. As Robert Reischauer of the Brookings Institution and former director of the Congressional Budget Office observed,

> My assumption is that the Republican leadership and the president are waiting for the other to cry uncle first. No one realistically believes we're going to live within the caps.

Still, whatever momentum had been created for environmental issues in April 1999 had been dampened by the beginning of the budget debate in May.[28]

The Global Future of the Environmental Movement

We no longer live in a world in which one nation can isolate itself from its global neighbors. This is particularly true in regard to the environmental crises that affect every living being on the planet. For example, global warming, destruction of the rain forests, depletion of the ozone layer, and losses of animal species and plant life that might have contributed immensely to medicine and the sciences threaten the health of the world's population. This interconnectedness is both regional and global, crossing national borders and continents, requiring that a nation's environmental policy must be international as well as domestic.

For the United States, global environmental issues present two distinct challenges: to protect the health of its citizens and to protect U.S. interests abroad. International treaties attempt to negotiate solutions to environmental problems that affect Americans directly and indirectly. For instance, there are and have been agreements dealing with the use of toxic chemicals, preservation of forests, release of numerous types of pollutants, global warming, population growth, and others. Vice President Gore clearly made the connection between global warming and the health of American citizens when he stated,

> Environmental problems such as global climate change, ozone depletion, ocean and air pollution, and resource degradation—compounded by an expanding world population—respect no border and threaten the health, prosperity, and jobs of all Americans. All the missiles and artillery in our arsenal will not be able to protect our people from rising sea levels, poisoned air, or foods laced with pesticides. Our efforts to promote democracy, free trade, and stability in the world will fall short unless people have a livable environment.
>
> We have an enormous stake in the management of the world's resources. Demand for timber in Japan mean trees fall in the United States. Greenhouse gas emissions anywhere in the world threaten coastal communities in Florida. A nuclear accident in Ukraine kills for generations. Over-fishing the world's oceans depletes resources for future generations. Our children's future is inextricably linked to our ability to manage the earth's air, water, and wildlife today.[29]

However, these concerns are not simply altruistic or preservationist in their approach, but take into account economic interests both domestically and internationally. Republican and Democratic administrations have sought solutions to environmental problems, while differing on costs and priorities, which Secretary of State Madeleine K. Albright argued, "protects our commercial interests . . . That makes business sense, environmental sense, scientific and medical sense." For instance, in May 1999 the Clinton administration opposed proposals by the European Union (EU) to limit what are known as "flexible mechanisms," under the Kyoto Climate Change Treaty of 1997, which enable industries to circumvent restrictions on carbon emissions. The administration argued that such flexibility was necessary to reduce costs to industry and protect the U.S. economy. It has also stated that developing countries must share the economic burden, arguing that within two decades the largest emitter of greenhouse gasses will not be the United States but China. Ten years after that, the developing countries will have become the source of the majority of such emissions.

This claim may be true, but in 1999 the United States contained one-twentieth of the world's population but generated one-fifth of all greenhouse gas emissions. This pollution was the result of a healthy industrialized economy, and no doubt U.S. international environmental diplomacy is based on a determination to preserve this condition. Peter Jorgensen, spokesman for acting EU environment commissioner Ritt Bjerregaard, criticized U.S. self-interest on this matter diplomatically, saying, "There is a different level of ambition between us and the Americans."[30] Europe's criticism of the United States is not uncommon on many issues and no nation has a monopoly on self-interest when it comes to international policies, but it is also true that the United States is often the most economically conservative voice among the developed nations when it comes to paying for solutions to global environmental crises.

Although the U.S. government recognizes that global environmental problems threaten Americans at home, it views this issue as a key to maintaining its influence abroad. Since the end of the Cold War, U.S. foreign policy has become increasingly aware that environmental problems often cause internal political and economic instability for nations and regions. This instability threatens U.S. interests and controlling it has become a major part of the foreign policy agenda. A State Department policy statement in 1999 emphasized this fact.

> The State Department now operates on the premise that countries sharing common resources share a common future and that neighboring nations are downstream and upwind, not just north and south or east and west, of each other. Threats to a shared forest, a common river, or a seamless coastline are forcing countries to expand their existing bilateral relationships to include environmental issues, and to create new regional frameworks to confront and combat shared environmental challenges.

As a result the State Department targeted five environmental problems that it deemed to be globally significant: climate change, toxic chemicals, species extinction, deforestation, and marine degradation. To pursue treaties and agreements with nations and regions particularly susceptive to these issues, the State Department set up "regional environmental hubs" in its embassies in Costa Rica, Uzbekistan, Ethiopia, Nepal, Jordan, and Thailand while making "environmental cooperation" an important part of the diplomatic agenda with countries such as Japan, India, Brazil, and China.[31]

Clearly the argument is that the diplomatic mechanism has been set in place for global environmental cooperation, but that is not really the point. The structure for such diplomacy already existed in the United Nations. However, the U.S. government had become sensitive to the criticism it had endured over the years from the United Nations, and many within the government believed that the United Nations is essentially anti-American. Also, within this global institution, the United States has only one vote in the General Assembly, a very powerful vote no doubt, but still susceptible to being outvoted on issues it deems particularly important to its interests. And these interests are essentially economic, particularly when it comes to the argument, often made by developing nations, that the United States should pay for the global environmental problems it is largely responsible for creating. Surprisingly, the U.S. government gave little support to a plan presented by the UN Development Program in May 1999, which proposed that a worldwide fund be set up to deal with global environmental crises. The plan estimated that a five-year commitment by donor nations to contribute 0.1 percent of their GDPs could raise $100 billion. By regionalizing its diplomacy, the United States avoids the awkwardness of such costly UN entanglements and can quietly negotiate agreements to its liking without the stage of well-publicized international meetings. At best, this means that U.S. foreign policy can use environmental issues to influence nations to make more responsible use of their resources for the betterment of the global community. However, it also means that foreign policy avoids a truly global approach to essentially a global problem and that diplomats can play on the peculiar strengths and weaknesses of nations and regions to forward U.S. interests, whether political or economic.

Conclusion

In the 1990s the environmental movement had truly become an institution, not just in the United States but globally. Is this a good thing? Without question the movement had made Americans more aware of their environment than at any time in their history and they are responding in unprecedented numbers. However, the sheer volume, complexity, and apocalyptic nature of the debate often left people confused and numbed. The issues seemed overwhelming and led many to seek comfort in solutions that were more perception than substance. In June 1999 scientists had begun studying a large haze of pollutants that collects over the Indian Ocean.[32] When they discovered that this filthy cloud deflected radiation and could lead to cooling, some viewed it as a possible solution to global warming. Clearly we cannot pollute our way out of global warming, and scientists were quick to observe that the soot drops from the atmosphere in weeks, while greenhouse gases remain for centuries. Still, the event exemplifies how the complexity of the environmental movement has created an anxious public, at times swamped by the debate, and prepared to grasp at anything that might be hopeful.

So, has the institutionalization of the environmental movement really accomplished anything? The answer may be comparable to our own democratic institutions. It is a system governed by many voices, based on compromises, and infuriatingly slow to many observers. Yet it seems to work. We can only hope that eventually the environmental movement will work. Unfortunately, unlike the workings of governments, there is a time limit to solving our domestic and global environmental problems.

Chapter Notes

1. "Club Endorses Bill Clinton," *The Planet* 3, no. 8, Nov. 1996.
2. "President Clinton's Fact Sheet on Joint Implementation," Oct. 22, 1997, http://www.whitehouse.gov/Initiatives/Climate/Jl.html.
3. William K. Stevens, "Greenhouse Gas Issue Pits Third World Against Richer Nations," *New York Times*, Nov. 30, 1997.
4. "Environment and the Economy: The Kyoto Protocol," *Business Roundtable*, June 22, 1998, http://www.brtable.org/document.cfm/161.
5. David Bacon, "Cottage Street Beats the Concrete Mountain," *EcoJustice Network*, April 9, 1997, http://www.igc.org/envjustice/communique/montana.html.
6. Ibid.
7. John H. Cushman, Jr., "Environmental Spending Decisions Colored by Compromise," *New York Times*, Oct. 16, 1998.
8. Laura Bly, "Ecological Changes Cloud Tahoe's Future," *USA Today*, July 25, 1997.
9. William K. Stevens, "As Alaska Melts, Scientists Consider the Reasons Why," *New York Times*, Aug. 18 1998.
10. John H. Cushman, "The Endangered Species Act Gets a Makeover," *New York Times,* June 2, 1998.
11. Ibid.
12. "U.S. EPA Announces 1997 Toxics Release Inventory," *PRNewswire*, May 13, 1998.
13. Karen L. Miller, "The Greening of the Web: Reduce, Reuse, Recycle, Research, React . . . and Buy," *New York Times*, Jan. 23, 1998.
14. Ibid.
15. Jason Chervokas and Tom Watson, "Timber Issue Offers Gauge of Internet Discourse," *New York Times,* May 30, 1997.
16. John Skow, "The Redwoods Weep: In California Ancient Forests, the Clash between Industry and Idealism Culminates in Tragedy," *Time*, Sept. 28, 1998.
17. John Cloud, "Fire on the Mountain: The Posh Ski Town of Vail Is Shaken by an Act of Apparent Ecoterrorism," *Time*, Nov. 2, 1998.
18. "University of Washington Students Urge Board of Regents to Divest of 'Egregious Eight' Contributors to Global Warming," *Business Wire*, May 13, 1999.
19. H. Josef Hebert, "Congress Embracing Land Conservation," *USA Today*, April 20, 1999.
20. "Gore Focuses on 2000 U.S. Presidential Campaign," *New York Times*, Jan. 14, 1999.
21. Paul Leavitt, "House OKs Standards for Beach Water Quality," *USA Today*, April 23, 1999, 8A.
22. Sam Howe Verhovek, "Salmon Put on U.S. List as at Risk," *New York Times*, March 16, 1999.
23. "1998 Report: 15 Most Endangered Wild Lands," *Wilderness Society*, http://www.wildemess.org/standbylands/15most/index.htm.
24. Ibid.
25. John Hughes, "Group: Sprawl Threatens Rivers, with Snake River Topping List," *USA Today*, April 12, 1999.

26. Todd Nissen, "Chairman Ford Defends Company Environmental Record," *Reuters*, May 13, 1999.
27. Jane Holtz Kay, *Asphalt Nation: How the Automobile Took Over America, and How We Can Take It Back* (New York: Crown, 1997), 34.
28. "Congress Gets Set to Confront Clinton Over Budget," Reuters, May 18, 1999.
29. U.S. State Department, "Letter from Vice President Albert Gore, Jr.," *Environmental Diplomacy: The Environment and U.S. Foreign Policy*, http://www.state.gov/ www/global/oes/earth.html, 1997.
30. Michael Mann, "EU Says U.S. Must Be More Ambitious over Climate," Reuters, May 18, 1999.
31. U.S. State Department, "Environmental Diplomacy at Work," *Environmental Diplomacy: The Environment and U.S. Foreign Policy*, http://www.state.gov/ www/global/oes/earth.html, 1997.
32. Dick Thompson, "What Global Warming? As the World Heats Up, the Public Simply Goes Cold," *Science*, 153, no. 24, June 21, 1999.

11

The Environmental Movement in the Post 9/11 World

As the people of the United States entered the twenty-first century they faced many serious issues but none seemed more alarming than the domestic and global challenges presented by the growing environmental crisis. Academics, politicians, and numerous other observers and commentators had been predicting that this would be the "century of the environment" when the nation's energies would be directed, in alliance with the nations of the world, at solving the numerous environmental problems that many believed were threatening the very existence of humanity. Then, the nation and the world changed on September 11, 2001, when terrorists destroyed the Twin Towers in New York City. Priorities also changed on that day as the "War on Terrorism" forced the United States to focus on the real and perceived threats in the Middle East and elsewhere. All other issues, including the environment, seemed to pale in comparison to this new global crisis.

The Presidential Election of 2000

The lead up to the political elections of 2000 was highly anticipated by environmentalists across the United States. For many, the elections were to be the springboard for making the United States the leader in the global effort to solve the global environmental crisis facing the world in the twenty-first century. Ballot initiatives across the nation targeted urban sprawl; the League of Conservation Voters named dozens of key races, pointing to Congress's failing scorecard when it came to the environment; and the prospect of having a bona-fide environmentalist, Vice

President Al Gore, as the next president mobilized national as well as grass-roots environmental groups in every state.

The Republican platform presented its party and its presidential candidate as a moderate in regard to the environment placing George W. Bush within "the proud tradition of Teddy Roosevelt, the first president to stress the importance of environmental conservation." However, it favored the states over the existing regulatory powers of the federal government for solving environmental issues crediting "their unique ability to solve problems at the local level." It further made it clear that environmental policy must be responsive to the needs of development and "an environment in which innovation can flourish," emphasizing that "just as environmental pollution affects our physical health, so too does the pollution of our culture affect the health of our communities."[1]

While the Republican Party may have attempted to present a more moderate approach to the environment, their candidate, George W. Bush, made it clear during his campaign that his administration would not support the proactive approach of existing government agencies and would roll back years of regulation. For example, he criticized the Clean Air and Clean Water Acts, "I don't think you can litigate clean air and clean water." He went further in declaring that Washington should "probe [the] EPA, not the oil refineries" and argued that the causes of global warming needed further study before any direct action could be taken. His views were consistent with the Republican Party's efforts to present itself as the party of deregulation in which "a new era of environmental protection" would increase state powers and lessen the "micromanagement" of Washington bureaucrats.[2]

In stark contrast to the Republicans, the Democratic Party began the campaign by highlighting environmental issues as a key to the election. This was not surprising considering Gore's reputation and long standing support for the environmental cause. As the author of *Earth in the Balance*, Gore had strong environmental credentials and as vice president had consistently lobbied for issues such as the Kyoto Protocol, Clean Air regulations, and restrictions on gas emissions. The Democratic Party platform boasted that the nation had "the cleanest environment in decades" and stressed the need for public transit and the protection of wetlands. In his acceptance speech Gore had declared "our children should not have to draw the breath of life in cities awash in pollution."[3] Even his running mate, Senator Lieberman, ranked high on environmental issues with a rating of 95 percent by the League of Conservation Voters as compared to Republican nominee Richard Cheney's 13 percent. In fact, environmental groups made their choice early and clear. Albert Gore was their man. The League of Conservation Voters stated that "When Al Gore wins, the planet wins," while the Sierra Club went further by declaring him the most pro-environment candidate of modern times.[4] In what was clearly a move toward the pragmatic, most environmental groups chose Gore over the

Green Party candidate, Ralph Nader, warning that Nader's candidacy would only damage the election of a more valid candidate

The most anticipated events of the elections were the televised debates between the presidential candidates. Environmental issues began as a key issue clearly defining the differences between the two candidates. In the first meeting Gore called for "new investments in clean coal technology" and domestic exploration, but not in what he termed "precious . . . environmental treasures." He also asked for tax incentives to put America on the "cutting edge of the new technologies" in "more efficient, cleaner energy." Bush replied by favoring "an active exploration program in America." He also came out "against removing dams in the Northwest" and in favor of coal mining. Both candidates pronounced themselves pleased with the debate. In their second meeting the environment was dealt with in more general terms. Gore stuck by his plea of nearly a decade ago for "the rescue of our environment." He asked America to take the "leadership role" on global warming and rapidly rising pollution levels: "The old argument that the environment and the economy are in conflict is really outdated." It marked a message he was to repeat on the campaign trail, saying that "we can create . . . technology to stop the pollution and lift standards of living at the same time." Bush countered that his state had cleaned some 450 abandoned industrial sites, and "not all wisdom is in Washington." He refused "the burden for cleaning up the world's air." The candidates then sparred over Bush's environmental record as Texas governor and the very reality of global warming. "Look," Gore concluded, "the world's temperature's going up, weather patterns are changing . . . and what are we going to tell our children?" In one more sign of a politer exchange, he summed it all up for both sides: "We differ on whether or not pollution controls ought to be voluntary." Bush ventured that "Some of the scientists, I believe . . . haven't they been changing their opinion a little bit?" However, by the third debate the environment had become a minor issue as both candidates avoided any strong comments on the issue while there were no questions from the audience regarding the environment.[5]

As it turned out the United States presidential election of 2000 was the closest Presidential election in United States history, decided by only 537 votes in the swing state of Florida. On election night, November 7, the media prematurely declared a winner twice based on exit polls before finally deciding that the Florida race was too close to call. It would turn out to be a month before the election was finally certified after numerous court challenges and recounts. In the end, George W. Bush won Florida's twenty-five electoral votes by a razor-thin margin of the popular vote in that state, and thereby defeated Al Gore. This election marked the fourth time in United States history that a candidate had won the Presidency while losing the nationwide popular vote. (The other times were the elections of 1824, 1876, and 1888.) In a nation so clearly divided on many key issues the election came down to a personality contest with the polls showing that voters agreed with Al Gore on the issues, but trusted George W. Bush more personally. However, for environmentalists the election of Bush was clearly a defeat. While pro-environmental candidates won in Washington and Michigan there were few others to boast of. The evidence seemed clear that the environmental movement had failed to garner the public support needed to put their candidate in office or to establish a nationwide environmental agenda.

It didn't take long for the Bush administration to begin making its environmental philosophy government policy. In accordance with the goals of the Bush administration's national energy plan, released in May 2001, federal agencies shifted their focus away from balanced resource protection. Instead, they were actively scouring public lands for energy development opportunities. The Bureau of Land Management (BLM) led efforts to open up enormous amounts of public lands to the energy industry. BLM data, released in early March 2001, showed that the number of leases for oil, gas, and coal mining on public lands increased by 51 percent—from 2.6 million acres in 2000 to 4 million acres in 2001.[6]

While environmentalists condemned Bush's environmental policies, his popularity with the general U.S. population remained strong. The Pew Research Center survey reported in April 2001 that 56 percent expressed approval for the way Bush was handling his job, while 27 percent said they disapproved. That mark was an improvement over Clinton's rating of 55 percent and 37 percent in April 1993—not only because fewer people disapproved of the current president, but also because a considerably larger number strongly approved of Bush than held very positive opinions of Clinton three months into his term (34 percent vs. 18 percent). The president's strong position with the public reflected continuing comfort with Bush personally, positive reaction to his handling of international issues and his tax proposals, combined with limited knowledge of unpopular administration decisions about the environment. The latter was particularly true considering environmental issues that seemed to be a minor issue to most Americans. Just 28 percent of poll respondents knew that Bush had decided not to restrict emissions of carbon dioxide from power plants and even fewer (20 percent) knew of his decision to withdraw support for the Kyoto agreement to combat global warming. This lack of awareness favored the administration because each of these decisions, when tested, was broadly unpopular. Future expectations of Bush varied across different policy areas. The public was more optimistic about Bush's ability to be successful in the foreign policy realm than they were about his ability to make progress on environmental protection. While more than half (55 percent) expected him to perform well in handling the nation's foreign policy, only 39 percent thought Bush was likely to make real progress in protecting the environment, and 54 percent thought he would not.[7]

The Post 9/11 World

Then, on that bright clear morning in September, 2001, two hijacked airliners destroyed the Twin Towers in New York City, another damaged the Pentagon, and a fourth, Flight 93, crashed in Pennsylvania near a forest, possibly heading for the White House. Approximately three thousand people died in the attacks and a number of buildings were damaged or destroyed. Nineteen men, all affiliated with the Islamic group al-Qaeda, had hijacked the commercial passenger jet airliners in a terrorist act against the United States. From that day on, "9/11" became a rallying cry for revenge and the "War on Terrorism." Seemingly overnight the nation turned its attention and energies toward this perceived threat and all other issues seemed to take a backseat to this crisis. In response, the United States, with the military support of NATO and the political support of much of the international community, invaded Afghanistan and overthrew the Taliban regime, which had supported and harbored Osama bin Laden, the leader of al-Qaeda and planner of the 9/11 attack. Then, in 2003, weapons of mass destruction were said to be hidden in Iraq, Saddam Hussein and Bin Laden were linked by the U.S. government and the media, and soon a war that almost everyone seemed to want was underway.

The need to maintain domestic security and the pursuance of the war on terrorism quickly put a strain on the nation's resources bringing into question the problem of just how much freedom should be given up to maintain freedom. The result was the Patriot Act and a quickly soaring national debt. Still, these sacrifices and others seemed necessary in the face of the threat emanating from the Middle East and elsewhere. Indeed, sacrifices would have to be made and one of the most important of these seemed to be that of environmental protection. There was no longer talk of the "century of the environment" but instead the government declared that the Alaska Wildlife Reserve must be opened to the oil industry in order to free the nation from its dependence on Middle East oil and that the resources of the nation needed to be utilized to fight a lengthy and costly, but ultimately just, war against "Terrorism."

During the Bush administration's first term in office the United States invaded Afghanistan in 2001, toppled Saddam Hussein in Iraq in 2003, and began a lengthy policy of suppression of insurgents in that country while continuing efforts to rebuild the Iraqi nation. For the Bush administration these acts were all part of its comprehensive war on terrorism, necessary to protect the nation, its interests and the people of the world who shared its determination to eliminate the terrorist threat. Not surprisingly, war dominated the headlines and the attention of most U.S. citizens resulting in much debate about the aims, methods, and strategies of government policies. There was certainly much to debate. After the initial military victories in Afghanistan and Iraq the administration became bogged down trying to rebuild an Iraqi government, settle sectarian conflict, and destroy the persistent Islamic extremist movement, which maintained a constant terrorist offensive against the U.S. presence in Iraq. While critics made charges of duplicity, inconsistencies, and profiteering supporters praised the administration for its strong and successful leadership.

While the U.S. public was preoccupied with the issues concerning the war on terrorism, the Bush administration intensified its efforts to deregulate environmental policies. There was nothing secretive or inconsistent in these efforts and were simply the continuation of Bush's stated goal to dismantle what he considered to be an over abundance, destructive and inefficient mountain of environmental laws and policies. In doing so he was aided by a growing number of presidential appointees at key federal agencies actively pursuing a deregulation environmental agenda, Bush's surge in popularity, and a news media distracted by the war on terrorism.

Once in office Bush had immediately begun appointing individuals who shared his pro-development and anti-regulation approach to environmental policy. Among them were Mark Rey, Undersecretary for Natural Resources and Environment, Department of Agriculture, a leading advocate of logging in national forests, who stated, "We should start with the premise that a policy cannot be good for the environment if it is bad for people"; Marianne L. Horinko, Acting Administrator, Environmental Protection Agency, who as president of the environmental consulting firm Clay Associates, represented industry clients regulated by the EPA; Thomas Sansonetti, Assistant Attorney General for Environment and Natural Resources, a member of the Federalist Society, a conservative libertarian property rights group, which had opposed federal regulations under many environmental laws; Allan Fitzsimmons, Wildlands Fuels Coordinator, Department of the Interior, who as an aide to the Assistant Secretary for Fish and Wildlife and Parks in 1986, wrote a memo suggesting that "public recreational benefit is the principal reason for conserving natural features"; and Bennett Raley, Assistant Secretary for Water and Science, Department of the Interior, who, as a lawyer, lobbyist, and property-rights activist in Colorado, represented irrigators, water districts, and property-rights groups. The list goes on of appointees who had close ties with industries regulated by and often at odds with government environmental agencies and who supported efforts to weaken environmental restrictions.[8]

Some of the most important environmental issues debated and acted upon during Bush's first term included proposals for oil drilling in the Alaska's Artic National Wildlife Refuge, passage of the Kyoto Protocol, and the theory of global warming. The issue of whether to tap Alaska's Arctic National Wildlife Refuge for oil and gas had been highly debated for more than two decades. For years, legislation to allow such drilling had been blocked in the Senate by filibusters spearheaded by Democratic senators. As a former oil man, Bush argued that drilling in the refuge would decrease U.S. dependence on foreign oil. His opponents cited reports, including one from the Congressional Research Service in 1998, which stated that the Arctic refuge would provide less than a six-month supply of oil—which would not be available for ten years. Regardless of the amount of oil and the length of time it would take to reach U.S. markets, the risk the drilling would pose to the area's ecological integrity and its diverse wildlife could not be easily denied. The Arctic Refuge is a nineteen million acre natural wonder containing marshes, lagoons, and rivers that run through the rugged foothills of the Brooks Range and the expansive icy waters of the Beaufort Sea. It is also the nation's largest wildlife preserve, home of 180 species of birds and 36 species of mammals, including 3 species of North American bears. Nine marine mammal species live along its coast and 36 fish species inhabit its rivers and lakes. The Bush administration argued that drilling would only take place on a small part of the preserve while opponents were suspicious of the administration's claims, countering that any drilling would damage breeding grounds and that the cost to the ecosystem was too high for such short-term rewards. The House of Representatives voted in 2000 to allow drilling but in April 2002 the Senate rejected it. The issue continued to be debated throughout Bush's first term with both sides maneuvering for support and promising to continue the fight into the future.

The White House decision to withdraw the United States from negotiation over the Kyoto Protocol in 2002 drew criticism from environmentalists but little attention from the general public. Kyoto would have created, among other issues, greenhouse gas rules and regulations. On July 25, 1997, before the Kyoto Protocol was finalized (although it had been fully negotiated, and a penultimate draft was finished), the U.S. Senate unanimously passed, by a 95–0 vote, the Byrd-Hagel Resolution, which stated the sense of the Senate was that the United States should not be a signatory to any protocol that did not include binding targets and timetables for developing as well as industrialized nations or "would result in serious harm to the economy of the United States." On November 12, 1998, Vice President Al Gore symbolically signed the protocol. Both Gore and Senator Joseph Lieberman indicated that the protocol would not be acted upon in the Senate until there was participation by the developing nations. The Clinton Administration never submitted the protocol to the Senate for ratification. Once he took office, Bush made it clear that he would not submit the treaty for ratification, not because he did not support the general idea, but because of the strain he believed the treaty would put on the economy; he emphasized the uncertainties which he asserted were present in the climate change issue. Furthermore, he was not happy with the details of the treaty. Specifically, he did not support the split between Annex I countries and others. Bush said of the treaty:

> This is a challenge that requires a 100 percent effort; ours, and the rest of
> the world's. The world's second-largest emitter of greenhouse gases is

China. Yet, China was entirely exempted from the requirements of the Kyoto Protocol. India and Germany are among the top emitters. Yet, India was also exempt from Kyoto. . . . America's unwillingness to embrace a flawed treaty should not be read by our friends and allies as any abdication of responsibility. To the contrary, my administration is committed to a leadership role on the issue of climate change. . . . Our approach must be consistent with the long-term goal of stabilizing greenhouse gas concentrations in the atmosphere.[9]

Another global environmental issue which attracted national attention during Bush's presidency was the issue of global warming. The term "global warming" is a specific case of the more general term "climate change." In principle, "global warming" is neutral as to the causes, but in common usage, "global warming" generally implies a human influence. The Earth's average near-surface atmospheric temperature rose 0.6 ± 0.2 degrees Celsius (1.1 ± 0.4 degrees Fahrenheit) in the twentieth century. The prevailing scientific opinion on climate change is that "most of the warming observed over the last fifty years is attributable to human activities." The increased amounts of carbon dioxide (CO_2) and fifty other greenhouse gases (GHGs) are the primary causes of the human-induced component of warming. They are released by the burning of fossil fuels, land clearing and agriculture, etc., and lead to an increase in the greenhouse effect.

The measure of the climate response to increased GHGs, climate sensitivity, is found by observational studies and climate models. This sensitivity is usually expressed in terms of the temperature response expected from a doubling of CO_2 in the atmosphere. The current literature estimates sensitivity in the range 1.5 to 4.5 °C (2.7 to 8.1 °F). Models referenced by the Intergovernmental Panel on Climate Change (IPCC) predict that global temperatures may increase by between 1.4 and 5.8 °C (2.5 to 10.5 °F) between 1990 and 2100. The uncertainty in this range results from both the difficulty of predicting the volume of future greenhouse gas emissions and the uncertainty about climate sensitivity.

An increase in global temperatures can in turn cause other changes, including a rising sea level and changes in the amount and pattern of precipitation. These changes may increase the frequency and intensity of extreme weather events, such as floods, droughts, heat waves, hurricanes, and tornados. Other consequences include higher or lower agricultural yields, glacier retreat, reduced summer streamflows, species extinctions and increases in the ranges of disease vectors. Warming is expected to affect the number and magnitude of these events; however, it is difficult to connect particular events to global warming. Although most studies focus on the period up to 2100, warming (and sea level rise due to thermal expansion) is expected to continue past then, since CO_2 has a long average atmospheric lifetime.

Only a small minority of scientists contested the view that humanity's actions have played a significant role in recent warming. However, the uncertainty is more significant regarding how much climate change should be expected in the future, and there is a hotly contested political and public debate over what, if anything, should be done to reduce or reverse future warming, and how to cope with the predicted consequences.

Bush and Changing Regulations

A review of Bush's first term demonstrates that he continually pursued a policy of deregulating and weakening environmental regulations. During his first three years in office there was a 75 percent decline in the number of federal lawsuits filed against companies violating national environmental laws as compared to the last three years of the Clinton administration. Civil citations for polluters were down 57 percent since 2001, and criminal prosecutions had fallen 17 percent. The pace of completed cleanups of Superfund hazardous waste sites, which increased dramatically in the later years of the Clinton era, had declined 52 percent since 2001, according to the EPA. Furthermore, the Bush administration refused to seek renewal of the Superfund clean-up tax on polluting industries, allowing the fund effectively to go bankrupt. As a result, the EPA reported thirty-four unfunded Superfund cleanups in nineteen states in 2004. There had also been a 52 percent decrease in EPA clean air inspections at refineries since 2001, and a 68 percent reduction in the number of notices of violations issued to refineries over the same period.[10]

Critics argued that the EPA and the regulatory system established to control and punish major polluters had been undermined by the administration resulting in a dramatic increase in pollution. After years of consistent decline, the 2004 inventory of industrial toxic releases showed an increase of 5 percent in the release of toxic substances into the air, water, and land. EPA data released in June 2004 documented toxic releases from industrial facilities of nearly 4.8 billion pounds. The EPA reported a 36 percent increase in annual beach closings due to unsafe water quality since 2001. Sewage contamination was an important and growing part of the problem. A total of 2,348 fish consumption advisories for mercury contamination were issued in 45 states in 2003. Seventy-six percent of fish samples from U.S. lakes were found to contain mercury levels unsafe for children three years old and younger to eat twice a week, according to the EPA. As a result it was believed that every year more than six hundred thousand newborns may have been exposed to levels of mercury exceeding EPA health standards while still in the womb. In September 2004, EPA's inspector general concluded that the agency was not making sufficient progress in reducing the pollutants that cause ozone smog in the nation's population centers. According to EPA data, 159 million Americans (55 percent of the population) lived in areas with hazardous smog levels and

100 million people live in areas that violate the EPA's new pollution standards for harmful soot. Perchlorate, a toxic rocket fuel additive, is leaching out from military dumps and contaminating the drinking water of more than 20 million Americans. More than 90 percent of lettuce and milk sampled nationwide showed levels of perchlorate that may be unsafe for children. Despite recommendations from scientific experts at the EPA to severely reduce perchlorate contamination, the Bush administration refused to take action. Nonetheless, in December 2004, after winning re-election in a campaign nearly devoid of any mention of environmental issues, Bush proclaimed that his environmental policies had "improved habitat on public and private lands."[11]

During Bush's second term there were several domestic issues which attracted and polarized the public's attention including partial birth abortion, federal funding of stem cell research, separation of church and state, same-sex marriage, and immigration. However, U.S. foreign policy and the war in Iraq continued to be the government's primary agenda as it expanded its strategy with the intention of preparing the nation for a lengthy global conflict referring to the war on terrorism as the "The Long War." This became the approach promulgated by both military and political leaders. In September 2006, the outgoing chairman of the Joint Chiefs of Staff, Air Force General Richard Myers, during his final news conference pointed out that political and economic measures, not just military ones, would be needed to win the war. Bush first officially presented this idea in his 2006 State of the Union speech: "Our own generation is in a long war against a determined enemy." The 2006 Quadrennial Defense Review Report (QDRR) of the U.S. Department of Defense headlined the section on the war's long-term goals with "Fighting the Long War." The report's preface starts with the phrase: "The United States is a nation engaged in what will be a long war." For the Bush administration the disaster of 9/11 had ignited a World War III in which the nation's resources would be mustered for the protection of the world's democratic institutions as defined by U.S. standards.

The Debate and the Gamble

Ironically, while the war in Iraq spiraled into sectarian violence, the conflict in Afghanistan continued with no clear ending, and global terrorism remained deadly, there were signs that the environmental crisis, which had taken a back seat to the war on terrorism, might threaten to make all these issues irrelevant. One of the most global and dangerous issues was that of global warming. In January 2006, the Prime Minister of Britain, Tony Blair, a close ally of the United States in the war on terrorism, declared "the risks of climate change may well be greater than we thought." In the foreword of a British government-commissioned report Blair wrote, "It is now plain that the emission of greenhouse gases, associated with industrialization and economic growth from a world population that has increased six-fold in 200 years, is causing global warming at a rate that is unsustainable." The report confirmed, what many scientists had been warning for decades, that over the next century, global warming was expected to raise ocean levels, intensify storms, spread disease to new areas and shift climate zones, possibly making farmlands drier and deserts wetter. In fact, the U.N.-backed Intergovernmental Panel on Climate Change found that global temperatures rose by about 1 degree during the twentieth century. Computer modeling predicted increases of between 2.5 degrees and 10.4 degrees by the year 2100, depending on how much is done to limit greenhouse gas emissions. Still, Blair was unable to overcome the Bush administration's antipathy to the Kyoto climate-change accord rejected by the U.S. government on the grounds it would damage the economy. Even British ministers had to admit that Britain was unlikely to meet its own target of cutting carbon dioxide emissions by 20 percent by 2010.[12]

U.S. sources confirmed the threat of global warning. A report published in 2006 by the Proceedings of the National Academy of Sciences warned that temperatures on Earth were just two degrees shy of an average temperature of 59 degrees Fahrenheit, which was what they believed the temperature was about a million years ago. NASA's James Hansen, along with colleagues from the University of California and Columbia University, cautioned "Humans are now in control of the Earth's climate, for better or worse." Based on a "business as usual" scenario in which greenhouse gasses continued to rise unabated, Hansen said the million-year-old record would be broken in about forty-five years. But he stressed we can't wait that long to cut greenhouse gas pollution, because of the decades it takes for the climate system to respond to changes. "We need to get started now," he said. "We can't wait another decade or two to take this seriously." The 2 degrees the scientists were talking about meant that by midcentury, the world would experience even more record heat waves, wildfires, more intense storms, and flooding. In other parts of the world, the increase may worsen drought conditions as more mountain glaciers and snow packs vanish, no longer sending water to the valleys below.

Despite these types of cataclysmic warnings, the Bush administration's view was that the type and degree of danger associated with global warming had yet to be defined, necessitating more research on the matter before a possibly economic crippling set of policies could be implemented to combat the issue. The debate over this issue, and Bush's ideological preference, was further publicized in 2006 when Fred Barnes, in his *Rebel in Chief: Inside the Bold and Controversial Presidency of George W. Bush,"* recalled a visit, set up by Bush's political advisor Karl Rove, by author Michael Crichton to the White House in 2004. He added that, "The visit was not made public for fear of outraging environmentalists all the more."[13] Environmentalists had long argued that Crichton's dismissal of global warming, coupled with his popularity as a novelist and screenwriter, had undermined efforts to pass legislation intended to reduce emissions of carbon dioxide, a gas that leading scientists said causes climate change. In the nonfiction sections of his 2004 book *State of Fear*, Crichton wrote that NASA's James Hansen's climate change calculations were "wrong by 300 percent." Shortly after the publication of Barnes' book Hansen retorted that Crichton had misrepresented his scientific work and had done so in testimony before Congress and in a meeting with President Bush— even though he was not a climate expert, charging that "He is propagating false information to the public."[14]

During Bush's second term both global and domestic environmental issues continued to be debated. Bush's critics often argued that his administration had eliminated or weakened environmental protection legislation that had been in place for over thirty years. Another common criticism was that Bush favored big business and that under his administration enforcement of anti-pollution laws has steadily and substantially declined. After it was reported in 2006 that U.S. Justice Department figures showed federal prosecutions for environmental violations had substantially decreased during Bush's first and second terms, Jeff Ruch, Executive Director of Public Employees for Environmental Responsibility, asserted: "This Bush administration can make no claim to law and order credentials when it comes to pollution. Corporate transgressors have growing reason for confidence that environmental violations will not trigger federal prosecution."[15] In response to these charges the Bush administration and its supporters have maintained a consistent philosophy defending deregulation and support for voluntary public and corporate action to battle environmental problems. The official White House Web page states these goals clearly:

- The focus is on results—making our air, water, and land cleaner. We need to employ the best science and data to inform our decision-making. Our policies should encourage innovation and the development of new, cleaner technologies. We should continue to build on America's ethic of stewardship and personal responsibility through education and volunteer opportunities, and in our daily lives.
- Opportunities for environmental improvements are not limited to Federal Government actions—states, tribes, local communities, and individuals must be included.[16]

Natural disasters like the Asian Tsunami of 2004 and the flooding of New Orleans by hurricane Katrina in 2005 caught the attention of the public and media but while concern for the fate of the victims was widely expressed, the environmental causes of these disasters seem to have been quickly relegated to the less popular arenas of academics and professional environmentalists. In the 2006 Congressional elections the issue of the environment fell far behind Americans' concerns about the economy, terrorism, and taxes. Encouraging to environmentalists was a *Los Angeles Times/Bloomberg* poll published on August 4, 2006, in which 56 percent of poll respondents said Bush was doing too little to protect the environment, a sharp increase from 2001 when only 41 percent said the president was not doing enough for the environment.[17] Yet, in polls that asked Americans to identify the most important campaign issues the environment was at the bottom of the list or not included at all. Clearly, when asked directly about environmental issues Americans wanted more to be done and were unhappy with the Bush administration's policies. However, there was no immediacy to this unhappiness. The attitude appeared to be one of, "It can wait."

Conclusion

Unfortunately, it may take the environmental equivalent of the 9/11 Twin Towers disaster to shift the public's attention toward a global and national threat which promises to make the present human vs. human conflicts irrelevant. Nature favors no ethnic, national, or religious group when it reacts to exploitation, pollution, and the abuse of the environment. Time is the currency we are using in our gamble that the potential environmental disasters we face will wait until our debating, negotiating, and interspecies squabbles abate long enough to allow us to turn our attention to energetically dealing with these issues. If time runs out and the bet is lost we may be forced to turn our resources toward solving these environmental issues only after a monumental and catastrophic crisis occurs. Optimistically, this might unite the world in a common cause but more realistically it may be that we have truly run out of time.

The polarization of the political arena in the United States has increased since 9/11 with the "blue/red" sections of the nation being more or less defined by liberal and conservative views. The theatres of war have increased as well with conflicts in Afghanistan and Iraq, increased tensions with North Korea and Iran over the danger of nuclear proliferation, and a growing fear that U.S. foreign policy has undermined the initial good will offered by most of the world after 9/11 and alienated many of its allies. Apparently the proliferation of global crisis has created more division than unity in both domestic and international affairs. Still it is clear that the United States has the power, both economically and militarily, to influence the future of the world and subsequently faces a great responsibility. The war on terrorism is a very real threat and must be dealt with but perhaps there is a correlation that can be made between this threat and that of the environmental crisis that continues to grow. Short-term and superficial efforts to deal with environmental issues have never solved major environmental threats. Only through education, long-term planning, and a willingness to change has any real success been achieved in the war against environmental destruction. This is a lesson that may also be applied to the war on terrorism. In doing so the United States may be elevated to a position in global leadership in which its power can be successfully directed towards solving both issues.

Chapter Notes

1. http://patriotpost.us/histdocs/platforms/republican/rep.2000.html.
2. http://www.haberarts.com/election.htm.
3. http://www.cnn.com/ELECTION/2000/conventions/democratic/transcripts/gore.html.
4. http://www.commondreams.org/news2000/0530-03.htm.
5. http://www.haberarts.com/election.htm.
6. The Pew Research Center, "Bush's Base Backs Him to the Hilt," April 26, 2001.
7. The Pew Research Center, "Bush's Base Backs Him to the Hilt," April 26, 2001.
8. Mother Jones, "The Ungreening of America," Sept./Oct. 2003.
9. http://www.whitehouse.gov/news/releases/2001/06/20010611-2.html.
10. http://www.environment2004.org/.
11. http://www.environment2004.org/.
12. http://www.usatoday.com/news/world/2006-01-30-blair-global-warming_x.htm.
13. *The New York Times*, "Bush's Chat with Novelist Alarms Environmentalists," Michael Janofsky, February 19, 2006.
14. http://abcnews.go.com/Technology/story?id=2489179&page=1.
15. *Environmental News Service*, "Environmental Enforcement Dropping Under Bush," Washington, DC, September 6, 2006.
16. http://www.whitehouse.gov/infocus/environment/.
17. http://environment.about.com/od/environmentallawpolicy/a/bush environment.htm.

Everything is connected to everything
else. Everything must go somewhere.
Nature knows best.
There is no such thing as a free lunch.
—Barry Commoner

Conclusion

D uring the introduction to my environmental history class I often paraphrase a cartoon I once saw. A bewildered-looking character is staring at the belching smokestacks of factories in the horizon and says,

> Today's problems should have been solved in the 1960s but in the '60s we were solving the problems of the 1930s, and in the '30s we were solving the problems of the 1890s.

The cartoon caught my attention, not only because of its humor, but also because of its historical perspective. The cartoon very succinctly expresses the idea that the environmental movement and the issues that pertain to it are linked to the past. The environmental movement is part of a long struggle to manage our natural resources more responsibly. What we decide to do about our environment today affects human existence forever, whether for good or bad. The United States has a history of great accomplishments, not least of which are a determination to overcome difficult problems and the wish to improve human life. Despite many obstacles, the people of the United States have accepted the daunting challenge of dealing with environmental decay and, with the often contentious behavior of an open society, have accomplished a great deal.

Yet the path the environmental movement will follow is still unclear. Lately, we have seen a backlash against the proliferation of environmental regulations that have intruded into almost every aspect of our lives since the first Earth Day in 1970. There is also increased apathy toward environmental issues, as economic concerns and the perception that we have done enough to protect nature weaken the fervor that once invigorated the environmental movement. Environmental protection was not a major issue for most of the nation's voters in the 1994 congressional elections. Also, many Americans think that environmentalists do not relate to the needs of humans and have put nature above people. This perception is clearly defined by historian Anna Bramwell.

> Ecologists believe in the essential harmony of nature. But it is a harmony to which man may have to be sacrificed. Ecologists are not man-centered or anthropocentric in their loyalties. Therefore, they do not have to see nature's harmony as especially protective towards or favoring mankind. Ecologists believe in an absolute responsibility for one's actions, and for the world in general. There is no God the Shepherd; so man becomes the shepherd. There is a conflict between the desire to accept nature's harmonious order, and a need to avert catastrophe because ecologists are apocalyptical, but know that man has caused the impending apocalypse by his actions. Ecologists are the saved.[1]

As momentum for their cause wanes, environmentalists battle their opponents' attempts to deregulate and weaken government environmental policies. However, both friend and foe have undermined the environmental movement's achievements. By April 1995 House Speaker Newt Gingrich, an avowed opponent of the environmental groups, selected fifteen committee chairs who scored less than 15 percent on the League of Conservation Voters environmental scorecard.[2] Even Bill Clinton, who was hailed in 1992 as the "real" environmental president, retreated from his strong advocacy of the environmental cause, disappointing many environmentalists. In July 1995 he created an uproar among environmental organizations when he signed the 1995 Budget Recession Bill, which lifted environmental laws that had protected damaged trees in national forests from cutting and logging. Environmentalists charged that it would lead to unrestricted logging in many healthy forests.[3]

Although President Clinton and the Democrats have not proposed dismantling as many environmental regulations as have their Republican counterparts, both concede that some reform is needed. The debate is just how far this reform should go. Carol Browner, director of the EPA, expressed many lawmakers' sentiments when she said in 1995,

> the past 25 years have left us with a complex and unwieldy system of laws and regulations and increasing conflict over how we achieve environmental protection. The result of this history? An adversarial system of environmental policy. A system built on distrust. And too little environmental protection at too high a cost.[4]

The debate has swung from the enthusiasm of the pro-environmental activism of the 1970s to the conservative backlash of the 1980s to the seeking of a middle ground in the 1990s. Balancing economic concerns with environmental crises has become the major point of contention and mobilized well-organized groups on both sides of the issues. Although there are strong proponents in both camps, most Americans appear to have been numbed by the complexity and rhetoric of the debate. They shy away from the extremists and are prone to disbelieve the doomsayers. Are we destroying our environment and thus ourselves or are we heading into poverty in our efforts to preserve nature? Neither scenario is acceptable, especially because there appears to be no clear solution to either. Therefore, we gain solace from the knowledge that the government seems to be actively doing something about the issue, we recycle our garbage, buy eco-friendly products, donate to Greenpeace, or simply deny that the crisis exists.

The summer of 1999 began with a heat wave that baked a third of the eastern United States and Canada, driving temperatures into the 90s and 100s. Scientists attempted to explain such rises in temperature as a result of global warming, reporting that heat-trapping greenhouse gases were at their highest levels in 420,000 years. Yet a survey by the American Geophysical Union found that Americans were less concerned than ever about combating global warming. John Immerwahr, the study's director, said, "The more we talk about global warming, the [more the] public's concern goes down." Peter Kelly, spokesman for the National Environmental Trust, argued that this apathy was due to the more than $13 million spent by opponents of the Kyoto Treaty to convince Americans that global warming "isn't a problem or that it's too expensive to fix."[5] It may be that such PR jobs can convince American to deny what the evidence tells them to believe or it may be that such global issues, so distant and overwhelming, create a hopelessness that produces indifference.

Yet the environmental movement continues its efforts, and with good reason. Since the arrival of Christopher Columbus in 1492, on average, one vertebrate is exterminated in North America each year, and that rate has been increasing in the last century. Harvard University biologist E. O. Wilson estimates that more than fifty thousand species worldwide have died annually and that 10 percent of all species now alive will be gone within twenty-five years.[6] Seventy percent of the world's marine fish stocks are overexploited. Furthermore, the EPA reports that a great deal of work is still needed to correct the nation's environmental problems.

> Twenty years after passage of the Clean Air Act, two in five Americans still live in areas where the air is dangerous to breathe. Fourteen years after Love Canal, one in four Americans lives within four miles of a toxic dumpsite. Asthma is on the rise. Breast cancer is on the rise.[7]

Added to this are the pressures of a world population that continues to multiply at an alarming rate. At the end of World War II, the earth's population was about 2 billion; by 1999, it reached 6 billion. It took hundreds of years to reach the 2 billion mark, but only fifty years to triple it. The result has been a rise in population that has crowded cities, overtaken green spaces, and created unprecedented demand for energy, food, and shelter. Forests four times larger than Switzerland are lost every year. The people of the world annually release 23 billion tons of carbon dioxide into the air, increasing the earth's temperature and threatening the health and habitat of animals, plants, and people. The difficulties of protecting an environment increasingly taxed by human demands involves a complex array of influences. Professor A. Falk of Princeton University and of the Center for Advanced Study in the Behavioral Sciences warned in 1970 that

> The planet and mankind are in grave danger of irreversible catastrophe. . . . Man may be skeptical about following the flight of the dodo into extinction, but the evidence points increasingly to just such a pursuit. . . . There are four interconnected threats to the planet—wars of mass destruction, over-population, pollution, and the depletion of resources. They have a cumulative effect. A problem in one area renders it more difficult to solve the problems in any other area. . . . The basis of all four problems is the inadequacy of the sovereign states to manage the affairs of mankind in the twentieth century.[8]

"Environmental Awareness" has indeed made Americans more sensitive to the connections between human living standards and the preservation of nature. Private and government groups are spending millions to promote their causes and have inundated the public to such a degree that the environmental issue has become an institution in American life. And yet, by the end of the twentieth century environmentalism can no longer be limited to local or even national borders, but must be seen as a global crisis. Activism cannot be restricted to governments, but must include global institutions, private businesses and industries, and nongovernmental organizations from large environmental groups to grass-roots groups all working to find effective solutions. Faced by such catastrophic disasters as global warming, depletion of the ozone layer, extinction of species, and other global crises, many American do feel hopeless and will continue to be indifferent until realistic solutions are found. Of course, there may be a catch-22 here, because it is unlikely that Americans will pressure their leaders to activate real solutions until they feel less hopeless.

The need for an energetic national strategy to combat the environmental crisis that loomed at the beginning of the twenty-first century was soon surpassed by the more immediate need to focus the nation's power against the threat of global terrorism. Unfortunately, it may take the environmental equivalent of the 9/11 Twin Towers disaster to shift the public's attention toward a global and national threat that promises to make the present human vs. human conflicts irrelevant. Nature favors no ethnic, national, or religious group when it reacts to exploitation, pollution, and the abuse of the environment. Time is the currency we are using in our gamble that the potential environmental disasters we face will wait until our debating, negotiating, and inter-species squabbles abate long enough to allow us to turn our attention to energetically dealing with these issues. If time runs out and the bet is lost we may be forced to turn our resources toward solving these environmental issues only after a monumental and catastrophic crisis occurs. Optimistically, this might unite the world in a common cause but it may also be that we have truly run out of time.

Chapter Notes

1. Anna Bramwell, *Ecology in the 20th Century* (New Haven: Yale University Press, 1989), 16.
2. Mark Dowie, "The Fourth Wave," *Mother Jones*, March/April 1995, 36.
3. Margaret Kriz, "Drawing a Green Line in the Sand," *National Journal*, Aug. 12, 1995, 2076.
4. Carol M. Browner, "The Earth Is in Your Hands," *EPA Journal*, winter 1995, 4.
5. Dick Thomson, "What Global Warming? As the World Heats Up, the Public Simply Goes Cold," *Science* 153, no. 24, June 21, 1999.
6. Paul Rauber, "An End to Evolution: The Extinction Lobby in Congress Is Now Deciding Which Species Will Live and Which Will Die," *Sierra*, Jan./Feb. 1996, 28.
7. Browner, "The Earth Is in Your Hands," 4.
8. John Fischer, "Survival U: Prospectus for a Really Relevant University," *The Environmental Handbook*, ed. Garrett De Bell (New York: Ballantine Books, 1970), 138.

Glossary

acid rain Rain with a high concentration of acids produced by gases of burning fossil fuels; destructive to plants, buildings, and so forth.

Adams, Ansel (1902–1984) San Francisco–born photographer who was recognized as a leader of modern photography for his sharp and poetic landscape photographs of the West. A leader of the Sierra Club, he fought to preserve Yosemite National Park and other wilderness areas.

Agricultural Adjustment Act Law passed in May 1933 that created the Agricultural Adjustment Administration (AAA), which was the most important early New Deal effort to combat the effects of the Great Depression on the nation's farms. The AAA tried to raise farm prices by restricting agricultural output. The Domestic Allotment Plan paid benefits for lowered crop production of staple crops such as wheat, cotton, corn, and tobacco.

alternative groups Organizations such as Friends of the Earth, Greenpeace, and Earth First! that take a more action-oriented approach to protect nature. They use protest to publicize environmental issues and to directly influence legislators and political policy making. They support civil disobedience and sometimes violence to promote their causes.

American transcendentalist movement American transcendentalists denied the existence of miracles, preferring a Christianity that rested on the teachings of Christ rather than on his supposed deeds. They rejected materialism and utilitarianism and were committed to intuition as a way of knowing, to individualism, and to belief in the divinity of both man and nature.

Animal Liberation Front (ALF) Organization established in 1979 that sometimes resorts to sabotage or other forms of coercion to protest the use of animals in medical experiments or killing them for their fur.

animism Religion based on the belief that a spirit or divinity resides within every object, controlling its existence and influencing human life and events in the natural world.

Arcadian myth Arcadia is a mountainous area in the center of the Greek Peloponnesus celebrated in ancient literature for its rustic simplicity. In the late nineteenth and early twentieth centuries, the myth of this ideal country living was popular in the United States, especially among urban populations.

Biodiversity Treaty Agreement signed at the Earth Summit in Rio de Janeiro in 1992; signer nations agreed to protect species of plants, insects, and microbes that are deemed essential for maintaining the world's atmosphere and soil and that may be used for cancer research.

Brower, David (1912–) Prominent environmentalist, twice elected a director of the Sierra Club (1941–1943, 1946–1953) and appointed executive director (1952–1969). He left to form Friends of the Earth and later the Earth Island Institute. He also narrated motion pictures on endangered wilderness areas and authored many books about nature.

California Desert Protection Act Law passed in 1994 that set aside millions of acres as protected wilderness in California.

Calvinism Protestant religious perspective associated with the work of John Calvin, who taught that wealth should not come between a person and God and that riches should be sought but not flaunted.

Cambridge Agreement Agreement by Puritans to leave England to escape persecution and seek religious freedom in Massachusetts.

Carson, Rachel Louise (1907–1964) Author of several scientific and popular articles and books about ecology and the environment. In *Silent Spring* (1962), she strongly criticized the indiscriminate use of DDT. The book helped stimulate environmental protection measures.

cash crops Crops cultivated for the purpose of reselling them for monetary reward rather than for personal sustenance.

Catlin, George (1796–1872) Foremost artist-chronicler of Native Americans in the nineteenth century.

civil rights movement Movement begun by African Americans in the 1940s and 1950s to combat racism. It was most prominent in the southern states where African Americans fought segregation. By the 1960s it had become a national movement to protect the individual rights of all Americans.

Civilian Conservation Corps (CCC) Group established in 1933 as a New Deal program to combat unemployment in the United States during the Great Depression. Unemployed, unmarried young men worked on conservation and resource-development projects, such as soil conservation, flood control, and forests and wildlife protection, in exchange for food, lodging, other necessities, and a small monthly salary. Abolished in 1942.

Clean Air Act Law passed in 1963 that established air-quality standards for six major pollutants: particulate matter, sulfur oxides, carbon monoxide, nitrogen oxides, hydrocarbons, and photochemical oxidants. Revised in 1970; expanded to 189 the number of controlled pollutants that cause smog and established standards to regulate their emissions; required factories and power plants to install smokestack filters to prevent the discharge of ash and other pollutants; forced automakers to equip cars with catalytic converters to reduce exhaust fumes; and required oil companies to remove lead from gasoline. Revised in 1990 to place stricter limits on the emissions of toxic air pollutants, but relied heavily on market incentives such as voluntary compliance credits and performance standards in an effort to protect industry and jobs.

Clean Water Act Law passed in 1972 that regulated the release of pollutants into waterways, storm sewers, and reservoirs, while mandating steps to restore polluted waters for recreational use.

clear-cutting   Process of harvesting all trees within an area at once, leaving an open, treeless plot of ground that can be seeded immediately, usually by seed drift from adjacent stands. Often, though, clear-cut land is left barren.

Comprehensive Environmental Response, Compensation, and Liability Act   Beginning in 1980, Congress appropriated money to a "Superfund" to be used by the EPA for hazardous waste cleanup.

conservation movement   Movement initially closely identified with the personality and politics of President Theodore Roosevelt. By the end of the nineteenth century, Americans were concerned with the rapid pace of social progress. They had seen the United States move quickly from a frontier to an industrial society, and the nation's much-cherished natural resources, especially its forests, appeared on the verge of extinction. Under Roosevelt's programs, the protection of forests, rangeland, and mineral and water resources began to evolve in piecemeal fashion.

conservationists   People who believe in the regulated exploitation of nature, or "right use." They recognize that human activities profoundly change the face of the earth and can irreparably damage or destroy the natural resources on which human well-being and survival depend.

Contract With America   Pamphlet published by the Republican Party before the 1994 congressional elections that outlined the Republican plan to establish a government based on family values, government deregulation, and individual freedoms.

Council on Environmental Quality   Organization established in 1969 as part of the National Environmental Policy Act to oversee government actions and provide environmental coordination.

Cove Mallard   Some 76,000 acres of federal timberland in the Nez Perce National Forest just outside Dixie, Idaho, that was designated in September 1993 by the U.S. Forest Service for logging. The area became a focus for the debate between environmentalists and those who felt the nation's resources should be used to supply jobs and products for human needs.

Dawes Severalty Act   Law passed in 1887 that stipulated that Native Americans give up tribal lands in return for individual land grants. It was intended to promote the integration of the Native Americans into the homesteading way of life. Its main effect was to open up the "Indian Territory" to white settlers.

DDT   A very active, broad-spectrum pesticide that is effective against beetles, moths, butterflies, flies, and mosquitoes, but virtually inactive against mites and ticks. DDT kills by acting as a nerve poison. Applying DDT to cultivated crops and livestock substantially increased yields. In 1962 Rachel Carson's *Silent Spring* raised fears that DDT was causing a dramatic decrease in the numbers of many bird species. It was found that the pesticide disrupts avian reproductive processes and causes birds to lay infertile or deformed eggs. DDT breaks down very slowly in the soil, so buildup in the food chain—the greater concentration of DDT as larger organisms eat smaller ones—also caused concern about how much DDT humans could safely ingest. Banned in the United States in 1972. U.S. chemical plants continued to manufacture DDT for several years. It remains in use globally, particularly as a way to control malaria.

deep ecology   A belief that nature has intrinsic value and should not be exploited for the needs of humanity. First used by Norwegian philosopher Arne Naess in the 1970s to illustrate the differences between those who sought to harmonize human activity with nature and those who viewed humans as the most important element in the human-nature relationship, deemed shallow ecology.

Deism (the Great Watchmaker Theory)   The belief that God is the creator of the world, but not its redeemer.

Department of Energy (DOE)   Cabinet department created by President Jimmy Carter in October 1977 to consolidate the activities of the Energy Research and Development Administration, Federal Power Commission, Federal Energy Administration, and elements of other agencies. The DOE was assigned a wide range of powers to set energy prices, enforce conservation measures, allocate fuel, and research new energy sources. It also directs nuclear-weapons research and development.

Desert Land Act   Law passed in 1877 that offered 640 acres at $1.25 an acre in states with little rainfall as long as the owner irrigated part of the land within three years.

direct-action groups   Another term for alternative groups.

Drake, Edwin Laurentine (1819–1880) Drilled the first successful oil well in the United States. After investing in the Pennsylvania Rock Oil Company, formed in 1854 to market surface oil found near Titusville, Pennsylvania, Drake went to Titusville (1857), where he leased land and formed the Seneca Oil Company as a subsidiary. After months of preparation and ridicule, he began drilling in June 1859, using techniques he learned observing the drilling of salt wells. On August 27, 1859, "Drake's Folly" began to produce twenty-five barrels of crude oil per day from 69 feet below ground.

Earth Day   First held on April 22, 1970, the event was largely campus-based and represented perhaps the apogee of the early years of the environmental movement. Since 1990, it has been celebrated nationally.

Earth Island Institute Environmental group formed by David Brower in the 1980s that publishes books on environmentalism and ecology and fights for the protection of wildlife and other natural resources.

Earth Summit   United Nations–sponsored event in 1992 in Rio de Janeiro, Brazil, at which the largest congregation of world leaders in history agreed on the broad principles that must guide environmental policies while still encouraging economic growth. Binding treaties commit most of the earth's nations to curb the emission of greenhouse gases and to protect endangered species.

eco-feminist movement   An egalitarian doctrine that espoused the oneness of humanity and nature and thus equality among the genders; it became an important part of the feminist agenda in the 1970s.

ecology   Scientific study of the inter-relationship of plants, animals, and the environment. Ecology principles are useful in many aspects of related fields of conservation, wildlife management, forestry, agriculture, and pollution control. The word ecology (derived from the Greek *oikos,* meaning "house," and *logos,* meaning "study of," is generally believed to have been coined by Ernst Haeckel, who used and defined it in 1869.

Econet Internet computer database, part of the San Francisco–based Institute for Global Communications, which allows those interested in environmental issues to discuss and share their views. http://www.igc.org/igc/econet.

eco-warriors People who protest and/or use violence to support the cause of environmentalism.

Emergency Planning and Community Right-to-Know Act Law passed in 1986 that required industries to report toxic releases and encouraged local communities to plan their responses to chemical emergencies.

Emerson, Ralph Waldo (1803–1882) Considered the leading exponent of American transcendentalism, he helped start the Transcendental Club in 1836 and published *Nature* (1836), which showed that all life is organic and that nature functions as a visible manifestation of invisible spiritual truths. His discussions of organic form (everything proceeds from a natural order that is followed but not imposed by man), self-reliance, optimism (evil does not exist as an actual force, being merely the absence of good), compensation, universal unity (or the Over-Soul), and the importance of individual moral insight influenced literature and philosophy of nineteenth-century America.

Endangered Species Act (ESA) Law passed in 1973 to protect the vital habitat of any species listed as threatened or endangered without considering the economic consequences of such action. Since 1973 it has been extended repeatedly.

Enlightenment Philosophic movement during the eighteenth and early nineteenth centuries in which reason, liberty, happiness, and science became the basis of intellectual and social thinking.

Environmental Action Organization formed in 1970 to coordinate Earth Day activities, it became an aggressive lobbying and public information group focusing on issues such as solid waste, and alerts voters to the "Dirty Dozen," companies with the worst pollution records.

Environmental Consortium for Minority Outreach Organization established in 1989 by leading environmental groups to attract and encourage the participation of racial and ethnic minorities in environmental organizations.

Environmental Defense Fund (EDF) Organization formed in 1967 to fight for conservation issues through the legal system and science.

environmental justice movement Movement that believes industrialists, government officials, and environmentalists have ignored the plight of urban minorities and low-income neighborhoods and that environmental racism has caused these communities to become disproportionately polluted by hazardous air and water toxins, congestion, and the nation's industrial waste dumps.

Environmental Policy Center (EPC) Organization created in 1972 by a group breaking from the League of Conservation Voters. EPC is an advocacy group of experts who support lobbyists and researchers with particular interests in water conservation. Later changed its name to the Environmental Policy Institute.

Environmental Protection Agency (EPA) Organization established in 1970 as an independent agency in the executive branch of the U.S. government to permit coordinated and effective government action on behalf of the environment.

Euro-Americans Established settlers of European origin.

eutrophication An aging process in the life cycle of a lake, pond, or slow-moving stream caused by the gradual accumulation in the water of the nutrients needed to sustain aquatic plants and animals, accompanied by an increase in the number of organisms in the water. As organic matter decomposes, the amount of dissolved oxygen in the lake decreases, and eventually the lake is overwhelmed by the plant life growing in its shallower waters or by silt, creating a marsh.

Friends of the Earth (FOE) Organization established by former Sierra Club leader David Brower in 1969 as a conservation group that would be more aggressive than traditional groups in defending environmental issues.

global warming Term used to describe the theory that global temperatures have been rising because of the increased levels of carbon dioxide in the atmosphere. This theory, also known as the greenhouse effect, argues that such pollutants create warm air that raise the temperature, causing the Antarctic icecap to melt and global sea levels to rise. This

theory also argues that because warm air can hold moisture, snowfall over Antarctica is increasing, enlarging the size of the continent.

gospel of success Nineteenth-century belief that equated material success with religious virtue.

Great Depression Economic collapse sparked by the stock market crash in October 1929. The economic crisis, exemplified by high unemployment and low production, continued throughout the 1930s.

Great Dust Bowl Popular name for the roughly 150,000-square-mile area that includes the Oklahoma and Texas panhandles and adjacent parts of Colorado, New Mexico, and Kansas. The area suffered severe drought between 1934 and 1937, and without the complex root system of grasses to anchor it, much of the soil was picked up by the winds. The resulting severe dust and sandstorms buried roads and houses, and clouds from the storms were observed hundreds of miles away. More than half the population (two hundred thousand people) fled the area.

Green Decade The 1970s, when support for environmental protection and legislation was at its peak.

green marketing Term that refers to the production and advertising of products that are said to be less harmful to the environment than previous or existing products.

greenhouse effect Popular environmental science term for the effect on surface temperatures by the earth's lower atmosphere gases—water vapor (H_2O), carbon dioxide (CO_2), and methane (CH_4). They keep ground temperatures at a global average of about 60 degrees Fahrenheit. Without them the average ground temperature would drop below the freezing point of water. As incoming solar radiation strikes the surface, the surface gives off infrared radiation, or heat, that the gases trap and keep near ground level. The effect is similar to how a green-house traps heat, hence the term.

green parties   Political movement that emphasizes environmental concerns. The central goal of green political activists is to link environmental issues with broader social issues of democracy, peace, social justice, and the changing of social values and economic relationships. The general message is that society must alter its living habits and priorities to protect nature and in turn enable nature's resources to improve everyone's lives. Its roots began in Australia in April 1972 when the United Tasmania Group (UTG) tried to halt the flooding of Lake Pedder. Unable to persuade the existing political parties to take up their cause, they decided to go directly to the people. Although their efforts failed to gain them any political power, their example encouraged others. Values was founded in New Zealand in 1972, and People (later called Ecology Party and finally Green Party) was founded in Britain in 1973. The Green Party forwarded a platform warning of the earth's limited resources and the dangers of pollution. While the political clout of green parties was minimal in the beginning, their debate did influence the creation of the United Nations Environmental Program in 1972, which was established to promote international awareness of global environmental problems.

Greenpeace   International organization founded in 1969 by Canadian environmentalists. It advocates direct, nonviolent action to halt environmental threats. Its confrontational tactics earned widespread publicity for its causes, which include ending commercial whaling and the slaughter of baby seals, halting the dumping of toxic wastes, and creating a nuclear-free world.

Greenwire   Internet computer database where you can read or download a survey of national and international environmental news. http://www.ecology.com.

habitat conservation plans (HCPs)   Binding, voluntary agreements in which a landowner adopts conservation measures, sometimes going beyond what the law strictly requires, in exchange for permission to develop some property, even if endangered wildlife and habitats are hurt.

Hetch Hetchy Valley   Valley carved by centuries of glaciers and the Tuolumne River that before 1913 was part of Yosemite National Park. Site of a struggle between pro- and antienvironmentalists.

Homestead Act   Law passed in 1862 that granted 160 acres of public land in the West as a homestead to anyone who paid a small filing fee, lived on the land for five years, and made certain improvements in order to receive clear title.

Ickes, Harold LeClaire (1874–1952) Secretary of the interior in the Franklin Roosevelt and Harry Truman administrations. He opposed exploiting limited natural resources in the United States by private interests and supported federal development of electric power in the public domain.

Industrial Revolution   Transformation between 1865 and 1900 of traditional social patterns and values into modern societies by industrialization of the economy.

Izaak Walton League   Organization created by sportsmen in 1922 and led by Will H. Dilg, to promote the protection of wildlife areas.

Joint Implementation Plan   Program established by U.S. government in 1997 to apply market-based approaches in an attempt to link international economic partnerships to promote low-cost reductions in greenhouse gas emissions.

Land and Water Conservation Fund   Suggested by President John F. Kennedy in 1962, the fund was established in 1965 to acquire land for national and state parks. In 1968 by a congressional amendment, it used federal revenues from offshore oil drilling to achieve this goal.

land jobbery   Illegally manipulating the established system to obtain extra land.

League of Conservation Voters   Organization created in 1970 by national environmental groups leaders to track voting records and policy decisions of members of Congress and the executive branch. The group also endorses and organizes electoral support for environmentally minded politicians while attempting to maintain a bipartisan approach.

Leopold, Aldo   (1886–1948) Environmentalist who aroused the first great public interest in wilderness conservation. He believed that undisturbed wilderness is a valuable asset and felt that people should enjoy wilderness areas but disturb them as little as possible. Although Leopold received worldwide acclaim as an authority on wilderness conservation, he was also an expert on wildlife management. His textbook *Game Management* (1933) has become a classic in the field. Leopold also wrote a number of essays on conservation,

published in *A Sand County Almanac* (1949) and *Round River* (1953).

Lite Greens   People who like the idea of protecting the environment but not at the cost of lowering their own standard of living.

Love Canal   Old canal bed near Niagara Falls, New York, that the Hooker Chemical and Plastics Corporation used as a chemical dump from the 1930s to 1952. The filled land was donated to the city in 1953, and a new school and a housing tract were built on it. In 1971 toxic liquids began leaking through the clay cap that sealed the dump, contaminating the area with at least eighty-two chemicals, including a number of carcinogens: benzene, some chlorinated hydrocarbons, and dioxin. Extremely high birth-defect and miscarriage rates developed, as well as liver cancer and a high incidence of seizure-inducing nervous disease among neighborhood children. The area was declared an official disaster area. The state paid $10 million to buy some of the homes and another $10 million to try to stop the leakage. About a thousand families had to be relocated. Hooker Chemical disclaimed responsibility. Portions of the site were cleaned up sufficiently by 1990 for houses located there to be put up for sale.

MacKaye, Benton   (1879–1975) Research forester in the U.S. Forest Service from 1905 to 1908, specialist for the U.S. Department of Labor from 1918 to 1919, one of the organizers of the Wilderness Society in 1935, and the author of many works on conservation issues.

mainstream groups   Organizations that work within the established political and economic systems with staffs of lawyers, lobbyists, scientists, economists, organizers, fund-raisers, publicists, and political operatives to influence environmental policies as well as the government agencies that regulate them.

Malthusian theory   Malthus said that the standard of living of the masses cannot be improved because the power of the population is indefinitely greater than the power of the earth to produce subsistence for humans. Neo-Malthusian theory states that the natural resources humans need for survival cannot last forever because of society's overconsumption.

Manifest Destiny   Term coined by Americans in the 1840s to describe an optimistic spirit of confidence in the righteousness of expanding the borders of the United States during the nineteenth century.

Marsh, George Perkins (1801–1882) Author of *Man and Nature, or Physical Geography as Modified by Human Action* (1864), which aroused great public interest in the problems of conservation, the basic principles of which he defined for the first time.

Marshall, Robert   (1901–1939) In 1933 appointed director of forestry in the Office of Indian Affairs, Department of the Interior. In 1935 he helped found the Wilderness Society. He also advocated public ownership of the nation's commercial timberlands.

Mayflower Compact   Preliminary form of government based on majority rule, drafted in 1620 by the Puritans at Plymouth, Massachusetts.

McCoy, Joseph   (1837–1915) He opened Northeast beef markets to Texas ranchers. With the help of surveyors, he laid out a trail from Corpus Christi, Texas, and convinced ranchers to drive their cattle to railroad shipping points in Abilene, Kansas, in 1867. He also helped open the Chisholm Trail.

monocultural husbandry   Farming method that depends on the cultivation of a single crop.

Montreal Protocol   Agreement signed in 1987 by the United States and twenty-three other countries, which pledged that by 1999 they would phase out production and use of CFCs (chlorofluorocarbons).

Muir, John   (1838–1914) Naturalist who emigrated from Scotland and worked toward gaining popular and federal support of forest conservation. His writings, including *The Mountains of California* (1894), *Our National Parks* (1901), *The Yosemite* (1912), and *Steep Trails* (1918), aroused much public interest. He was also a founder and the first president of the Sierra Club.

Nader, Ralph   (1934–) Lawyer and since the mid–1960s a leading figure in the consumer protection movement. Author of *Unsafe at Any Speed* (1965), which maintained that defective design was a common cause of auto accidents and injuries. He testified before Congress on auto safety, influencing them to bring car design under federal control with the National Traffic and Motor Vehicle Safety Act of 1966. Also helped pass such legislation as the Wholesome Meat Act (1967) and natural gas pipeline safety and radiation hazards control. Set up study groups of college students (called Nader's Raiders), who investigated government regulatory agencies. In 1971 he founded a consumer lobbying group, Public Citizen, Inc., which, with other Nader-affiliated groups, monitor tax reform, health issues, and congressional activities, lobby for new legislation, and finance legal action.

National Audubon Society   Organization founded in 1905 and named for the ornithologist John James Audubon that seeks to promote the conservation of wildlife and of natural environments. The national group developed from the New York Audubon Society, which was founded in 1886 to protect wild birds.

National Environmental Policy Act (NEPA)   Law passed in 1969 to coordinate government environmental departments in an effort to allay public concern. It required environmental impact statements for federally funded construction projects and established the Environmental Protection Agency.

National Park Service   National-park movement began in the United States in 1870 when a group of explorers recommended that a portion of the upper Yellowstone River region be set aside to protect its geothermal features, wildlife, forests, and unique scenery for future generations. The idea of preserving land for public use was not new, for there had long been public parks, but Yellowstone, established in 1872, set the pattern for preserving large, undisturbed ecosystem as national parks. Overseeing such a growing, complex domain proved so difficult at first, that from 1886 to 1916, the U.S. Army administered and protected the parks. In 1916 Congress created the National Park Service, part of the Department of the Interior, to oversee the park system, which gradually grew in diversity by the addition of historic and prehistoric sites, battlefields, parkways, hiking trails, seashores, lakeshores, rivers, recreation areas, memorials, scientific reserves, and so on.

National Wildlife Federation   Conservative organization established 1936 by Jay N. Darling, supported by sportsmen, to protect wilderness areas for hunting and fishing. Similar to right-use philosophy of progressive conservation movement.

Nelson, Gaylord   Wisconsin senator who organized the first Earth Day in 1970 and remains a leading supporter for environmental causes, such as clean water.

New Deal   President Franklin D. Roosevelt's program (1933–1939) of relief, recovery, and reform aimed at solving the economic problems created by the Great Depression.

New World   The Americas.

Ocean Dumping Act   Law passed in 1972 to regulate the intentional disposal of material into the ocean and authorize related research.

Old World   The known world before the discovery of the Americas.

OPEC   Organization of Petroleum Exporting Countries formed by Iran, Iraq, Kuwait, Saudi Arabia, and Venezuela on September 14, 1960. Qatar joined in 1961, Indonesia and Libya in 1962, Abu Dhabi (now part of the United Arab Emirates) in 1967, Algeria in 1969, Nigeria in 1971, Ecuador and Gabon in 1973.

ozone layer   Layer of the upper atmosphere lying 12 to 15 miles above the earth's surface and named for the unstable form of oxygen called ozone that is concentrated in this layer. The ozone layer absorbs ultraviolet radiation from the sun, which would be destructive to all life-forms if it reached the earth's surface at unprotected levels. For example, the incidence of human skin cancers and cataracts would increase, and food production would decrease.

paganism   Nature-based religion whose followers believed humans and the natural world were spiritually connected, dependent on each other, and had a common bond.

People for the Ethical Treatment of Animals   Organization established in 1980, dedicated to the protection of animals, particularly regarding their use in scientific experiments; closely associated with the Animal Liberation Front.

Pinchot, Gifford   (1865–1946) Public official who made his greatest contributions to the conservation movement during Theodore Roosevelt's presidency (1901–1909) as a publicist for the progressive conservation movement. Named head of the U.S. Forest Service in 1905.

plantation system   Large, self-contained farms.

Pollution Prevention Act   Law passed in 1990 that encouraged companies to reduce pollutant generation by cost-effective changes in production, operation, and raw material use.

Powell, John Wesley   (1834–1902) Geologist, ethnologist, and anthropologist. In 1869 he and eleven others, financed by the Smithsonian Institution, explored the Green and Colorado river canyons. He was appointed first director of the U.S. Bureau of Ethnology in 1879 and later director of the U.S. Geological Survey, 1881–1892. His writings include *Exploration of the Colorado River of the West and Its Tributaries* (1875), *An Introduction to the Study of Indian Languages* (1877), and *Report on the Lands of the Arid Regions of the United States* (1878).

preservationists   People who believe nature must be protected for its own sake not merely for its uses.

Progressive Era   Period between 1900 and the 1920s during which the U.S. government became increasingly active in both domestic and foreign policy. Progressive, reform-minded political leaders sought to extend their vision of a just and rational order to all areas of society.

radon   A radioactive gas.

Reclamation Act   Law passed in 1902 (also known as the Newlands Act) that established the Bureau of Reclamation in the Department of Interior and began a federal program to fund dam and canal construction, and development of water power projects in the seventeen western states.

Renaissance   Period of rebirth of learning and fresh enthusiasm for scholarship that transformed western Europe during the fourteenth and fifteenth centuries.

Renaissance Man   A person who is accomplished in a variety of pursuits.

Resource Conservation and Recovery Act   Law passed in 1976 to regulate the disposal and treatment of solid and hazardous wastes.

romantic era   Intellectual movement that flourished in Europe and to a lesser degree the United States in the early nineteenth century. Romantic thought often features an organic conception of individual life, society, and the interconnections of humanity, nature, and divinity.

Roosevelt, Franklin Delano (1882–1945) Elected the thirty-second president of the United States (1933–1945) for an unprecedented four terms, he led the nation through two of its most critical events—the Great Depression and World War II. He developed the New Deal programs to provide relief and economic recovery during the Depression. Roosevelt died in office in April 1945, shortly before Allied victory was achieved.

Roosevelt, Theodore (1858–1919) Became the twenty-sixth president of the United States after President William McKinley was assassinated on September 14, 1901; he was elected to the office in 1904, serving until 1909. As president and political leader, Roosevelt was an articulate spokesperson for the aspirations and values of progressivism, the reform movement that flourished in the United States from 1900 to World War I.

Sagebrush Rebellion Movement started in the western U.S. that opposed federal government regulation and protection of wildlife and wilderness. Originated in 1979 when the Nevada legislature passed the Sagebrush Rebellion Act, which authorized the state to sue for possession of federal lands. The motivation for the act was the deterioration of rangeland suitable for the support of livestock. Ranchers blamed the Wild Horse and Burro Act, passed by the federal government in 1971, which caused the tripling of the wild horse population in its first six years.

Schurz, Carl (1829–1906) German emigrant who was appointed secretary of the interior by President Rutherford B. Hayes, Schurz worked for Native American rights and conservation, and instituted the merit system in his bureau.

scientific revolution Period during the seventeenth and eighteenth centuries when the rational nature of the universe was emphasized over blind faith.

Sea Shepherd Conservation Society Organization established in 1977 by Paul Watson, a former Greenpeace member, to use force, such as blowing up whaling ships, to promote environmental issues.

Sierra Club Social organization devoted mainly to two programs: participation in wilderness activities such as mountain climbing, backpacking, and camping, and protection of the wilderness environments through political action. It was founded on June 4, 1892, by 162 Californians, mostly university-trained individuals and faculty members, with John Muir as president.

Social Darwinism Belief that societies, like organisms, evolved by a natural process through which the most fit members survived or were most successful. The theory went hand in hand with political conservatism; the most successful social classes were supposedly composed of biologically superior people.

Soil Conservation Act Law passed in 1935 that established the Soil Conservation Service to manage water and soil conservation in the nation.

Southwest Research and Information Center (SRIC) Organization created in Albuquerque, New Mexico, in 1971, that combines the knowledge of environmental experts with community groups to support and promote local environmental issues.

sustainable development Management of human use of the environment so it can yield the greatest benefit to current generations, while maintaining its potential to meet the needs and aspirations of future generations, a tenet of the modern conservation movement.

Taylor Grazing Act Law passed in 1934 to limit grazing in designated districts on the Great Plains, an attempt to prevent soil erosion.

Taylorism Scientific management methods of Frederick Winslow Taylor

(1856–1915). In 1881 he began the first time-and-motion studies in factories to discover the most efficient method of managing machines and workers.

Tennessee Valley Authority (TVA) Federal agency created in May 1933 as a major feature in Franklin D. Roosevelt's New Deal to foster development in the Tennessee River Valley and adjacent territories. The TVA extends over large areas in Tennessee, North Carolina, Virginia, Georgia, Alabama, Mississippi, and Kentucky.

thermal pollution Discharge of waste heat by the dissipation of energy into cooling water and into nearby waterways. Main sources are fossil fuel and nuclear electric power facilities and, to a lesser degree, cooling operations of industrial manufacturers, such as steel foundries and chemical producers. Heated water discharged into a waterway often causes ecological imbalance, sometimes killing many fish near the source. The higher temperature increases chemical-biological processes and decreases the ability of the water to hold dissolved oxygen. These thermal changes limit or change the type of fish and aquatic life able to grow or reproduce, causing rapid and dramatic changes in biologic communities near heated discharges.

Thoreau, Henry David (1817–1862) Author best known for *Walden* (1854), an account of his experiment with simple living, and for the essay "Civil Disobedience" (1849). His doctrine of passive resistance influenced Mahatma Gandhi and Martin Luther King, Jr. Essentially a philosopher of individualism, Thoreau placed nature above materialism in private life and ethics above conformity in politics.

Three Mile Island The most serious U.S. commercial nuclear reactor failure occurred on March 28, 1979, at the Three Mile Island reactor near Harrisburg, Pennsylvania.

Timber and Stone Act Law passed in 1878 that sold 160 acres of forest-land for $2.50 an acre.

Timber Culture Act Law passed in 1873 that gave western homesteaders additional 160 acres of land if they grew trees on 40 acres, an attempt to improve land in drier areas.

Toxic Substances Control Act Law passed in 1976 to regulate the use of toxic wastes.

trap out To deplete a river or stream of wildlife, such as beaver, by trapping incessantly.

Turner, Frederick Jackson (1861–1932) American historian whose "frontier thesis" also known as the "Turner thesis," strongly influenced the writing of U.S. history. At a meeting of the American Historical Association in 1893, Turner presented his famous thesis in a paper entitled "The Significance of the Frontier in American History." He argued that the existence of free land and the advance of settlement west had exerted a crucial influence on the development of American institutions and character.

U.S. Fish and Wildlife Service Agency founded in 1940 that guides the conservation and management of the country's bird, mammal, and fish populations.

utilitarian movement Nineteenth-century movement based on a theory in moral philosophy by which actions are judged as right or wrong according to their consequences.

Valley of Drums In 1978 some hundred thousand hazardous-waste-leaking barrels were discovered here, in West Point, Kentucky.

western public domain Lands in the western United States that are not privately owned but are the property of the nation.

Wilderness Act Law passed in 1964 to preserve wilderness areas and set up the mechanism for the future preservation of such lands.

Wilderness Society Organization created in 1935 by Aldo Leopold and Robert Marshall to fight for the protection of wilderness areas. It didn't tap the new energies of the environmental movement of the 1960s and 1970s, but instead maintained its focus on implementing the Wilderness Act and protecting the Alaskan wilderness.

wise-use movement Organizations that advocate using the environment to support human needs and deregulating government legislation that restricts industry and exploitation of natural resources.

Glossary entries compiled from: Henry Clepper, ed., *Leaders of American Conservation* (New York: Ronald Press, 1971); Douglas H. Strong, *The Conservationists* (Menlo Park, Calif.: Addison-Wesley, 1971); and *The New Grolier's Multimedia Encyclopedia.*

Bibliography and Suggested Readings

A Centennial Celebration 1892–1992. San Francisco: Sierra Club Books, 1992.

Ambrose, Stephen. *Undaunted Courage: Meriwether Lewis, Thomas Jefferson, and the Opening of the American West*. New York: Simon and Schuster, 1996.

Ayres, Robert U. and Udo E. Simonis, eds. *Industrial Metabolism: Restructuring for Sustainable Development*. New York: United Nations Publications, 1994.

Bacon, David. "Cottage Street Beats the Concrete Mountain." *EcoJustice Network*. http://www.igc.org/envjustice/communique/montana.html. April 9, 1997.

Begley, Sharon. "And Now, the Road from Rio." *Newsweek*. June 22, 1992.

———. "The Grinch of Rio." *Newsweek*. June 15, 1992.

Benenson, Bob. "House Passes Property Rights Bill." *Congressional Quarterly Weekly Report*. March 4, 1995.

———. "Water Bill Wins House Passage, May Not Survive in Senate." *Congressional Quarterly Weekly Report*. May 20, 1995.

Bly, Laura. "Ecological Changes Cloud Tahoe's Future." *USA Today*. July 25, 1997.

Boyer, Paul S. *The Enduring Vision*. Lexington, Mass.: D. C. Heath, 1995.

Bramwell, Anna. *Ecology in the 20th Century: A History*. New Haven: Yale University Press, 1989.

Browner, Carol M. "The Earth Is in Your Hands." *EPA Journal*. Winter 1995.

Bullard, Robert D. *People of Color Environmental Groups 1994–1995 Directory*. Georgia: Environmental Justice Resource Center, Clark Atlanta University, 1996.

Business Roundtable. "Environment and the Economy: The Kyoto Protocol." http://www.brtable.org/document.cfm/161. June 22, 1998.

Business Wire. "University of Washington Students Urge Board of Regents to Divest of 'Egregious Eight' Contributors to Global Warming." May 13, 1999.

Carroll, Charles F. *The Timber Economy of Puritan New England*. Providence: Brown University Press, 1973.

Carson, Rachel. *Silent Spring*. New York: Houghton Mifflin, 1962.

Chervokas, Jason, and Tom Watson. "Timber Issue Offers Gauge of Internet Discourse." *New York Times*. May 30, 1997.

Clepper, Henry, ed. *Leaders of American Conservation*. New York: Ronald Press, 1971.

Clifford, Frank. "Bill Would Limit Federal Power Over Environment." *Los Angeles Times*. Dec. 28, 1994.

Cloud, John. "Fire on the Mountain: The Posh Ski Town of Vail Is Shaken by an Act of Apparent Ecoterrorism." *Time*. Nov. 2, 1998.

Coates, Peter. *Nature: Western Attitudes Since Ancient Times*. University of California Press, 1998.

Collins, Craig. "The Green Knight." *Mother Jones*. Jan./Feb. 1993.

Cone, Marla. "Federal Suit Over DDT Dumping Is Dismissed." *Los Angeles Times*. March 23, 1995.

Conlin, Joseph R. *The American Past*. Fort Worth, Texas: Harcourt Brace, 1993.

Cooper, Mary H. "Environmental Movement at 25." *CQ Researcher.* March 31, 1995.
———. "Jobs vs. Environment." *CQ Researcher.* May 15, 1992.
Cronon, William. *Nature's Metropolis: Chicago and the Great West.* New York: W. W. Norton, 1991.
Crosby, Alfred W. *Ecological Imperialism: The Biological Expansion of Europe, 900–1900.* Cambridge: Cambridge University Press, 1986.
Cushman, John H., Jr. "Congress Forgoes Its Bid to Hasten Cleanup of Dumps." *New York Times.* Oct. 17, 1994.
———. "The Endangered Species Act Gets a Makeover." *New York Times.* June 2, 1998.
———. "Environmental Spending Decisions Colored by Compromise." *New York Times.* Oct. 16, 1998.
Darnovsky, Marcy. "Stories Less Told: Histories of US Environmentalism." *Socialist Review.* Oct. 1, 1992.
Davidson, James West, and Mark Hamilton Lytle. "The Invisible Pioneers." *After the Fact.* New York: Alfred A. Knopf, 1986.
De Bell, Garrett. "The Recovery of the Cities." *The Environmental Handbook,* ed. Garrett De Bell. New York: Ballantine Books, 1970.
De Feis, George L. "Sustainable Development Issues: Industry, Environment, Regulation and Competition." *Journal of Professional Issues in Engineering Education and Practice* 120, no. 2. April 1994.
DeMont, John, with William Lowther. "A Bigger, More Influential Greenpeace Begins Its Third Decade." *Maclean's.* Dec. 16, 1991.
Diamond, Irene and Gloria Orenstein, eds. *Reweaving the World: The Emergence of Ecofeminism.* San Francisco: Sierra Club Books, 1990.
———. "Two Feminists Discuss the Emergence of Ecofeminism." *Major Problems in American Environmental History,* ed. Carolyn Merchant. Lexington: Mass.: D. C. Heath, 1993.
Dowie, Mark. *Losing Ground: American Environmentalism at the Close of the Twentieth Century.* MIT Press, 1995.
———. "The Fourth Wave." *Mother Jones.* March/April 1995.
Ember, Lois R. "EPA Administrators Deem Agency's First 25 Years Bumpy But Successful." *C&EN.* Oct. 30, 1995.
EPA Journal. "Presidential Earth Day Address." April/June 1993.
Fischer, John. "Survival U: Prospectus for a Really Relevant University." *The Environmental Handbook,* ed. Garrett De Bell. New York: Ballantine Books, 1970.
Flores, Dan. "Bison Ecology and Bison Diplomacy: The Southern Plains from 1800 to 1850." *Journal of American History.* Sept. 1991.
Friedenberg, Daniel M. *Life, Liberty, and the Pursuit of Land.* New York: Prometheus Books, 1992.
Gordon, John Steele. "The American Environment: The Big Picture Is More Heartening Than All the Little Ones." *American Heritage.* Oct. 1993.
Gottlieb, Robert. *Forcing the Spring: The Transformation of the American Environmental Movement.* Washington, D.C.: Island Press, 1993.
Graham, Frank, Jr. *Man's Dominion: The Story of Conservation in America.* New York: M. Evans, 1971.
———. *Since Silent Spring.* Boston: Houghton Mifflin, 1970.
Hardin, Garrett. "The Tragedy of the Commons." *Science* 162. December 13, 1968.
Hays, Samuel P. *Conservation and the Gospel of Efficiency: The Progressive Conservation Movement, 1890–1920.* Cambridge: Harvard University Press, 1959.
Healy, Melissa. "Partisan Politics Swamps Environmentalists." *Los Angeles Times.* Oct. 17, 1994.
Hebert, H. Josef. "Congress Embracing Land Conservation." *USA Today.* April 20, 1999.
Holden, Constance. "Animal Rightists Trash MSU Lab." *Science.* March 13, 1992.

Hughes, John. "Group: Sprawl Threatens Rivers, with Snake River Topping List." *USA Today*. April 12, 1999.

Hurley, Andrew. *Environmental Inequalities: Class, Race, and Industrial Pollution in Gary, Indiana 1945–80*. Chapel Hill: University of North Carolina Press, 1995.

Hynes, H. Patricia. *The Recurring Silent Spring*. New York: Pergamon Press, 1989.

Johnson, Jeff. "Clinton Offers Regulatory Reforms as Congress Hammers Out Bills." *Environmental Science and Technology* 29, no.5. May 1995.

———. "Environment Emerges as Key Issue in 1996 Election." *Environmental Science and Technology* 29, no.12. Dec. 1995.

Johnson, Lyndon B. "Natural Beauty—Message from the President of the United States." *Congressional Record*. 89th Congress, 1st Session, vol. 111, pt. 2. Feb. 8, 1965.

Kay, Jane Holtz. *Asphalt Nation: How the Automobile Took Over America, and How We Can Take It Back* New York: Crown, 1997.

Knickerbocker, Brad. "Environmentalism Extends Its Reach." *Christian Science Monitor*. Jan. 1993.

Kriz, Margaret E. "Warm-Button Issue." *National Journal*. Feb. 8, 1992.

———. "A New Shade of Green." *National Journal*. March 18, 1995.

———. "Drawing a Green Line in the Sand." *National Journal*. Aug. 12, 1995.

———. "The Vice President Gores the Opposition." *National Journal*. Oct. 14, 1995.

Lawrence, Jennifer. "Green Products Sprouting Again." *Advertising Age*. May 10, 1993.

Leavitt, Paul. "House OKs Standards for Beach Water Quality." *USA Today*. April 23, 1999.

Leopold, Aldo. *A Sand County Almanac and Sketches Here and There*. New York: Oxford University Press, 1949.

Lewis, Martin W. "The Green Threat to Nature." *Harper's Magazine*. Nov. 1992.

Lichter, S. Robert. "Liberal Greens, Mainstream Camouflage." *Wall Street Journal*. April 21, 1995.

Linden, Eugene. "The Green Factor." *Time*. Oct. 12, 1992.

Long, David R. "Pipe Dreams: Hetch Hetchy, the Urban West, and the Hydraulic Society Revisited." *Journal of the West*. July 1995.

Mann, Michael. "EU Says U.S. Must Be More Ambitious over Climate," Reuters, May 18, 1999.

Marsh, George P. *Man and Nature; or, Physical Geography as Modified by Human Nature*. New York: Charles Scribner, 1864.

Marshall, Robert. "The Problem of the Wilderness." *Scientific Monthly* 30. 1930.

Mathews, Jessica Tuchman, ed. *Preserving the Global Environment: The Challenge of Shared Leadership*. New York: W.W. Norton, 1991.

Merchant, Carolyn. *The Death of Nature: Women, Ecology, and the Scientific Revolution*. San Francisco: Harper and Row, 1980.

———. *Ecological Revolutions: Nature, Gender, and Science in New England*. Chapel Hill: University of North Carolina Press, 1989.

———. *Major Problems in American Environmental History*. Lexington, Mass.: D.C. Heath, 1993.

Miller, Karen L. "The Greening of the Web: Reduce, Reuse, Recycle, Research, React . . . and Buy." *New York Times*. Jan. 23, 1998.

Muir, John. *Our National Parks*. Boston: Houghton Mifflin, 1901.

———. *The Yosemite*. New York: Century, 1912.

Nash, Roderick. *The American Environment: Readings in the History of Conservation*. London: Addison-Wesley, 1968.

New York Times. "Bill Clinton, Environmentalist?" Jan. 5, 1993.

———. "Gore Focuses on 2000 U.S. Presidential Campaign." Jan. 14, 1999.

Newman, Alan. "Clinton's Budget for the Environment." *Environmental Science and Technology*. 1993.

Nissen, Todd. "Chairman Ford Defends Company Environmental Record." Reuters. May 13, 1999.

Opie, John. *Nature's Nation: An Environmental History of the United States*. Holt, Rhinehart and Winston, 1998.

Pinchot, Gifford. *Breaking New Ground.* New York: Harcourt, Brace and World, 1947.

———. *The Fight for Conservation.* New York: Harcourt, Brace, 1910.

The Planet. "Club Endorses Bill Clinton." Vol. 3, no. 8. Nov. 1996.

Ponting, Clive. *A Green History of the World.* London: Penguin Books, 1991.

Powell, John Wesley. *Exploration of the Colorado River of the West and Its Tributaries.* Washington, D.C., 1875.

Public Citizen Global Trade Watch. "NAFTA Agreement." http://www.citizen.org/pctrade/nafta/reports/5years.htm#environment. Dec. 1998.

Rauber, Paul. "An End to Evolution: The Extinction Lobby in Congress Is Now Deciding Which Species Will Live and Which Will Die." *Sierra* 80. Jan./Feb. 1996.

———. "Eco-Thug: Helen Chenoweth." *Sierra* 81. May/June 1996.

Reichhardt, Tony. "Clinton Announces Package of Environmental Reforms." *Nature.* April 29, 1993.

Riesch, Anna Lou. "Conservation under Franklin Roosevelt." In *The American Environment: Readings in the History of Conservation,* ed. Roderick Nash. London: Addison-Wesley, 1968.

Roche, Vaughn. "At Loggerheads in the Wilderness." *Washington Post.* Sept. 4, 1993.

Roosevelt, Theodore. "Opening Address by the President." *Proceedings of Governors in the White House,* ed. Newton C. Blanchard. Washington, D.C.: Government Printing Office, 1909.

Sanoff, Alvin P. "The Greening of America's Past." *U.S. News and World Report.* Oct. 19, 1992.

Scarce, Rik. *Eco-Warriors: Understanding the Radical Environmental Movement.* Chicago: Noble Press, 1990.

Scheffer, Victor B. *The Shaping of Environmentalism in America.* Seattle: University of Washington Press, 1991.

Schmidt, Peter, Jr. *Back to Nature: The Arcadian Myth in Urban America.* New York: Oxford University Press, 1969.

Schneider, William. "A Firm Stand on Wrong Issue in Rio?" *National Journal.* June 20, 1992.

Shabecoff, Philip. *A Fierce Green Fire: The American Environmental Movement.* New York: Hill and Wang, 1993.

Silver, Timothy. *A New Face on the Countryside: Indians, Colonists, and Slaves in South Atlantic Forests, 1500–1800.* Cambridge: Cambridge University Press, 1990.

Skow, John. "The Redwoods Weep: In California Ancient Forests, the Clash between Industry and Idealism Culminates in Tragedy." *Time.* Sept. 28, 1998.

Standing Bear. *Land of the Spotted Eagle.* Lincoln: University of Nebraska Press, 1978.

Stevens, William K. "As Alaska Melts, Scientists Consider the Reasons Why." *New York Times.* Aug. 18 1998.

———. "Greenhouse Gas Issue Pits Third World Against Richer Nations." *New York Times.* Nov. 30, 1997.

Stewart, Frank. *A Natural History of Nature Writing.* Washington, D.C.: Island Press, 1995.

Strong, Douglas H. *The Conservationists.* Menlo Park, Calif.: Addison-Wesley, 1971.

Swain, Donald C. *Federal Conservation Policy, 1921–1933* 76. Berkeley: University of California Publications in History, 1963.

Thomson, Dick. "What Global Warming? As the World Heats Up, the Public Simply Goes Cold." *Science* 153, no. 24. June 21. 1999.

Thoreau, Henry David. "Walking." *Excursions, The Writings of Henry David Thoreau* 9. Boston: Riverside Edition, 1893.

Turner, B. L., ed. *The Earth as Transformed by Human Action: Global and Regional Changes in the Biosphere over the Past 300 Years.* Cambridge: Cambridge University Press, 1993.

Turner, Frederick Jackson. *The Significance of the Frontier in American History,* ed. Harold P. Simonson. New York: Frederick Unger Publications, 1963.

Udall, Stewart L. *The Quiet Crisis.* New York: Holt, Rinehart and Winston, 1963.

Underwood, Joanna D. "Going Green for Profit." *EPA Journal.* July/Sept. 1993.

U.S. State Department. "Letter from Vice President Albert Gore, Jr." *Environmental Diplomacy: The Environment and U.S. Foreign Policy.* http://www.state.gov/www/global/oes/earth.html. 1997.

———. "Environmental Diplomacy at Work." *Environmental Diplomacy: The Environment and U.S. Foreign Policy.* http://www.state.gov/www/global/oes/earth.html. 1997.

Verhovek, Sam Howe. "Salmon Put on U.S. List as at Risk." *New York Times.* March 16, 1999.

Vollers, Maryanne. "Greening the White House." *Audubon.* May/June 1995.

Welford, Harrison. "On How to Be a Constructive Nuisance." *The Environmental Handbook,* ed. Garrett De Bell. New York: Ballantine Books, 1970.

White, Lynn, Jr. "The Historical Roots of Our Ecological Crisis." *Science* 125. March 10, 1967.

Wilderness Society. "1998 Report: 15 Most Endangered Wild Lands." http://www.wildemess.org/standbylands/15most/index.htm.

Wildlife Digest. "Trends, Issues, Views and News." Nov. 1988.

———. "Trends, Issues, Views and News." Nov. 1989.

Worster, Donald. *Dust Bowl: The Southern Plains in the 1930s.* Oxford University Press, 1979.

———. *Nature's Economy: The Roots of Ecology.*

Index